Women in British Politics, 1760–1860

The Power of the Petticoat

Edited by

Kathryn Gleadle
British Academy Post-Doctoral Research Fellow
Department of Politics and Modern History
London Guildhall University

and

Sarah Richardson
Lecturer
Department of History
University of Warwick

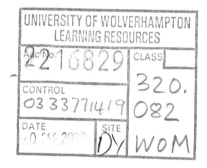

First published in Great Britain 2000 by
MACMILLAN PRESS LTD
Houndmills, Basingstoke, Hampshire RG21 6XS and London
Companies and representatives throughout the world

A catalogue record for this book is available from the British Library.

ISBN 0–333–77141–9 hardcover
ISBN 0–333–77142–7 paperback

First published in the United States of America 2000 by
ST. MARTIN'S PRESS, INC.,
Scholarly and Reference Division,
175 Fifth Avenue, New York, N.Y. 10010

ISBN 0–312–23356–6

Library of Congress Cataloging-in-Publication Data
Women in British politics, 1760–1860 : the power of the petticoat / edited by
Kathryn Gleadle and Sarah Richardson.
    p.   cm.
Includes bibliographical references and index.
ISBN 0–312–23356–6 (cloth)
1. Great Britain—Politics and government—19th century. 2. Women in politics–
–Great Britain—History—19th century. 3. Women in politics—Great Britain–
–History—18th century. 4. Great Britain—Politics and government—1760–1820.
I. Gleadle, Kathryn. II. Richardson, Sarah, 1964 May 11–

DA530 .W57   2000
941'.0082—dc21
                                                               00–022313

This book is printed on paper suitable for recycling and made from fully managed and sustained
forest sources.

10   9   8   7   6   5   4   3   2   1
09 08 07 06 05 04 03 02 01 00

Printed and bound in Great Britain by
Antony Rowe Ltd, Chippenham, Wiltshire

In memory of Tom Green

Contents

List of Figures

Acknowledgements

The editors wish to thank the participants of the conference held at the University of Warwick in May 1998, 'The Power of the Petticoat: Women in British Politics, 1780–1860', from which many of the chapters are drawn. We would particularly like to thank all those who gave papers at the conference, and to Maxine Berg, Anna Clark, Peter Mandler and Jane Rendall for their insightful comments and support. The conference was partially funded by a grant from the Humanities Research Centre at the University of Warwick. Special thanks are due to Jem, Rowan and Tess for their cheerful encouragement and to their heroic carer, who wishes to remain anonymous.

Notes on the Contributors

Elaine Chalus is a Lecturer at Bath Spa University College. She is co-editor (with Hannah Barker) of *Gender in Eighteenth-Century England: Roles, Representations and Responsibilities* (London: Longman, 1997) and author of *Women in English Political Life, 1754–1790* (Oxford: Oxford University Press, forthcoming).

Matthew Cragoe is a Lecturer at the University of Hertfordshire. His recent works include *An Anglican Aristocracy: The Moral Economy of the Landed Estate, 1832–95* (Oxford: Oxford University Press, 1996).

Kathryn Gleadle holds a British Academy Post-Doctoral Research Fellowship in the Department of Politics and Modern History at London Guildhall University. She is the author of *The Early Feminists: Radical Unitarians and the Emergence of the Women's Rights Movement, 1831–51* (Basingstoke: Macmillan, 1995).

Clare Midgley is a Senior Lecturer in the Department of Politics and Modern History at London Guildhall University. Her previous publications include *Women against Slavery: The British Campaigns, 1780–1870* (London and New York: Routledge, 1992) and *Gender and Imperialism* (Manchester: Manchester University Press, 1998).

Simon Morgan has recently completed a D.Phil. thesis at the University of York entitled 'Middle-class Women and Public Identities in Leeds and the West Riding of Yorkshire, *c.* 1830–1860'.

Sarah Richardson is a Lecturer in the Department of History at the University of Warwick. She is co-editor (with Anna Clark) of *History of the Suffrage, 1760–1867*, 6 vols (London: Pickering and Chatto, 1999).

Anne Stott is an Associate Lecturer for the Open Univeristy. She is currently working on a biography of Hannah More.

Nadia Valman is the Ian Karten Research Fellow at the Parkes' Centre for Jewish/Non-Jewish Relations in the Department of English at the University of Southampton. She has published widely on Victorian Jewish literature and is editor of *Jewish Culture and History*.

Introduction
The Petticoat in Politics: Women and Authority[1]

Kathryn Gleadle and Sarah Richardson

In December 1832, the borough of Ripon in Yorkshire was contested for the first time for over one hundred years. In the aftermath of the Reform Act expectations were high that the proprietorial influence of the Aislabie family of Studley Royal could be thrown off and that the election would launch a new era of democratic politics.[2] The Liberal candidates centred their campaign on the unnatural and illegal influence of the owner of the Studley Royal estate and proprietor of many burgage plots in Ripon. However, this traditional claim of 'old corruption' was given an alternative spin because it was a woman, Elizabeth Sophia Lawrence, who had sole control of the estate and therefore could influence borough politics. In a series of speeches, one of the Liberal challengers, Richard Crompton Staveley, utilised a particularly evocative image to draw attention to the role of this female, political power:

> At your request, I now stand before you (ladies, I am sorry to say it) to do away with petticoat influence. Men could no longer bear it, that one immense blue petticoat should cover the whole town of Ripon and exclude from its inhabitants those bright rays of light and liberty which are now shining forth in all their glory from one end of the borough to another.[3]

The petticoat as a metaphor for women's authority over men had been a favourite symbol in political propaganda from the early eighteenth century. Significantly, the image was used to depict female influence in the realm, as well as women's dominance within the home. It would be wrong to assume, however, that these portrayals of female power were invariably and simplistically misogynist. Staveley, for example went on to acknowledge his debt to the 'many ladies sporting my colours today' (who had organised together to raise a subscription for his expenses).

1

He also recognised the importance of 'petticoat influence . . . [as] an indispensable item in our domestic happiness'.[4] However, petticoat government in the public sphere was not invariably constructed as a neat binary opposition to a more acceptable form of petticoat government within the domestic setting. The petticoat was a much contested and shifting metonym whose meaning could alter across different ideological constituencies. In times of political crises, moreover, the petticoat could acquire new resonances of anxiety and tension.

Some of these nuances are captured in the changing use of the petticoat within the political literature of Queen Anne's reign. John Dunton's pamphlet, *Petticoat Government*, for example, which dated from the beginning of Anne's reign, spoke benignly of the two spheres of female government: 'By Petticoat Government, I mean when Good Women Ascend the Throne, and Rule according to Law, as is the case of the present Queen. Again, by Petticoat Government, I mean the discreet and housewifely Ruling of a House and Family.'[5] On her accession to the throne Queen Anne, it has recently been noted, carefully constructed her public image as the unthreatening and homely 'nursing mother' of the people, making full use of court ceremony and ritual, and therefore petticoat government was treated positively by Dunton.[6] As her reign continued and Anne surrounded herself with female favourites, a more satirical use was made of the phrase – as can be seen in the titles of these anonymous pamphlets which propagated a fear of feminine influence: *The Prerogative of the Breeches: an Answer to Petticoat-Government, Written by a True-born English Man* (1702) and *The Petticoat Plotters or the D——ss of M——h's Club* (1712).[7]

The metonymic employment of the petticoat to represent an unwarranted interference in politics by royal women went on to reach its zenith during the Wilkite campaigns against the Earl of Bute in the 1760s. Jackboots and petticoats signifying Bute and his supposed paramour, the Princess Dowager, were hung from scaffolds (and subsequently burned) throughout the country during the 1760s with the icons also being liberally sprinkled throughout prints and pamphlets (see Figure 1).[8] The use of the petticoat, a particularly intimate item of women's clothing, added the spice of sexual impropriety to the already potent recipe of illicit behaviour in high places: an image that was imitated in the pictures and prints circulating during the Westminster election of 1784, where the Duchess of Devonshire played a prominent public role.[9] The imagery surrounding women's political involvement was highly complex and did not rely upon a straightforward allusion to petticoat government. The 'female' petticoat was frequently used in counterpoint to the 'male'

The Rape of the Petti-coat.

He valiantly seiz'd the Petti-coat and Boot at the Portal of his own Mansion.

Daily adv.

Figure 1 *The Rape of the Petticoat*, 1768. The print depicts the Lord Mayor of London removing a boot (representing the Earl of Bute) and a petticoat (representing the Princess Dowager) from a gibbet outside the Mansion House.

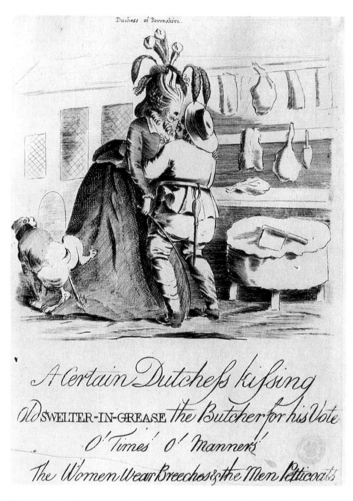

Figure 2   *A Certain Duchess Kissing Old-Swelter-in-Grease the Butcher for his Vote,* 1784.

breeches. Satirists might portray female incursions into political space not as petticoat government but as an inversion of gender roles with women wearing the breeches and men the petticoats (see Figure 2). However, the two symbols could be juxtaposed to create more positive representations of female behaviour. For example, Burnet in his *History of My Own Time* claimed that one of Cromwell's daughters, Lady Falconbridge, was considered to have been a more worthy successor to the Protectorate than either of her two brothers; and that a saying went of

the Cromwell children that 'those who wore the breeches deserved petticoats better, but if those in petticoats had been in breeches they would
have held faster'.[10]

A further public scare about petticoat government emerged during the
turbulent May days of the Reform Bill crisis in 1832. A rumour began to
circulate that Queen Adelaide, hitherto considered as an unremarkable,
dutiful consort to the more colourful William IV, had intervened in
the crisis in order to turn her husband against the Reform Bill. It
was alleged that she plotted variously with her daughters, the Earl of
Munster (William's illegitimate son) and the Duke of Wellington to
resist the Whig government's plans to create peers in order that the
Reform Bill would pass through the House of Lords and become law:

> The Queen and the Princesses have in fact never ceased tormenting
> his Majesty with all manner of sinister reports and forebodings as to
> the evils which will result from Reform. It is proper that the nation
> should know, without disguise or reserve, that the Queen has done
> more injury to the cause of Reform than any person living.[11]

At once the nation was flooded with prints, pamphlets, newspaper reports
and broadsheets inflaming the public's fear of the foreign, the feminine and of unfettered influence. The populace were reminded of the
Queen's German origins and a Reform meeting in Newcastle upon Tyne
taunted her with the fate of Marie Antionette, a parallel that had already
been drawn by Adelaide herself.[12] Allegations of petticoat government
abounded. A scurrilous pamphlet, entitled *A Secret History of the Late
Petticoat Plot Against the Liberties of the People* which was rushed into
print in 1832 and allegedly written by a member of the queen's household, was typical.[13] An engraving of a Reform meeting at the Mixed
Cloth Hall in Leeds during the crisis has resonance with the Boot and
Petticoat hysteria of 1762. Members of the Leeds Reform Association
stand aloof on a platform surrounded by an angry crowd displaying
banners proclaiming 'No petticoat government', some with pictorial representations of the Queen and Wellington, others carrying effigies of
Adelaide, which later would be burned. That the Queen had the potential influence to scupper the Reform Bill was not in doubt in the radical
press and rapidly led to the expression of republican sentiments:

> we are monarchists, . . . but if monarchy can only subsist with Welling-
> tons, Cumberlands, Lyndhursts, ambitious bastards [Munster], and
> German women for its ministerings and its love, and with rotten

boroughs, enormous pensions, and desolating taxes for its append-
ages ... let Monarchy go to the right about, and the lesser evil of Repub-
licanism become dominant in England ... [14]

The accession of Queen Victoria provided another cultural moment in
which the trope of the petticoat became invested with anxieties concerning the potency of female political power. A comic ballad dating
from 1837, entitled 'Petticoats is Master', warned the country's male citizens of the threat which a female monarch posed to their liberties and
happiness. It suggested that women might now associate together to
pass laws to their own advantage (particularly with regard to their
access to drink!):

> Now all married men, I'd have you look out,
> Or the Petticoats surely will bang you about,
> For the women have got the right side of the Queen,
> So success to the Petticoats, wherever they're seen.[15]

While the ballad itself is preoccupied with the implications of a female
monarch and raises the spectre of a nationwide sisterhood controlling
the polity, the accompanying illustration refers purely to women's
dominance within the home. It neatly encapsulates, therefore, the contemporary associations between women's power within the household
and its potential ramifications on the political stage. In this, the ballad
was exemplary. The contingency between women's domestic and public power was frequently alluded to throughout this period. In 1870
Justin McCarthy's article 'The Petticoat in the Politics of England'
noted that although women may not legally possess the vote, they
held the whip-hand in domestic and public politics. Popular allegations
of women's 'petticoat government' over their husbands were certainly
common. Witness William Cobbett's comments of a man who, 'being
under strict petticoat government ... was compelled to get home that
night'.[16] Of course, petticoat government need not necessarily allude to
women's political authority. Images of dominant wives tapped into a
vibrant popular tradition of mocking the figure of the hen-pecked husband, and, as Anna Clark has richly illustrated, were implicated in a
broader discourse of 'battling for the breeches' within plebeian marriages.[17] Another popular ballad (again entitled, *Petticoats is Master*)
encouraged wives whose husbands denied them their rights to 'wap
him round and round about, / Nor flinch an inch, but make him shout, /
Oh! Petticoats is Master!'[18] Yet it would be wrong to assume that the

petticoat image was a response purely to the conflict of personalities and gender relations within contemporary families. As the examples cited above indicate, the persistent connections made between petticoat government at home and in the realm suggest profound disquiet over the wider potentialities of female authority, (and significantly *Petticoats is Master* was itself a product of the Queen Caroline crisis). One context for dismantling such tensions is provided in Chapters 1 and 8 of this volume, which demonstrate that late eighteenth- and nineteenth-century electoral politics were often preoccupied with the explicitly political influence that wives might exert over their husbands.

The common hostility towards women's political involvement was reflected in the frequent use of the petticoat as a term of abuse for female politicians. Typical examples include: the well-known description of Mary Wollstonecraft by Horace Walpole as 'that hyena in petticoats'; Fielding's assertion in a *Grub-Street Opera*, that 'petticoat government is a very lamentable thing indeed'; and Addison's description of 'A seminary of petticoat politicians who are to be brought up at the feet of Madam de Maintenon'.[19] In 1849 *Blackwood's Magazine* went as far as to invent a new term for a group of female politicians, calling them a 'petticoatery', a pun on the terms petticoat and coterie.[20] These allusions to women politicians were not accidental. Contemporaries often seemed to have made a distinction between 'legislators' and 'politicians'. Legislators were defined in the narrow sense as being Members of Parliament; whereas politicians were characterised more broadly as being those who were highly active and extremely knowledgeable in the field of politics.[21]

In radical circles, which explicitly encouraged female political involvement, the petticoat could be applied as a term of respect. Sarah Jane Maling, the member of a radical salon in late eighteenth-century Suffolk, was known as a 'Tom Pain [*sic*] in petticoats' for her skill in political debate.[22] The Friends of the Oppressed, an association of radical women who campaigned for the freedom of the press, talked with indignation of the government's response to their activities, 'Will they add to the cruelty and injustice inflicted daily upon destitute cripples and starving old men by entering upon a war against *petticoats*?'[23] The trope was also used as a shorthand for describing women's engagement in other forms of public protest, as this incident from August 1837 aptly illustrates:

A petticoat victory. On Friday last, by order of the Poor Law Guardians for Redruth Union, the overseers and their assistants proceeded to remove the paupers from Stithians to Illogan. The clothes were packed and ready for starting, when a strong body of about two hundred females, commanded by an old weather-beaten female veteran, rushed from behind an embankment, and proceeded to contest the removal with the overseers, who, not willing to risk so formidable a charge, instantly retreated, in doing which the overseer was taken a prisoner, and after being roughly handled was securely packed in his own cart and allowed to escape, whilst the victorious party repaired to a neighbouring beer-shop exalting in their triumph.[24]

On occasions the very materiality of women's intimate garments and their implications for political authority was emphasised as the image of Elizabeth Lawrence's petticoat physically blocking out the 'light of liberty' testifies. Elaine Chalus has forcefully argued for the recognition that eighteenth-century politics suffused all aspects of the social lives of the elite and that female fashion and dress could be used in order to signify allegiance to particular party political or royal factions.[25] Ribbons and cockades were displayed on the clothing of women (and men) of all classes in society: caps, dresses and even petticoats were adorned in appropriate colours during election contests to occasionally sensational effect.[26] Female radical reformers frequently dressed in white at mass meetings to convey their purity and respectability; Irish republicans wove strips of green silk into their clothes as a symbol of their nationalist principles.[27] Such preoccupations and practices confirmed contemporary tendencies to elide discursively women's political engagement with aspects of the female body and female dress. In recent years scholars such as Linda Colley, Kathleen Wilson and Nicholas Rogers have also drawn attention to the multivalent and nuanced representation of women within political discourses. For example, political corruption was frequently portrayed in popular literature as a wanton or debauched woman, contrasted with the unimpeachable female figure of Britannia.[28]

The recourse to the image of 'petticoat government' within such a wide range of genres suggests a contemporary cognisance that women had the potential to exploit various sites of power. This volume, by concentrating upon the myriad expressions of upper- and middle-class women's political activity, considers the ways in which their engagement was both widely acknowledged yet highly contested.[29] Politics is here defined broadly and inclusively. As feminist political scientists have argued, definitions of what construes the political are inherently problematic, often being themselves derived from a particular ideological viewpoint. Political history is frequently dominated by the concerns of 'high politics'. Although women regularly engaged with parliamentary agendas, this is a strategy which can be blind to the often informal, domestic and issue-based contribution of women.[30] This perception has recently led to an emerging literature on women's involvement in such issues as vegetarianism, animal rights, alternative medicine and consumerism (although many of these insights have yet to be applied to late eighteenth-century and early Victorian Britain).[31] This is not to say that women's potential for political involvement was unrestricted. It goes without saying that they did not have the same opportunities as their male contemporaries, but we should also recognise that the barriers against their activities were not as inflexible as has been commonly assumed.[32] The boundaries between public and private worlds merged and overlapped. Contemporary issues could be renegotiated within the home, leading to discrete avenues for political expression, such as consumerism and ideologically-motivated methods of child-rearing.[33] Equally, women's predominance in the domestic environment could legitimate their involvement in campaigns which were centred around a moral imperative, such as the campaigns against *sati* and the Corn Laws, and for minority rights.[34] This did not, however, preclude women from making an active contribution in a wide range of more conventional political arenas, including electoral events, political trials and imperial governance.[35]

The reconfiguration of the potential sites for women's political expression also demands a fresh approach to the models conventionally employed for understanding women's activity. For example, many studies of political women have focused upon the achievements and philosophies of individuals.[36] Whilst some such studies make little attempt at theorisation, recently this 'great women of history' approach has received more nuanced treatments. Barbara Caine used the framework of individual biography to make searching critiques of the development of individual feminisms. Sandra Stanley Holton has based her insightful account of the suffrage movement around the particular contribution made by seven, lesser-known, but still exceptional individuals, to throw into relief new patterns and strands to the suffrage movement.[37] In this volume only one chapter concentrates upon a single individual: Anne Stott's consideration of the politics of Hannah More. However, Stott's chapter is concerned not to detail the 'achievements' of Hannah More, but rather to place her within the context of middle-class loyalist women and to consider the ways in which such women were able to contribute to the political culture of the day. Similarly, Gleadle's discussion of communitarian feminists focuses not upon Anna Wheeler, but upon the diverse and often 'hidden' means whereby early socialist women influenced contemporary radical culture; Richardson's chapter also includes many well-known examples of female political endeavour, including

Harriet Martineau and Sarah Austin, but it decentres their exceptionality, being concerned to investigate some of the many ways in which middle-class and elite women were able to contribute to the fabric of radical political life.

Other treatments of women's political involvement have tended to focus upon the family, rather than the individual, as the unit of study. According to Sally Alexander, writing of the working-class experience, 'Women fell under the protection of their fathers, husbands or Parliament and were denied an independent political subjectivity'.[38] Studies of elite women's political involvement within the family context have often been similarly pessimistic. Both Gerry Maguire and Pat Jalland have considered the ways in which women were able to play a supportive role to politically active husbands. Maguire offers a bleak perspective of women's scope for political agency in this situation, assuming that their influence was limited, being utterly dependent upon their relationships with men. Pat Jalland's account is more attuned to the personal variations which complicated women's political identity, although she too concludes that political women, 'had no role in political decision-making, even indirectly, and their influence on political issues was negligible'.[39] Recently, a more sophisticated understanding of the political role of aristocratic women has been offered by K. D. Reynolds. Using the sociological concept of the 'incorporated wife', Reynolds notes that in their political activities, women worked, if not on terms of equality with their husbands, then in 'active partnership with them'. According to Reynolds, hackneyed portrayals of 'separate spheres' bore little relation to the duties and engagements undertaken by aristocratic women. Moreover, it was women, rather than men, who had most to lose by the democratisation of the state, for this threatened the informal channels of influence and patronage by which they sought and promoted familial interests.[40] Reynolds's thesis is further elaborated when placed alongside Elaine Chalus's articulation of women's role in 'social politics'. For Chalus, elite women's participation in the political process is highlighted by their involvement in the assemblies, balls, dinners, treating and visits which were essential for the promotion of the family political interest.[41] Recent research has also suggested the importance of social politics in underlining the civic consciousness of urban women.[42]

The concept of women's sociability is central to many of the contributions to this volume. Whether it was campaigning in pressure-group politics; managing political salons; organising bazaars; attending chapel and enjoying lectures; or canvassing at elections, women's familial and community relationships played a crucial role in facilitating their participation

in public affairs. Nevertheless, they demonstrate sensitivity to the patriarchal family models within which most of the subjects were situated;
(the contributions on pressure-group politics in Chapters 4–6 also note
the extent to which conventional family norms were projected within the
discourse of these movements). Yet, an emerging theme is the extent to
which acquiescence in more traditional family structures had little
impact upon the development of individual political identities. This is
in contrast to Reynolds, who maintains that women's political involvement was a functional phenomena – they sought to protect the political
interest and views of their husbands and families. Many of the chapters
here go much further than Reynolds in their insistence that female
political engagement was often ideologically driven. Whether this is due
to the greater focus upon middle-class women, requires further invest-
igation.

The contributions of Elaine Chalus and Matthew Cragoe (Chapters 1
and 8) are also suggestive of new paradigms for assessing women's political commitment within the family context. In Victorian politics and
social comment, it was commonplace to argue that women had no need
of the vote, for they were already represented politically, either by their
husbands, or by their brothers and fathers. As James Mill famously
declared, when discoursing on the distribution of political rights, 'One
thing is pretty clear, that all those individuals whose interests are
indisputably included in those of other individuals, may be struck off'.[43]
Subsequent commentators have invariably taken such arguments to be
symptomatic of a patriarchal backlash against the threat of female
enfranchisement. However, it is possible that such comments reflected
a social reality, as some contemporaries may have seen it. Many women
may have genuinely believed themselves to be represented by their Member of Parliament and to have positioned themselves as political constituents. Cragoe's depiction of the franchise as a form of 'family property'
and Chalus's analysis of women's importance in certain franchises are
perhaps indicators that the concept of virtual representation was an
important source of women's political identity. The deputations of large
numbers of female constituents, during this period, to present their
local Member of Parliament with gifts of thanks for his services, serve to
strengthen such an hypothesis.[44]

The study of the community also offers new approaches to the study
of women's political involvement. To date, such considerations have
been confined to the experience of working-class women;[45] the implications of community involvement for elite and middle-class women,
save for that of philanthropy, have yet to be investigated. This volume

offers some initial insights into the possibilities of such an approach. The literal understanding of community, as practised in the early socialist movement (see Chapter 7) may be compared to the expansive concept of community articulated in Chapters 4 and 5. Clare Midgley and Nadia Valman both demonstrate that the perception of the community was central to the political consciousness of campaigning women. Was the community to be conceptualised only as white, British and Christian, or should it also incorporate those of other religions and races?

The importance of religion in structuring and motivating women's political consciousness is a consistent theme of this volume. There has been a tendency to assume that women's religious affiliations were an inevitable corollary to the evangelical injunctions that women might construe their own, apolitical discursive space. This was a space in which issues of morality, nurturing and spirituality were to be especially privileged and which would allow engagement in philanthropic activities. But philanthropy has, to date, been largely portrayed as a female phenomenon which operated in parallel to (and not in tandem with) affairs of the political nation.[46] Clare Midgley's previous work on the anti-slavery movement made a vital contribution in suggesting the fluid links which might exist between philanthropic campaigning and political aims.[47] Since then, a growing interest in the Unitarian movement has highlighted the rich connections between rational religion, gender and politics.[48] This tradition is reflected in Chapters 4 and 6, which allude to the importance of dissenting chapels as a site for women's political activism. Chapters 2 and 4 also underline the importance of evangelical discourses in drawing women into fields of political engagement. The concept of divine providence emerges here as a powerful motivation for women's participation in loyalist and imperialist politics. However, as Nadia Valman (Chapter 5) powerfully suggests, non-Christian religions have remained, until now, wholly neglected in recovering the political lives of British Victorian women.

Whilst accepting the importance of religious communities, it is also possible to problematise other ways of understanding the community. In particular, sociological analyses have stressed that a 'community' need not be confined to a geographical locality, nor need a community be defined in terms of face-to-face contact.[49] The electorate, for example, may be viewed in this light and this raises interesting implications for women's involvement in the electoral process.[50] As Sarah Richardson (Chapter 3) demonstrates, educated, middle-class women were highly adept at building their own intellectual and political communities. These were networks which might extend across the Atlantic, as well as to the Continent in geographical scope, but could be tightly linked to ideological and political activity. Yet, this chapter, (as many others in the book) recognises that women's political behaviour must be understood not only in the context of female association (as one tradition of feminist scholarship has stressed)[51] but should also be analysed with reference to mixed-sex networks.[52]

The reconstruction of women's political networks raises significant questions concerning the nature of the sources one might employ. The retrieval of extensive correspondence networks, for example, has brought to light the political interests of a host of lesser-known women.[53] The broadening of the concept of the political also calls for a reappraisal of the genres which might serve to reconstitute women's political engagement. Whereas many studies have concentrated upon the explicitly political writings of well-known figures, such as Mary Wollstonecraft and Catherine Macaulay,[54] in recent years, attention has turned to the diverse *oeuvre* produced by female intellectuals. Gary Kelly has analysed how even the minor writings of Mary Wollstonecraft, ostensibly works of fiction or pedagogy, help to explicate her political critique of the social system.[55] For Anne K. Mellor, drawing upon critiques of Habermas, the fluorescence of women's writing from the late eighteenth century produced an alternative, female counter-public sphere. This may be discerned in works of dramatic fiction, for example, such as the plays of Joanna Baillie, which constructed an alternative, female vision of the state.[56] In this volume such an approach is pursued by Anne Stott, who suggests that the loyalist and conservative Hannah More was able to articulate her political views within such genres as the advice book written for Princess Charlotte. This is a strategy which leads to a great enrichment of our understanding of the workings of the contemporary political and cultural scene. A further implication of exploring alternative genres is that it promises to bring to light a number of little-known or forgotten writers. This is important, for it underlines the point that women's political interest should not be seen as an exceptional phenomena, limited to the 'big names' which recur so often.[57] In Chapter 5 of this book, Nadia Valman demonstrates that it is necessary to turn to alternative genres – in this case domestic fiction – to understand the ways in which women managed to articulate political views and to highlight the widespread contribution which contemporary women made to political debate.

Women's willingness to exploit the many sites of political expression discussed in this volume – through fiction, salons, friendship networks, influence over husbands at election times, not to mention their role in pressure group movements and electoral politics – provide a central context for understanding contemporary fears of women's authority. Indeed, behind the image of the petticoat lay an accepted perception (frequently emerging as a deep-seated anxiety) that women did possess the potential for political influence: whether derived from their sexuality or their social status, their electoral practices or their sheer physical force. The ubiquitous references to petticoat government within the home also indicated that, contrary to the dictates of contemporary ideology, women might exert their tempers and personalities, but equally their ideals and beliefs within the domestic situation. In investigating some of the forgotten aspects to women's political engagement and in acknowledging that this might encompass both public and domestic pursuits, the chapters in this book capture the 'power of the petticoat' in all its varied manifestations.

Notes

1. This introduction reflects the views of the editors and does not necessarily represent those of the contributors.
2. For further detail on this election contest see Sarah Richardson, 'The Role of Women in Electoral Politics in the West Riding of Yorkshire during the 1830s', *Northern History*, 32 (1996), pp. 133–51, and her 'Independence and Deference: a Study of the Electorate of the West Riding of Yorkshire, 1832–1841' (unpublished Ph.D. thesis, University of Leeds, 1995).
3. Yorkshire Archaeological Society, Staveley MSS, DD115/26, campaign speech by Staveley.
4. Ibid.
5. J. Dunton, *Petticoat Government* (London, 1702), p. 70.
6. Sara Mendelson and Patricia Crawford, *Women in Early Modern England, 1550–1720* (Oxford: Oxford University Press, 1998), pp. 363–5, and R. Bucholz, '"Nothing but Ceremony": Queen Anne and the Limitations of Royal Ritual', *Journal of British Studies*, 30 (1991), pp. 288–323.
7. *The Prerogative of the Breeches: an Answer to Petticoat-Government, Written by a True-Born English Man* (London, 1702); *The Petticoat Plotters or the D——ss of M——h's Club* (London, 1712); and see also *Petticoat Government, in a Letter to the Court Ladies by the Author of the Post-Angel* (London, 1702).
8. Kathleen Wilson, *Sense of the People: Politics, Culture and Imperialism in England, 1715–1785* (Cambridge: Cambridge University Press, 1995), pp. 213–27; Linda Colley, *Britons: Forging the Nation, 1707–1837* (New Haven, CT, and London: Yale University Press, 1992).
9. Colley, *Britons*, pp. 244–8.
10. Gilbert Burnet, *History of My Own Time*, 2 vols (London, 1724), vol. i, p. 83.
11. *Morning Chronicle*, 9 May 1832, cited in J. R. M. Butler, *The Passing of the Great Reform Bill*, 2nd edn (London: Frank Cass, 1964), p. 379.

12. A meeting of the National Political Union in London concluded with three groans for the King and the German Queen (see ibid., pp. 381 and 404). A confidant of the Queen wrote: 'The Queen's fixed impression is that an English revolution is rapidly approaching, and that her own fate is to be that of Marie Antoinette, and she trusts she shall be able to act her part with more courage' (ibid., p. 379).

13. *A Secret History of the Late Petticoat Plot Against the Liberties of the People by an Officer of Her Majesty's Household* (London: W. P. Chubb, 1832?).

14. *Poor Man's Guardian*, 19 May 1832, cited in Butler, *The Passing of the Great Reform Bill*, p. 404.

15. Cited in Anna Clark, *The Struggle for the Breeches: Gender and the Making of the British Working Class* (London: Rivers Oram Press, 1995), p. 254. The ballad goes on to say, 'we'll settle the men, and let them know that now the Queen reigns that petticoats is master'.

16. William Cobbett, *Rural Rides in the Counties of Surrey, Kent, Sussex . . .* , 2 vols (London: William Cobbett, 1830), vol. i, p. 365.

17. Clark, *Struggle for the Breeches*.

18. Ibid., pp. 167–9.

19. Horace Walpole to Hannah More, 26 January 1795; Henry Fielding, *Grub-Street Opera,* act I, scene i; *Spectator*, 305 (1712), p. 4.

20. The article described an attempt by women to impose their Anglo-Catholic views on the Anglican Church: 'the whole coterie (which, in this instance is an undiluted petticoatery)' (*Blackwood's Magazine*, LXV (1849), p. 680).

21. Cited in Juliet Gardiner, *The New Woman: Women's Voices, 1880–1918* (London: Collins & Brown, 1993), p. 12.

22. Cited in Kathryn Gleadle, 'British Women and Radical Politics in the Late Nonconformist Enlightenment, *c.* 1780–1830', in Amanda Vickery (ed.), *Women, Privilege and Power: British Women and Politics, 1780–1998* (Stanford, CA: Stanford University Press, forthcoming).

23. Ruth and Edmund Frow, *Political Women, 1800–1850* (London: Pluto Press, 1989), p. 64.

24. *The Times*, 19 August 1837.

25. Elaine Chalus, '"Invited in the Political Way": Women, Social Politics and Political Society in Eighteenth-Century England', *Historical Journal* (forthcoming). We would like to thank Elaine Chalus for permission to cite this paper prior to publication.

26. The clothing of the Duchess of Devonshire attracted much attention. See Amanda Foreman, *Georgiana, Duchess of Devonshire* (London: HarperCollins, 1998), pp. 76 and 218.

27. Malcolm I. Thomis and Jennifer Grimmett, *Women in Protest, 1800–1850* (London: Croom Helm, 1982), p. 100, and Maria Luddy, *Women in Ireland, 1800–1918: A Documentary History* (Cork: Cork University Press, 1995), p. 250.

28. Wilson, *Sense of the People*, pp. 212–28; Colley, *Britons*, for example p. 341; Nicholas Rogers, *Crowds, Culture and Politics in Georgian Britain* (Oxford: Clarendon Press, 1998), p. 221.

29. Although this book focuses upon middle class and elite women, some chapters also give examples of working-class women's political involvement.

30. See, for example, Vicky Randall, *Women in Politics: An International Perspective* (Basingstoke: Macmillan, 1987).

31. Mary Ann Elston, 'Women and Anti-Vivisection in Victorian England', in
     Nicolaas Rupke (ed.), *Vivisection in Historical Perspective* (London: Routledge,
     1990), pp. 259–94; Hilda Kean, *Animal Rights: Political and Social Change in
     Britain since 1800* (London: Reaktion Books, 1998); Leah Leneman, 'The
     Awakened Instinct: Vegetarianism and the Women's Suffrage Movement in
     Britain', *Women's History Review*, 6 (1997), pp. 271–88; Susan E. Cayleff,
     Wash and Be Healed: The Water-Cure Movement and Women's Health (Phil-
     adelphia, PA: Temple University Press, 1987); Jane B. Donegan, *'Hydropathic
     Highway to Health': Women and Water Cure in Antebellum America* (New York:
     Greenwood Press, 1986); Matthew Hilton, 'The Politics of Consumer Society',
     History Workshop Journal, 45 (1998), pp. 290–6, and see also Chapter 7 in this
     volume.
32. The thesis of women's increasing exclusion from the world of politics has
     been discussed extensively. See, for example, Leonore Davidoff and Cather-
     ine Hall, *Family Fortunes: Men and Women of the English Middle Class, 1780–
     1850* (London: Hutchinson, 1987); Catherine Hall, 'Private Persons versus
     Public Someones: Class, Gender and Politics in England', in Catherine Hall,
     White, Male and Middle-Class. Explorations in Feminism and History (Cam-
     bridge: Polity Press, 1992), pp. 151–71; Joan Landes, *Women and the Public
     Sphere in the Age of the French Revolution* (Ithaca, NY, 1987); see also Eileen
     Janes Yeo (ed.), *Radical Femininity: Women's Self-Representation in the Public
     Sphere* (Manchester: Manchester University Press, 1998), introduction.
33. Gleadle, 'British Women and Radical Politics'.
34. See Chapters 3–7 below.
35. See Chapter 1; Frow and Frow, *Political Women, 1800–1850*, pp. 3–15; and
     Susan Staves, 'Investment, Votes, and "Bribes": Women as Shareholders in
     the Chartered National Companies', in Hilda L. Smith (ed.), *Women Writers
     and the Early Modern British Political Tradition* (Cambridge: Cambridge Uni-
     versity Press, 1998), pp. 259–78.
36. See, for example, Brian Harrison, *Prudent Revolutionaries: Portraits of British
     Feminists between the Wars* (Oxford: Clarendon Press, 1984); Mary Cullen
     and Maria Luddy (eds), *Women, Power and Consciousness in 19th-Century Ire-
     land* (Dublin: Attic Press, 1995) and Margaret Forster, *Significant Sisters: The
     Grassroots of Active Feminism, 1839–1939* (Harmondsworth: Penguin, 1986).
37. Barbara Caine, *Victorian Feminists* (Oxford: Oxford University Press, 1992);
     Sandra Stanley Holton, *Suffrage Days: Stories from the Women's Suffrage Move-
     ment* (London and New York: Routledge, 1996).
38. Sally Alexander, 'Women, Class and Sexual Difference in the 1830s and
     1840s: some Reflections on the Writing of a Feminist History' (1984), reprinted
     in Sally Alexander, (ed.), *Becoming a Woman: And Other Essays in 19th- and
     20th-Century Feminist History* (London: Virago, 1994), p. 125.
39. G. E. Maguire, *Conservative Women: A History of Women and the Conservative
     Party, 1874–1997* (London: Macmillan Press, 1998); Pat Jalland, *Women, Mar-
     riage and Politics, 1860–1914* (Oxford: Clarendon Press, 1986), p. 204; a brief
     consideration of the influence of politicians' mistresses and royal consorts
     may be found in P. J. Jupp, 'The Roles of Royal and Aristocratic Women in
     British Politics, *c.* 1782–1832', in Mary O'Dowd and Sabine Wichert (eds),
     Chattel, Servant or Citizen: Women's Status in Church, State and Society (Belfast:
     The Institute of Irish Studies, The Queen's University, 1995), pp. 103–13.

40. K. D. Reynolds, *Aristocratic Women and Political Society in Victorian Britain* (Oxford: Clarendon Press, 1998).
41. Elaine Chalus, '"That Epidemical Madness": Women and Electoral Politics in the Late Eighteenth Century', in Hannah Barker and Elaine Chalus (eds), *Gender in Eighteenth-Century England: Roles, Representations and Responsibilities* (London and New York: Longman, 1997), pp. 151–78. See also B. J. Harris, 'Women and Politics in Early Tudor England', *Historical Journal*, 33 (1990), pp. 259–81.
42. Rosemary Sweet, 'Women and Civic Elites in the Eighteenth Century'. Paper delivered at '"On the Town": Women in Urban Life in Eighteenth-Century England, *c.* 1660–1820', conference held at the University of Leicester, 29 May 1999. We would like to thank Rosemary Sweet for discussion on this issue.
43. Quoted in William Thompson, *Appeal of One Half the Human Race, Women, Against the Pretensions of the Other Half, Men, To retain them in Political and thence in Civil and Domestic Slavery*, ed. Dolores Dooley (Cork: Cork University Press, 1997, first published 1825), p. 61.
44. See Gleadle, 'British Women and Radical Politics'.
45. John Bohstedt, 'Gender, Household and Community Politics: Women in English Riots, 1790–1810', *Past and Present*, 120 (1988), pp. 88–122; E. P. Thompson, 'The Moral Economy of the English Crowd in the Eighteenth Century', *Past and Present*, 50 (1971), pp. 76–136; Clark, *Struggle for the Breeches*.
46. This is implicit in Catherine Hall, 'The Early Formation of Victorian Domestic Ideology', in Hall, *White, Male and Middle Class*, pp. 74–92, and F. K. Prochaska, *Women and Philanthropy in Nineteenth-Century England* (Oxford: Clarendon Press, 1980).
47. Clare Midgley, *Women against Slavery: The British Campaigns, 1780–1870* (London and New York: Routledge, 1992). See also Louis and Rosemary Billington, '"A Burning Zeal for Righteousness": Women in the British Anti-Slavery Movement, 1820–1860', in Jane Rendall (ed.), *Equal or Different: Women's Politics, 1800–1914* (Oxford: Basil Blackwell, 1987), pp. 82–111.
48. Kathryn Gleadle, *The Early Feminists: Radical Unitarians and the Emergence of the Women's Rights Movement, c. 1831–51* (Basingstoke: Macmillan, 1995); Gleadle, 'British Women and Radical Politics in Late Nonconformist Enlightenment', and Ruth Watts, *Gender, Power and the Unitarians in England, 1760–1860* (London and New York: Longman, 1998).
49. For an overview of approaches to the historical community see Alan Macfarlane, *Reconstructing Historical Communities* (Cambridge: Cambridge University Press, 1977), Chapter 1.
50. For discussion of the electorate as a community, see J. Clyde Mitchell (ed.), *Social Networks in Urban Situations: Analyses of Personal Relationships in Central African Towns* (Manchester: Manchester University Press, 1969); and A. C. Mayer, 'The Significance of Quasi-Groups in the Study of Complex Societies', in M. Banton (ed.), *The Social Anthropology of Complex Societies* (London and New York: Tavistock Publications, 1968). For illustrations of women's role in the electoral process see Chapters 1 and 8 below.
51. See, for example, Blanche Weisen Cook, 'Female Support Networks and Political Activism: Lilian Wald, Crystal Eastman, Emma Goldman', *Chrysalis*, 3 (1977), pp. 43–61; Philippa Levine, *Feminist Lives in Victorian England: Private Roles and Public Commitment* (Oxford: Basil Blackwell, 1990).

52. This is an approach pursued in Angela V. John and Claire Eustance (eds), *The Men's Share? Masculinities, Male Support and Women's Suffrage in Britain, 1890–1920* (London and New York: Routledge, 1997); Gleadle, *The Early Feminists*; and Caine, *Victorian Feminists*.

53. See, for example, Chapters 2 and 3, and also Marjorie Reeves, *Pursuing the Muses: Female Education and Nonconformist Culture, 1700–1900* (London: Leicester University Press, 1997).

54. Among recent contributions one might cite Bridget Hill, *The Republican Virago: The Life and Times of Catherine Macaulay, Historian* (Oxford: Clarendon Press, 1992); Wendy Gunther-Canada, 'The Politics of Sense and Sensibility: Mary Wollstonecraft and Catherine Macaulay Graham on Edmund Burke's Reflections on the Revolution in France', and J. G. A. Pocock, 'Catherine Macaulay: Patriot Historian', both in Smith (ed.), *Women Writers and the Early Modern British Political Tradition*; Miriam Brody, 'The Vindication of the Writes of Women: Mary Wollstonecraft and Enlightenment Rhetoric', in Maria J. Falco, *Feminist Interpretations of Mary Wollstonecraft* (Pennsylvania State University Press, 1996), pp. 104–23.

55. Gary Kelly, *Revolutionary Feminism: The Mind and Career of Mary Wollstonecraft* (Basingstoke: Macmillan, 1992); see also his *Women, Writing and Revolution, 1790–1827* (Oxford: Clarendon Press, 1993). Another example of a woman who combined political and educational practices is Anna Laetitia Barbauld. See Grace A. Ellis, *A Memoir of Anna Laetitia Barbauld*, 2 vols (Boston: J. R. Osgood, 1874).

56. Anne K. Mellor, 'Joanna Baillie and the Counter-Public Sphere', *Studies in Romanticism*, 33 (1994), pp. 559–67.

57. For example, Ann Shteir's fascinating survey of botany in Georgian and Victorian Britain has highlighted how even women's botanical writing may be scrutinised for its gendered and political meanings. Ann B. Shteir, *Cultivating Women, Cultivating Science: Flora's Daughters and Botany in England, 1760 to 1860* (Baltimore, MD, and London: Johns Hopkins University Press, 1996).

1
Women, Electoral Privilege and Practice in the Eighteenth Century

Elaine Chalus

The electoral status of women prior to the Reform Act in 1832 and the extent to which they were involved in electoral politics have thus far received little attention from historians of politics and women. Indeed, women's formal political involvement still tends to be equated with an ability to vote, a qualification which would certainly no longer be applied to eighteenth-century men as a group.[1] It has often been acknowledged that there were some elite women who controlled or managed political interests for themselves or for family members; moreover, recent research has shown that there were also many others who took part in the overall electoral process with varying degrees of commitment and interest.[2] This chapter examines women's place in electoral politics, through a study of the franchise prior to Reform and women's involvement in controverted election cases, and reveals that women in some boroughs had electoral privileges that accorded them a degree of formal political recognition right up to municipal and corporation reform in 1835. It also reveals that, as witnesses in the House of Commons in cases of controverted elections, women's political word could carry legal weight. As onlookers or participants in electoral events, or as long-standing members of local communities who were repositories of electoral memory, women's testimonies helped to determine the outcomes of elections and the nature of franchises – formal contributions in even the most narrowly defined notions of political history.

By applying a broader, more inclusive, understanding of politics to women, albeit predominantly to the women of the political elite, historians have begun to uncover a vibrant and highly politicised society, where women's involvement was far more widespread and integrated than previously imagined. Women took part in a range of politicised activities, extending from writing, publishing and debating, through membership of charities and joint-stock companies, to the more 'traditionally' political areas of social politics, patronage and electoral politics. While not all women were involved in politics, their involvement was *real* and, on the whole, accepted by contemporaries. At times, it was even expected or required. It is exactly this juxtaposition of ongoing, actual female political involvement with idealised notions of domestic femininity and a desire for a 'purified', masculine polity that needs further examination in order to explain what Hilda Smith has so aptly termed the 'confused realities' of early modern female political involvement.[3]

While eighteenth-century women's political status might be thought to be clear, it was never entirely unambiguous. There were always a small number of women who were peeresses in their own right, but they did not sit in the House of Lords. And, while some women at the other end of the social spectrum might vote at the parish level, the women of the electorate seem not to have voted in parliamentary elections. Constraints against women voting were customary, though not legal: women in England and Wales were not legally disenfranchised until the Reform Act of 1832, and did not lose their electoral privileges until the Municipal Corporations Act of 1835.[4] Moreover, idiosyncrasies in regional customs and diversity in borough practices make it impossible to conclude without question that women *never* voted. Derek Hirst's work on the seventeenth century has revealed instances of women who believed that they had the *right* to vote in parliamentary elections, of candidates who tried to poll them, and of election officials who were ready to accept their votes. These practices appear to have fallen out of favour in the eighteenth century, possibly as a result of growing concerns about female propriety among the middling sort and the increasing refinement and codification of electoral practices.[5]

Prior to the reforms of the 1830s, it is arguable that women's electoral involvement was facilitated or legitimated by certain types of franchise and the way they were interpreted in the locality.[6] At the very least, at a time when the vote was seen as a form of personal or familial property and, in some instances, was the direct result of property ownership, female property-owners formed a small but undeniable political constituency.

The nature and extent of the electoral privileges of women who owned property to the value of 40s. freehold in the forty English counties – and thus met the requirement of the county franchise – has received almost no attention from historians. While the Forty Shilling Freeholder Act of 1430, which set the legal framework of the county franchise up to 1832, ensured that the level at which the franchise was set was uniform, it was often creatively interpreted. Local practices and inter-pretations determined which other specific forms of property constituted the equivalent of a land-tax qualification, thereby conferring the right to vote.[7] To compound matters, there was no official register of voters, or even an easy way to prove qualifications. Thus, in practice, the franch-ise varied, even for men. Little is yet known about how single women or widows who technically met the franchise requirement were treated. Since county voters were expected to benefit directly from their free-holds, however, it is possible that they did not share the electoral privil-ege of their counterparts in boroughs where the vote was similarly attached to property. What is known is that husbands voted 'in right of' their wives, and were regularly recognised as doing so, personally and officially.[8]

In close election contests, marriages might even be encouraged and expedited by patrons, candidates or agents in order to increase the number of their voters. Two days before the poll was due to open for the Oxford-shire election of 1754, Lady Susan Keck sent a couple to Oxford. As she pointedly reminded the New Interest's agent in Oxford, he was to ensure that the marriage took place and defray whatever costs it incurred: 'I send you my Bridegroom and Bride I desire you will instantly take out a Licence and Marry them forthwith; you are to pay everything; This makes the Bridegroom a Voter therefore never see my face if they are not married.'[9] Sir Roger Newdigate's notes on the extended parliament-ary deliberations that followed from the eventual double return in this contest suggest that it was assumed that the 'right' to vote could be lost if the marriage broke down and the couple separated. Ed Spragg's vote, for instance, was objected to because, he had voted on an estate that had been and remained the property of his estranged wife, who had been a widow at the time of their marriage. Not only was the estate assessed in her name, but she also received the rent and profits. The most telling argument, however, seems to have been that she had turned Spragg out and had a bond against him.[10] Although Newdigate's notes shed no light on whether women such as Mrs Spragg could then appoint more distant relatives, tenants or neighbours as proxies to vote in their stead, they do suggest that a number of other familial voting combi-nations existed. These included sons voting on their mothers' estates, a son-in-law voting on his wife's mother's estate, a father voting on his daughter's estate and a nephew voting on his aunt's estate. While these votes were open to challenge, it is highly unlikely that such voting practices were either innovative or unique to Oxfordshire, and, in a less heated election, they might well have been accepted without question.[11]

There was even more variation in the franchises that operated in the 203 English boroughs. These differed widely in size, in the character of their electorates and in the extent of their independence. Just as some approached universal male suffrage while others never had more than a handful of voters, so too were some fiercely independent while others were under tight proprietorial or patronal control. Qualifications for enfranchisement were neither uniform nor clearly gendered, and, even among those boroughs which ostensibly had the same franchises, unresolved local disputes about the legal constitution of the electorate, or peculiarities in local electoral custom, could result in uncertainties which could be exploited in the event of a contest.

In the eleven potwalloper or householder boroughs (twelve after 1768), the franchise was in all inhabitant householders; only those receiving poor relief or alms were excluded. In the ninety-two freeman boroughs, the right to vote lay in the freemen, but was frequently complicated both by differing local criteria for the creation of freemen and variations in the franchise (for example, in resident freemen only, in freemen paying scot-and-lot, or in assorted combinations of freemen, freeholders, householders and burgage holders). Similar local stipulations could also qualify the electorate in the thirty-seven scot-and-lot boroughs, where the franchise was otherwise determined by all those inhabitant householders who paid the poor rate. In the twenty-nine burgage boroughs, the franchise appeared equally simple: the right to vote was in the ownership of burgages – pieces of ancient property which were customarily assumed to have had the franchise. However, lack of documentation and reliance upon custom and local memory meant that what constituted a burgage and what residence requirements (if any) were to be applied could be open to debate, especially in boroughs where elections were infrequent. The six freeholder boroughs were an offshoot of burgage boroughs, in that the franchise also rested in the ownership of property: freeholds, in this case.

The parliamentary historians Edward and Annie Porritt pointed out at the turn of the twentieth century that, women's electoral involvement in some boroughs (particularly householder and scot-and-lot boroughs) might be limited to influence and acting as 'the channels between the bribers and the bribed', but that women in freeman and burgage boroughs (treating the freeholder and burgage boroughs as one) had 'places recognized by custom and by the determination of election committees'. These, the Porritts concluded, amounted to official electoral privileges, with those privileges in burgage boroughs being the most direct and valuable.[12]

Considering that the freeman, burgage and freeholder boroughs as a group comprised 125 out of the total of 203 English boroughs, this is a striking conclusion. Not only does it suggest that the potential for recognised female electoral involvement was much higher than historians have previously assumed, but in re-opening the vexed question of the nature of women's political involvement as a whole it also raises larger questions about the definitions of, and relations between, the eighteenth-century extra-parliamentary and parliamentary nations. The very difficulty of categorising women's political involvement as public or private, direct or indirect, formal or informal, reveals their shortcomings as analytical tools and emphasises interconnections on the ground. Were women formally or informally involved in politics if they met all of the necessary requirements to vote (except gender), if they could assign their votes to men of their choice, and if, as a result, they were canvassed in the same way as their male counterparts? Were they members of the parliamentary or the extra-parliamentary nation?[13]

In the ninety-two freeman boroughs, the extent of women's electoral privileges and the ways in which they were administered varied somewhat according to local practice, but followed a general pattern. Women who were the daughters of freemen (or, occasionally, their widows) had the right to make their husbands freemen and voters. In boroughs such as Bristol, Grimsby, Ludlow, Maldon and Wells, this process was straightforward; in others, it was more complicated. In Hertford, the privilege was limited to the eldest daughters of freemen who had no sons, whereas in Dover, men retained their freeman status only in their wives' lifetimes.[14] While there is no easy way to measure the effect that this privilege had on levels of women's politicisation and activity, it certainly operated to give them local status and an undeniable platform for wielding influence over their husbands' votes. It also had additional personal benefit, as it was an acknowledged, if intangible, supplement to a woman's value in marriage, a fact that was not lost on contemporaries:

> I am a Countryman of small Fortune, who accidentally fell in Love with a Freeman's Daughter of your City. The Agreeableness of her person, and the Recommendation of her being a good Manager in her Father's Family, together with the Certainty of my being distinguished by the honourable Title of a *Free-Burgess* of BRISTOL, soon prevailed on my Love, my Industry, and Ambition to determine my Choice.[15]

The contest which occurred in Bristol in 1754 placed this electoral privilege on centre stage. In an attempt to control the outcome of the election, a by-law was passed that attempted to limit the number of non-resident voters. Only the daughters of Bristol freemen who remained inhabitants of the city were to be allowed to make their husbands voters. This resulted in an election address, (cited above) aimed directly at 'the Free-women of Bristol'.[16] The address drew upon the traditional political rhetoric of urban independence and placed the women firmly within its remit, reminding them that if they allowed the historical privileges of their 'Sisters' to be illegitimately removed by this product of 'Arbitrary Power', they were accepting the first step in a campaign to remove all female privileges – thereby emasculating the borough by prohibiting their honest and independent freemen husbands from voting.[17] The married 'Free-women' of Bristol were therefore given two charges: they were to use their interest with their husbands to ensure that non-resident women's privileges were restored; and they were to ensure that their husbands voted for the candidate who represented liberty and honourable independence:

> Will your Husbands, Ladies, who addressed the H[onoura]ble House of C[ommo]ns against the *General Naturalization* and *Jew Bills*, suffer this Partiality of Behaviour? And will *you* not rouse them out of their Lethargy? Remember your *Sisters* in the *Country*. Make it a Point for them, the Free-Electors of BRISTOL to redress their Wrongs If Mr. N[ugen]t be not to be depended on, as from the Hint just given is too clear. – Why then, I think, you must try what Sir JOHN PHILLIPS can do *elsewhere*. – Entreat that real, that resolute Champion of Liberty; and doubt not his Resolution, if he promises, to espouse your Cause. Make *This, one Condition* of your Husbands Votes and Interest.[18]

Although it was rare to seek female political support so openly in print, this address reflects two persistent eighteenth-century beliefs about women and politics: that women with political interests retained political *influence* even after marriage; and that women's influence over men's votes was *real*. Agents and candidates ignored it at their peril. Lord Townshend, recording the support of voters in Tamworth in 1765, knew only too well that it was necessary to have wives and daughters on side in order to secure men's votes. An initial pledge of support could have little meaning if the man's wife was adamantly opposed. Despite two previous canvasses of one voter, and an initial pledge of support, it was not until the third canvass that Townshend seemed secure of the vote, commenting laconically 'his Wife in better Humour'.[19]

Few candidates appear to have taken women's privileges in freeman boroughs as far as John Huske did in Maldon in 1763. Described by a historian of the borough as 'a tough, unscrupulous adventurer from New Hampshire', Huske was a friend of John Wilkes, who helped him canvass the borough. Huske conducted a ruthless campaign against the sitting member, Bamber Gascoyne, and won the seat through the support of the Corporation and the creation of freemen, despite having the Government interest against him.[20] His reported method of canvassing the freemen was effective, but unconventional. As the *Chelmsford Chronicle* reminded readers, when eulogising him years later, he had focused on the women who had the right to make freemen, rather than on their husbands:

> The novelty of this mode raised the curiosity of the ladies, in a company of which, he was one day asked, Why he never solicited the men, as was most customary on such occasions: To which he replied, I have ever, ladies, entertained the highest opinion of your sex, especially in the power and influence you have over us; but, in this respect, I think myself highly justified in asking you, ladies, rather than your husbands, as it is to you they owe such a privilege, and it is but justice that you should have some influence in the disposal of it.

This anecdote, and the accompanying sexual innuendo that Huske wanted to be the women's 'little member',[21] may be apocryphal, but were not out of keeping with Huske's character. By stripping away the male façade of eighteenth-century politics, and bluntly acknowledging the reality of female influence, he would have been playing up to beliefs that were widely held.

Women's electoral privilege in freeman boroughs may have sanctioned the use of female influence, but it did not give them a more direct electoral role. It was in burgage and freeholder boroughs that women were the most frequently, visibly and directly involved in electoral politics.[22] There, the right to vote was attached to the ownership of the relevant form of property; consequently, women who inherited or purchased burgages in the twenty-nine English burgage boroughs, or freeholds in the six freeholder boroughs, technically possessed the same right to vote as men.[23] This involved two groups of women directly in local electoral politics: the women of the electorate, who might own or purchase individual burgages; and the women of the political elite, who might own or purchase enough of the burgages to have a significant or controlling interest in the borough.[24] It was among the former that the tension between gender and politics in the eighteenth century was the most obvious. While these women's right to vote was recognised, they were prevented by custom from exercising it. Instead, a practice grew up whereby they were allowed to appoint a man to vote in their stead. Among the latter, women seem to have operated in conjunction with their agents in the same way as men: they acquired boroughs if and when available, and ensured that appropriately minded tenants were installed, complete with any necessary paperwork, in time to meet the borough's residence requirements (if any) prior to an election.

Evidence survives of candidates trying to use the votes of widowed burgage holders to their advantage in seventeenth-century Knaresborough and Richmond. It was only after the disqualification of widows' votes in Richmond in 1678 that the practice of the 'discreet transfer' of women's right to vote emerged in burgage boroughs.[25] By the second half of the eighteenth century, this practice had become customary. Evidence of men voting on their wives' and mothers' burgages can be found as early as 1699 in Pontefract and Corfe Castle, and the practice continued well into the nineteenth century.[26] Writing in 1816, for example, T. B. Oldfield named the Hon. Charles Anderson Pelham as having the most political influence in the borough of Yarmouth, Isle of Wight, where he held twelve burgages in the right of his wife.[27] The amount of influence that wives retained over the way their husbands voted ranged widely, but marriage certainly curtailed women's ability to exercise their electoral privilege to its full extent. Like women in freeman boroughs, they were unable to withdraw the right to vote from their husbands and assign it elsewhere as long as their marriages lasted. This was exactly where unmarried women and widows who were burgage holders benefited. They were not only expected to appoint men to vote for them – family members, distant relations, tenants or neighbours, as long as they met local requirements – but they could also change their assignations if they wished.[28]

The limitations imposed by surviving sources and a recognition of constantly changing patterns of landownership in the eighteenth century make attempts at quantifying women's overall burgage and freehold ownership extremely difficult. While certainly a minority interest, women could form a significant minority, as revealed by a report from Lord Irwin for the borough of Horsham in 1764. Horsham was a burgage borough with a notoriously complicated variety of votes. At mid-century, it had eighty-three votes, nineteen of which were in women.[29] The trend towards elite consolidation of power over these sorts of boroughs in the late eighteenth and early nineteenth centuries undoubtedly had an impact on small owners, male and female alike, but to what extent it eroded women's electoral privilege has yet to be studied.

Although the right to assign a vote was a formality for those women who were uninterested in politics or whose boroughs were uncontested, it could be turned to real advantage by women who were politically inclined or particularly astute. The ability to choose voters whose views tallied with their own provided women with a means of expressing their own political opinions, albeit at one remove. The ownership of property, especially burgages, also gave women status in the community. With the approach of elections, if there was even the hint of a contest, this political status could be turned to financial advantage. Like their male counterparts, they were courted by politicians hoping to make votes and, depending upon the virulence of the contest, might command significant sums for their political support. As early as 1747, for example, the deliberations on the controverted Westbury election reveal a widowed burgage holder, Mrs Cockle, being given the vast sum of £100, 'as a consideration' for her 'Assignment'.[30] Not all transactions were so blatant or so lucrative. As in other boroughs, 'considerations' might come in the form of debts being paid or written off, favours being proffered or promises given. And, of course, for those women and men who were willing to trade future political interest for immediate financial gain, there was always the possibility of the ultimate 'consideration', that of taking advantage of a bidding war by contending political interests and selling up to the highest bidder.[31]

At the level of the political elite, burgage ownership was one way of establishing or securing a family's political interest. Some burgages were passed down through women, others were managed by women for underage sons, while yet others were owned and contested by women. In the second half of the century, Lady Andover nominated to one of the seats at Castle Rising; when her daughter married, the burgages, and the political interest, formed part of her portion.[32] Similarly, Sarah Richardson's recent work on Elizabeth Lawrence, the early nineteenth-century proprietor of the borough of Ripon, reveals a woman who inherited her controlling political interest from female relatives. As Richardson has demonstrated, Lawrence operated in the same way as a male borough patron, showing her commitment to the borough through regular displays of charity and benevolence, frequent treating, and continuous involvement in civic politics.[33]

Splitting burgages between co-heirs could be a risky business if the co-heirs (and/or their spouses) were politically ambitious. Rivalry between different branches of a family could upset the balance of power in a borough and set off tremendous and enduring political contests as in the conflict over the borough of Downton. This began with Lord Feversham's death in 1763, when his estate was divided between a distant cousin, Thomas Duncombe, and his two daughters. Duncombe acquired the settled estate, but one of the daughters, Anne, Lady Radnor, acquired a portion of the burgages at Downton. When an injunction trying to force the sale of these burgages was overturned in Chancery, the struggle for control of the borough began in earnest. The conflict was not settled with Duncombe's death. He bequeathed his estate in Downton to his daughter, who was married to Robert Shafto. Shafto contested the borough against the other 'family' interest in 1780. As late as 1790, control of the borough was still unsettled.[34]

Of course, proprietorship was no guarantee of uninterrupted electoral peace. Women did fight, sometimes fiercely, to maintain or increase their, or their family's interest, in burgage boroughs. In East Grinstead at the beginning of the nineteenth century, the widowed duchess of Dorset's control extended to ownership of twenty-nine of the thirty-six burgages and the appointment of the borough's returning officer (the Bailiff) at her annual court. Still, she had to contend with a challenge from a radical candidate in 1802.[35] Widows with political aspirations for their underage sons seem to have been especially keen to preserve their sons' inheritance. Even Sir James Lowther, the boroughmonger of the century, owed some of his political interest to his mother's efforts during his minority. The young Sir James had been left sixty-seven burgages in the borough of Appleby, where an established compromise operated to share the representation with the Thanets, the other leading political family. When the Thanets broke the compromise by having a candidate of their own elected as mayor out of turn in 1751, Katherine Lowther acted quickly in order to prevent the Thanets from gaining control of the borough. Between 1751 and the contested election of 1754, she purchased another twenty-seven burgages. Although she did not capture the Thanets' seat (it may not have been her intent), she did succeed in holding her own family's seat. She also put enough pressure on the Thanets that they renewed the political compromise.[36]

One of the most heated battles for control over a burgage borough in the late eighteenth century pitched the widowed Lady Irwin against the eleventh duke of Norfolk in Horsham in Sussex.[37] The Irwin family had controlled the borough since the 1720s, but the death of Lord Irwin in 1778 without a male heir left Lady Irwin in control. Matters remained calm until the 1780s, when the young duke of Norfolk converted to Anglicanism and decided to become politically active. That Lady Irwin was a staunch supporter of the Administration, and had placed both seats at the disposal of the Administration in the 1780 and 1784 elections, and Norfolk was a Foxite Whig, only exacerbated matters. Further complications arose because voting qualifications in Horsham were so difficult to ascertain. The burgages were diverse and poorly recorded: houses, barns, stables, fields, and an unverifiable assortment of small plots of land, all possessed votes.[38] In the lead-up to the 1790 election, a purchasing war ensued between Lady Irwin and Norfolk. Owners of burgages were targeted by both parties and the price of houses with attached votes was reported to have risen 'near a thousand per cent'.[39] It is a testimony to Lady Irwin's success that, by the time of the election, Norfolk's only chance of defeating her rested on putting his steward in charge of a Court Baron packed with his supporters, called for the same day as the election, which refused to recognise any of her new votes.[40] When Lady Irwin lost the election as a result, she promptly petitioned and succeeded in having her candidates seated.[41] The irregularities of the contest were such, however, that nine separate actions at law resulted, the last of which was finally settled twelve years after the election.

While it might be argued that the electoral battle was inherently unequal, given Norfolk's status and the depth of his purse (he spent £70,000 on the borough), the fact that one of the two principals was a woman seems not to have been an issue. Party considerations, self-interest, greed, and a general desire for change, were the central concerns of the voters. As to the proprietors, Lady Irwin was certainly a match for Norfolk in terms of electioneering strategy and practice.[42] She was also determined to hold on to the borough, fighting yet another contest against Norfolk in 1806. Once again her candidates were defeated, only to be re-seated on petition. In fact, Norfolk only gained control of the borough after Lady Irwin's death in 1807: he then bought the Irwin interest outright – for the record sum of £91,475.[43]

While women's electoral privileges granted them varying degrees of official recognition and they were frequently involved in the practice of electioneering,[44] it is with their involvement in the formal legal processes which were used to challenge and resolve electoral outcomes – the post-election scrutinies that took place in the locality and the deliberations that followed petitions to Parliament – that their part in the making of electoral history is most clearly recorded. While the women of the political elite secured witnesses and forwarded useful, perhaps even crucial, evidence to the men conducting the proceedings, their involvement is only revealed anecdotally in the sources. Thus, in 1754, we find

Lady Parker, the young wife of one of Oxfordshire's New Interest's candidates, procuring witnesses to 'regularify' New Interest votes. Similarly, Lady Susan Keck sends two 'informations' to Sanderson Miller at the beginning of the parliamentary deliberations in January 1755, instructing him to deal with them with 'the utmost expedition', as 'such sort of things we shall begin with first in the House'.[45] Although elite women do not appear to have testified in controverted election cases, they were far from invisible. Indeed, by the 1760s it had become positively fashionable for women from the opposing sides to attend the deliberations in the Commons to support their sides.[46] Lady Mary Coke, for example, records attending the Commons at least eight times over the Cumberland election in 1768, usually as part of a group of eight or nine women.[47]

Before George Grenville's act of 1770, proceedings on controverted elections were heard by a committee of the whole House and took up inordinate amounts of time at the beginning of every new parliament. Particularly violent contests often resulted in long parliamentary battles and scores of witnesses. Deliberations on the 1754 Oxfordshire election alone occupied the Commons for the better part of three days a week between January and April 1755.[48] Grenville's act devolved the responsibility for settling election outcomes on to carefully chosen select committees. Whether this put a stop to elite female attendance is difficult to tell, but it did not affect the practice of calling female witnesses.

Coverage of controverted elections is far from complete, but witnesses' depositions for a significant number survive in the *Commons Journals* and in the separately published reports on controverted elections which began to emerge in the late eighteenth century. These provide an intriguing, almost unrivalled, perspective on the political culture of the electorate, as well as significant information about women's place therein. Mustered as witnesses by the opposing sides (by agents and candidates, as well as by local landowners and patrons), men and women from the ranks of the electorate and below were transported to the proceedings, where they were housed and fed, and their costs covered, for the duration of their stay. This was an expensive undertaking, but candidates were not allowed to shirk their responsibilities.[49]

In general, the testimonies of male and female witnesses were very similar: both gave evidence to prove or disprove votes, to establish the nature of electoral dealings with regard to the actions of specific individuals (usually regarding partiality, bribery or corruption), and to determine the local understanding and practice of the franchise. Testimonies were gendered to the extent that specialist legal knowledge, when required, was provided by men, while women were more likely to provide knowledge of local custom and electoral practice over time (for which they may have had a demographic edge).

While it is often impossible to determine the motivations of witnesses, the truthfulness of their statements or the extent to which they were coached, the efforts which were put into securing them and supporting them in London, and the energy with which causes were argued, demonstrates the importance accorded them by contemporaries. The existence of women's testimonies casts into sharp relief the tensions and ambiguities surrounding women's place in eighteenth-century politics. Their very presence as witnesses is a tacit recognition of the fact that women were seen as political actors when it was expedient to do so. That their political word was granted legal weight and used in the codification of politics is also telling.

Depositions given in controverted election cases reinforce the notion that women acted as agents or intermediaries for their husbands, serving as safe conduits for offers, suggestions and bribes.[50] They also confirm that contemporaries believed women to possess influence over men's votes. When this was the case, their electoral support was sought directly. Promises of improved financial situations or future financial security for the woman's family appear to have been the most common lures. In the case of the Morpeth election in 1769, Jane Atkinson testified that the returning officer 'came to her and told her, if she could persuade her Husband, who was a Mandamus Man, to give a Vote in the *Carlisle* Interest, he should have a Tide Waiter's Place of £40 a year, and said now was the Time to make her Fortune; – that she should never want for any Thing'.[51]

What is most important, however, is that women's depositions reveal that they acted as repositories of local electoral memory. This sort of personal knowledge was particularly important in determining borough franchises or the validity of individual votes at a time when documentary evidence was frequently either scarce or contradictory (a legacy, in part, of the political manoeuvring of James II) and when there were often long gaps between elections. While both old men and old women served in this capacity, women's longevity seems to have played to their advantage. Indeed, this may have been one of the few times that being an old woman was desirable in the eighteenth century. Given the stated ages of some female witnesses, it is even possible that their ages were occasionally exaggerated for impact. Their memories of the past were regarded as useful if the issue was the 'general reputation of the borough as to the right of voting'.[52] Then, drawing upon their own memories, their knowledge of their community over time, and their understanding of the way that the franchise had been interpreted in the past, they provided the Commons with an oral history (or contesting oral histories) of a borough.

In 1785, for example, the deliberations over the Saltash election revolved around whether the right of election was in the corporation or in the burgages. Of the nine witnesses called in, two were women, Jane Reanes, aged eighty-one, and Joan Dunn, aged fifty-four. Between them, they gave details on the voting practices that had been used in the 1722 and 1741 elections, respectively. They also provided their interpretation of the franchise, dwelling in this instance on their lack of familiarity with the term 'freeburgess'. Reanes claimed the right 'to be in *freeholders, if they lived in houses of their own, and in sworn freemen also* – described a freeholder to be one who had a *house of land*; had heard such persons called by the name of *freeholders*, and by no other'. In her 'younger days', she said, freeholders had always voted. Dunn reported having 'frequently heard it said' that freeholders and sworn freemen had a right to vote; like Reanes, she claimed never to have heard of freeburgesses and only to have heard of burgage tenants recently. She also pointed out that locally freeholders were generally referred to as freemen, even if they had not been sworn: her father had been introduced as such when he had voted in 1741.[53]

Women's testimonies were also useful in elections for boroughs where the vote was attached to property in some way. In potwalloper or householder boroughs, it was necessary to prove that a voter was capable of sustaining himself. He had to have a fireplace in which to cook (by extension, his dwelling-place had to have a chimney) and he had to live in what was a household in itself, not an electorally convenient partition of one (that is, it had to have a separate doorway and a history of being a separate home).[54] These were just the sort of details that long-standing members of a community could provide.

The Bramber election of 1768 provides a good example of such a case.[55] The (eventually successful) case depended upon the petitioners being able to prove the partiality of the constable, qualify two of their own votes and disqualify seven of the sitting members' votes. In order to do this, they had to establish that the right of election in the borough rested in persons 'inhabiting in ancient Houses, or in Houses built on ancient Foundations, paying Scot and Lot'. The personal and political memories of women, ranging ostensibly in age between sixty-four and ninety-one, played a large part in constructing the cases on each side.

This case also acts as a snapshot of a society in transition between oral and written cultures. The weight that was attached to local, anecdotal

knowledge, expressed orally, even in the presence of valid legal documents, was manifest in the qualification of Richard Holland's vote.
Two witnesses were called: Elizabeth Thomas, who indicated that she
had known some of the buildings in question for seventy years; and an
attorney, John Gates. Thomas testified first and drew on her memory
and knowledge of the community to provide the traditional burden of
proof:

> she knew the House *Richard Holland* lived in; that *William Cook* lived
> there before him; that the Persons who have lived in that House
> voted for it – that *Holland* was a Servant to Mr. *Lidbetter* before he
> came to live in that House, and continued to be so – that he came to
> be there Three Days before the Election – that *Cook* died about a Week
> before the Election, and his Widow gave Possession of the House to
> *Holland*, and did not live there herself at the Day of the Election –
> that she had some Goods in the Houses [*sic*] and so had *Holland*; he
> brought in a Bed and Bedstead, which was put up, and other Goods;
> and that there was no other Bed in the House – that he came into the
> House on purpose to live there.

All that then remained to secure the qualification was for Gates to present a written agreement between Holland and Widow Cook, which
demonstrated that he would be paying the poor rate, and a rental agreement between Holland and the marquis of Granby, the landlord.[56]
  Securing the disqualification of the seven votes depended entirely on
testimonies based on personal memory and local electoral practice. In
particular, the witnesses sought to prove that the houses upon which
the votes had been given did not, and had not in the past, complied
with the franchise. In total, the petitioners' counsel called ten witnesses,
six of whom were women; the sitting members' counsel responded in
kind. Special effort was taken to disqualify votes by demonstrating that
the voters' houses had only become houses in living memory. Mary
Chipper, aged ninety-one, testified that she had known Joseph French's
house, the Malt House, for sixty years. She maintained that it had been
a working malt house until the reign of Queen Anne and that an attempt
to vote from it had been disallowed in the past. Similarly, Elizabeth
Simmons, aged eighty-three, stated that while John Emery's house, the
Smith's Forge, had been a house in her lifetime, she could remember
her father speaking of it as a working smithy.
  Determining the legitimacy of Charles Best's vote was more complicated and somewhat more open to interpretation, as he had voted on half

of a house which, it was claimed, had had a vote in the past. The arguments used against his vote were given cumulative weight by the testimonies of three female witnesses, Mary Thorpe, Hannah Taverner and Elizabeth Thomas. Thorpe, aged sixty-four, established that the house had been one dwelling with one vote in her lifetime: her father had lived in the entire house and had voted for it. At that time, though, it had had only one door and one staircase, which made a strong case against its legal viability as a separate dwelling. Taverner corroborated this by testifying that she also remembered the house when Thorpe's family had lived there. She was able to provide additional details, however, by roughly establishing the timing of the partition and the belief that it possessed a vote. By the time her husband had lived in the house thirty years earlier, it had been divided and both halves had voted. Thomas provided the clinching argument. Her husband had lived in the parlour end of the house (the end which Best presently occupied), but his vote had been disallowed because the house was deemed to have only one vote. This was because the house was not truly divided: all, she claimed, that separated the two halves downstairs was a board partition, whereas upstairs it was not divided at all.[57]

To return, then, to the questions which opened this essay, what light has this study of electoral privilege and practice thrown on women's electoral status and their involvement in electoral politics prior to Reform? I have argued that, although denied by custom from voting, eighteenth-century women were by no means completely excluded from formal political involvement. In freeman, burgage and freeholder boroughs, women possessed recognised electoral privileges until 1835. As vote-makers and signifiers of political entitlement in freeman boroughs, they were bearers of status and figures of political influence. As possessors of votes in burgage and freeholder boroughs, they could be political figures in their own right. These privileges involved women of the electorate, not just the women of the political elite, upon whom most of the recent research into eighteenth-century women's involvement in politics has focused. This is particularly marked in the deliberations that followed controverted elections. It is here, more clearly than anywhere else, with women's appearance as witnesses in Parliament, that they made political history. As the repositories of electoral memory and local custom and knowledge, women could and did play a significant part in determining the outcomes of elections or the nature of borough franchises. Ironically, they were real participants, not only in eighteenth-century politics, but also in the codification process which in 1832 would deny them and define the polity as masculine.

Acknowledgements

I would like to thank Hannah Barker, Kathy Gleadle, Paul Langford, Sarah Richardson, Roey Sweet, Stephen Taylor, and the participants of the 'Power of the Petticoat' conference for helping me to develop the ideas found in this essay. I would also like to thank the Rector and Fellows of Exeter College, Oxford, for permission to consult the Bray Papers. Permission to use the Du Cane Manuscripts is courtesy of the County Archivist at the West Sussex Record Office. The funding for the initial research was provided by the Social Sciences and Humanities Research Council of Canada.

Notes

1. Although, for instance, recent and important publications by Kathleen Wilson and Nicholas Rogers cast new light on the political activities of 'the people' or 'the crowd', and are sensitive to gender, revealing aspects of women's political involvement, they assume women's exclusion from formal political participation: Kathleen Wilson, *Sense of the People: Politics, Culture and Imperialism in England, 1715–1785* (Cambridge: Cambridge University Press, 1995); Nicholas Rogers, *Crowds, Culture and Politics in Georgian Britain* (Oxford: Clarendon Press, 1998).
2. For an introduction to the involvement of the eighteenth-century female political elite in the electoral process, see my '"That Epidemical Madness": Women and Electoral Politics in the late Eighteenth Century', in Hannah Barker and Elaine Chalus (eds), *Gender in Eighteenth-Century England: Roles, Representations and Responsibilities* (London: Longman, 1997), pp. 151–78. For a more in-depth exploration of their overall political involvement, see my *Women in English Political Life, 1754–1790* (Oxford: Oxford University Press, forthcoming).
3. Hilda L. Smith, 'Introduction', in Hilda L. Smith (ed.), *Women Writers and the Early Modern British Political Tradition* (Cambridge: Cambridge University Press, 1998), pp. 9–12.
4. H. J. Hanham (ed.), *The Nineteenth-Century Constitution: Documents and Commentary* (London: Cambridge University Press, 1969), pp. 264–5. Interestingly, the Scottish version of the Representation of the People Act (1832) refers only to 'Person', not 'Male Person'. See also Derek Hirst, *The Representative of the People? Voters and Voting in England under the Early Stuarts* (Cambridge: Cambridge University Press, 1975), p. 19; James Vernon, *Politics and the People: A Study in English Political Culture, c. 1815–1867* (Cambridge: Cambridge University Press, 1993), p. 39.
5. Hirst, *Representative of the People?*, pp. 18–19.
6. The following paragraphs draw upon John Brooke, *The House of Commons, 1754–1790: Introductory Survey* (London: Oxford University Press, 1964), pp. 1–50; Sir Lewis Namier and John Brooke, *The House of Commons, 1754–1790*, 3 vols (London: HMSO, 1964), vol. i; Frank O'Gorman, *Voters, Patrons, and Parties: The Unreformed Electoral System of Hanoverian England, 1734–1832* (Oxford: Clarendon Press, 1992), pp. 27–67; Edward Porritt with Annie G. Porritt,

The Unreformed House of Commons: Parliamentary Representation before 1832, 2 vols (Cambridge: Cambridge University Press, 1909), vol. i. Borough franchises were notoriously difficult to define, a fact that is reflected in historians' differing methods of categorising and counting them.

7. I would like to thank Stephen Taylor for helping me to clarify my thinking about county politics and for sharing his insights into the interplay between electoral law and local practice in the counties.

8. T. B. Oldfield, *The Representative History of Great Britain and Ireland: Being a History of the House of Commons and the Counties, Cities, and Boroughs of the United Kingdom from the Earliest Period*, 6 vols (London: Baldwin, Cradock and Joy, 1816), vol. iii.

9. Exeter College Archives, Oxford, Oxfordshire Parliamentary Elections, Bray Papers (hereafter BP), L.IV.7.C/32: Lady Susan Keck to Revd Thomas Bray [recd 15 April 1754].

10. Warwickshire County Record Office, Warwick, CR136 B.2524 B/8, 11 January 1755 VII, no. 320, Parliamentary notes on the Oxfordshire Election of 1754 by Sir Roger Newdigate.

11. Ibid., B.2524–9.

12. Porritt and Porritt, *Unreformed House of Commons*, vol. i, pp. 39–41

13. Ibid., Brooke, *House of Commons, passim*.

14. J. Cowley (ed.), *Orders and Resolutions of the House of Commons on Controverted Elections and Returns*, 2nd edn (London: J. Stagg and D. Browne, 1736), pp. 23, 107–8, 159–60; Porritt and Porritt, *Unreformed House of Commons*, vol. i, p. 78.

15. 'The Dundry Petition: Or the Countryman's Humble Address to the Free-Women of the City of Bristol', in *The Bristol Contest: Being a Collection of all the Papers Published by Both Parties, on the Election, 1754* (Bristol [1754?]), pp. 54–6. My thanks to Madge Dresser for bringing this to my attention.

16. Ibid.

17. This appeal to urban independence and traditional rights – in this case the argument that a by-law made by the modern corporation could not legally modify a privilege granted to the 'Married Daughters of Freemen of the City of Bristol' by Elizabeth I – was both part of the rhetoric of urban borough politics and the reality of their expression. For a closer examination of the link between civic pride and political independence, for men, if not for women, see Rosemary Sweet, 'Freemen and Independence in English Borough Politics, *c.*1770–1830', *Past and Present*, 161 (1998), pp. 84–175.

18. 'Dundry Petition', p. 55.

19. Brit. Lib., Add. MS 45112, fos 17d–18, Tamworth Poll Book. The assumption that wives could have influence over their husbands' votes was reflected in electioneering practices and was satirised in contemporary writing: see, for example, *The Humours of a Country Election* (London: J. Roberts, 1734); *The Connoisseur* (1754). I explore the subject of influence in '"But his wife governed": Women and the Politics of Influence in Eighteenth-Century England' (forthcoming); see also my 'That Epidemical Madness'. For the nineteenth century, see Chapter 8.

20. John Raymond Smith, 'The Borough of Maldon, 1688–1768' (unpublished M.Phil. thesis, University of Leicester, 1981), p. 150. Even Namier and Brooke described it as a 'brazen and skilful campaign': Namier and Brooke, *House of Commons*, vol. i, p. 280.

21. *Chelmsford Chronicle*, 10 December 1773.
22. Porritt and Porritt, *Unreformed House of Commons*, vol. i, p. 41.
23. Brooke, *House of Commons*, p. 44; Namier and Brooke, *House of Commons*, vol. i, p. 31.
24. The Porritts present a similar breakdown: Porritt and Porritt, *Unreformed House of Commons*, vol. i, p. 41.
25. Hirst, *Representative of the People?*, pp. 18–19.
26. Ibid.
27. Oldfield, *Representative History of Great Britain and Ireland*, vol. iii, p. 570.
28. Porritt and Porritt, *Unreformed House of Commons*, vol. i, p. 40.
29. William Albery, *A Parliamentary History of the Ancient Borough of Horsham, 1295–1885, with Some Account of Every Contested Election*, intro. Hilaire Belloc (London: Longmans, 1927), pp. 93–7.
30. *Commons Journals*, xxv (1745–50), p. 577.
31. See, for example, n. 37 below.
32. Oldfield, *Representative History of Great Britain and Ireland*, vol. iv, p. 271.
33. Ibid., p. 308. Sarah Richardson, 'The Role of Women in Electoral Politics in Yorkshire during the 1830s', *Northern History*, 32 (1996), pp. 133–51.
34. Alexander Luders, *Reports of the Proceedings in Committee of the House of Commons upon Controverted Elections (1785–1790)*, 3 vols (London, 1825), vol. i, p. 114; Namier and Brooke, *House of Commons*, vol. i, pp. 32–3.
35. Oldfield, *Representative History of Great Britain and Ireland*, vol. v, p. 59; O'Gorman, *Voters, Patrons and Parties*, p. 305.
36. Brian Bonsall, *Sir James Lowther and Cumberland & Westmorland Elections, 1754–1775* (Manchester: Manchester University Press, 1960), pp. v, 15–35. Katherine Lowther's involvement in Appleby was not unique; she was also involved in a battle of burgage purchases with Lord Egremont in the borough of Cockermouth in 1756: ibid., pp. 37–42.
37. West Sussex Record Office, Chichester (hereafter WSRO), Add. MS 5190–5203, Horsham election, 1790; Albery, *Parliamentary History of the Ancient Borough of Horsham*, pp. 120–253.
38. O'Gorman, *Voters, Patrons, and Parties*, p. 35; Albery, *Parliamentary History of the Ancient Borough of Horsham*, pp. 75, 114–253; L. B. Namier, *The Structure of Politics at the Accession of George III* (London: Macmillan, 1957), p. 135; Namier and Brooke, *House of Commons*, vol. i, p. 393.
39. *Sussex Advertiser*, 8 September 1788, as quoted in Albery, *Parliamentary History of the Ancient Borough of Horsham*, p. 130. In order to have new burgesses placed on the burgage roll, they had to be admitted at a Court Baron. While Lady Irwin amassed an additional thirty-six burgesses which would have consolidated her control over the borough between 1774 and 1787, no Court Baron was held in that period, so they remained unrecorded.
40. WSRO, Add. MS 5192 [unfoliated], 'Memm. of What passed on the Election of two Members for Horsham on Saturday 19 June 1790'.
41. Lady Irwin's candidates – her son-in-law, Lord William Gordon, and James Baillie, a West India merchant – achieved 20 and 19 votes respectively against Norfolk's candidates, Timothy Shelley and Wilson Braddyll, who secured 25 and 24 votes each: *Commons Journals*, xlvi (1790–1), pp. 28–9, *passim.*
42. Albery, *Parliamentary History of the Ancient Borough of Horsham*, p. 242.

43. Ibid., p. 253.
44. For more detailed discussion of social politics, see my 'That Epidemical Madness'; also my '"Invited in the Political Way": Women, Social Politics and Political Society in Eighteenth-Century England', *Historical Journal* (forthcoming).
45. BP, L.IV.7.C/76, Mary, Lady Parker to Revd Thomas Bray, St James's Square, 21 December 1754; 'Lady Susan Keck to Sanderson Miller, Great Tew, 9 January 1755', in *An Eighteenth-Century Correspondence*, ed. Lilian Dickins and Mary Stanton (London: John Murray, 1910), p. 247. For Lady Susan Keck's interest in the scrutiny that followed the 1754 Oxfordshire election and for her efforts in securing witnesses for the subsequent, equally political, coroner's inquest and Rag Plot, see BP, L.IV.7.C/32, Lady Susan Keck to Revd Thomas Bray [n.d., recd 15 April 1754].
46. Lady Caroline Fox deplored the new fashion: see 'Lady Caroline Fox to Lady Emily Kildare, 10 Dec. [1768]', in *Correspondence of Emily, Duchess of Leinster (1731–1814)*, ed. Brian Fitzgerald, 3 vols (Dublin, 1949–57), vol. i, p. 556.
47. See her journal entries for 28 November–15 December 1768: *The Letters and Journals of Lady Mary Coke*, 4 vols (Edinburgh: privately printed, 1889–96), vol. ii, pp. 416–28.
48. *Commons Journals*, xxvii (1754–7); R. J. Robson, *The Oxfordshire Election of 1754* (London: Oxford University Press, 1949), p. 147.
49. As early as 1715, a successful petition to the Commons by the widow Anne Cater and her co-petitioners, John Purton, James Coot and Stephen Norman, had awarded witnesses compensation for 'their reasonable Charges'. As this also demonstrates, women's involvement as witnesses was not a mid-century innovation. See Cowley, *Orders and Resolutions*, p. 124 (8 September 1715).
50. See, for example, *Commons Journals*, xxix (1761–4), pp. 124–5; xxxii (1768–70), p. 313. For the continuation of such beliefs into the nineteenth century, see Chapter 8.
51. *Commons Journals*, xxxii (1768–70), p. 270.
52. Luders, *Reports of the Proceedings in Committee of the House of Commons upon Controverted Elections*, vol. ii, p. 138.
53. Ibid., pp. 140, 146, 153.
54. Porritt and Porritt, *Unreformed House of Commons*, vol. i, p. 31.
55. For the coverage of the Bramber election, see *Commons Journals*, xxxii (1768–70), pp. 209–17.
56. Ibid., p. 210.
57. Ibid., pp. 210–11.

2
Patriotism and Providence: the Politics of Hannah More

Anne Stott

It is increasingly recognised that Hannah More cannot be seen as merely the reactionary antithesis of Mary Wollstonecraft.[1] To Mitzi Myers, Susan Pedersen, Gerald Newman and Beth Fowkes Tobin, she is a cultural revolutionary in the name of Evangelical religion and bourgeois values.[2] For Kathryn Sutherland she represents a new 'tory' or counter-revolutionary feminism.[3] To historians of British loyalism during the Revolutionary and Napoleonic Wars, she typifies a nuanced conservatism forced to negotiate with the challenges thrown up by radical propaganda.[4] This chapter will seek to develop the revisionist case by examining some hitherto neglected aspects of Hannah More's political engagement. It will show that, for all her debt to Edmund Burke's conservatism, she was never his uncritical disciple. Far from representing the antithesis of Wollstonecraft's Enlightenment values, she acknowledged the significance of the rationalist tradition, particularly for the educative role of women. Through her involvement with the Evangelical Clapham Sect and her political writings, she affirmed a role for women outside the domestic sphere. As the self-appointed mentor of the young Princess Charlotte, she set out a vision of a nation that had attained greatness under the leadership of providentially chosen women. Even in her very conservative old age, she continued to advocate some liberal causes, including the campaign for Greek independence.

However, the purpose of the chapter is not to claim Hannah More as an original thinker in the canon of political thought; but rather to use More as an illustration of the variety of ways in which women were able to engage in contemporary politics. Far from being psychologically immured in a separate de-politicised sphere, middle-class and elite women participated energetically in public debates and political causes.[5]

While not aiming at political power for themselves, patriot and loyalist women deployed a series of versatile strategies to facilitate their interaction with public debates. One of the sites of this political engagement was contemporary elections.[6] More's earliest known intervention in an election occurred in 1774, when she and her four sisters aided Burke's campaign in Bristol; they entertained him at their house in Park Street, made him a cockade and presented him with a wreath at the end of the campaign.[7] More's motives were probably a combination of friendship for Burke, whom she had come to know earlier in that year, and dislike of his Wilkite opponents. From 1787, the approximate year of her Evangelical conversion, she was closely involved with William Wilberforce and his parliamentary group, the Clapham 'Saints', whose members included Henry Thornton, Thomas Babington, James Stephen and the Charles Grants, father and son, and who sought the moral and spiritual regeneration of society through political action.[8] Until Wilberforce's vote in favour of Catholic relief in 1813, she identified with every aspect of his political programme including his campaign for the reformation of manners, his support for Pitt's opposition to the radicals and, most notably, his support for the abolition of slavery. Fears that Wilberforce might lose his seat in 1807 to the Whig candidate, Lord Milton, 'flushed my Pulse back again up to a hundred, and my apothecary told me he shou'd send me double Doses of opium till the Contest was over'.[9] More sent £50 to aid his very expensive struggle.[10] Her main correspondent was Henry Thornton's wife, Marianne, who kept her in touch with the details of the campaign, the predictions (sometimes gloomy, but increasingly hopeful) of Wilberforce's prospects and the amount of money being raised.[11] His campaign was funded by locally based committees. A letter from Mrs Thornton to More asks her to 'thank Mrs Patty and Mrs Sally [two of More's sisters] for their exertions among the Bristolians'.[12]

It was, of course, Wilberforce's campaign for the abolition of slavery with which Hannah More most identified. The emerging debates on abolition had opened up a new area of political involvement for women. In 1788 More, and the more radical Helen Maria Williams and Anna Laetitia Barbauld, timed the publication of their anti-slavery poems to coincide with Sir William Dolben's Slave Limitation (or Middle Passage) Bill.[13] Less well known is women's involvement in the Evangelical petitioning campaign to open up India to Anglican missionaries, in the teeth of considerable hostility from the East India Company. More was prominent in this agitation. In response to Wilberforce's plea in March 1813 that she 'stir up a petition in Bristol, and in any other place', she recruited

Elizabeth De Quincey (née Penson) the mother of Thomas. In April she wrote,

> I hope you will think we have done wonders in Bristol, considering the shortness of the time. I next thought of Manchester. I named to a very sensible neighbour, Mrs. Quincey, late of Manchester, your idea about getting petitions for Christianising India; she sent me the inclosed [*sic*], desiring me to get a Frank, and sent it, but we are both so afraid we have not correctly met your wishes that I think it safer to trouble you to read it.[14]

The wording of the letter shows that More (understandably) did not feel confident about her ability to draw up a petition without the help of an experienced parliamentarian. But it also shows that, provided the cause was good, neither she nor Wilberforce saw anything transgressive in a woman petitioning parliament.[15] More was equally ready to intervene in contemporary debates about elections. Her distrust of the electoral process was reflected in many negative comments, such as her complaint in 1795 about the unruly process of nominating a member for Somerset.[16] In 1818 she was again lamenting the 'scenes of drunkenness, perjury and all manner of vices' associated with 'the approaching Septennial Saturnalia'.[17] Such behaviour was the reverse of the orderly, domesticated, feminised society she set out in the *Cheap Repository Tracts* (1795–8). For this reason, among others, she opposed demands for more frequent elections. As she asserted in her post-war ballad 'Fair Words and Fine Meanings':

> What would annual parliaments add to our quiet?
> Would idleness, drunkenness check the wild riot?
> One long Saturnalia would fill human life
> One uproar eternal, one durable strife.[18]

She also wrote a Cheap Repository ballad in 1796 to be sung to a popular tune during elections, which criticised their licentious nature:

> And here is a deal of treating
> Which the law forbids to be done,
> And here is the Publican cheating
> And setting down two for one
>
> And here is a man in vogue, Sir,
> That filthy song who sung,

Now I know the fellow's a rogue, Sir
As great as ever was hung.[19]

Hannah More confided to her diary a regrettable tendency to be 'warm' in politics, something that was reflected in her prose writings, where she made her main political contributions.[20] Her partisanship was conventional and instinctive. A moralist rather than a philosopher, she had no fully thought-out theory of the nature of the state or the role of the citizen. In 1783 she told Ann Kennicott that her friend Josiah Tucker, Dean of Gloucester and political controversialist, had 'sent me a Ms. to read full of good sense and knowledge of his subject, but unfortunately he expects me to understand it too'.[21] Her arguments were rooted in a belief in the ancient constitution and in Britain's destiny as a nation providentially chosen to guide the rest of the world. The High Church *British Critic* praised her 'strong and unalterable attachment to the civil and ecclesiastical constitution of her country'. The *Christian Observer*, house journal of the Clapham Sect, commended the *Hints Towards Forming the Character of a Young Princess* for taking 'a firm position on all the standard *common-places*... of liberty and the English constitution'.[22]

It was because of her firm belief that Britain after the Glorious Revolution was a guiding light to the rest of the world that she could understand, and to some extent share, the initial enthusiasm for the French Revolution. 'What English heart did not exult at the demolition of the Bastile?' she wrote in the *Remarks on the Speech of M. Dupont*.[23] However, More shared in the outrage that followed the executions of the king and queen and the fates of their children. These events were vividly reported in the British press and read with horrified eagerness by women such as Hester Thrale Piozzi and the bluestocking, Elizabeth Montagu.[24]

In the wake of these developments, many British literary women began to contribute to the ensuing propaganda war on both the loyalist and radical sides of the debate. Popular anti-Jacobin tracts and ballads were composed by a number of women. These included the well-known Piozzi but also others, such as 'Fidelia', who wished to remain anonymous.[25] Other women also corresponded with John Reeves' Association for the Preservation of Liberty and Property, offering their support; for example, Sarah Trimmer, who wrote outlining plans for poor-relief; Anne Kane, who offered to distribute loyalist pamphlets through her library and stationer's shop; and 'A Female' who proposed to write on the repatriation of subversive foreigners.[26]

One of the leading female initiatives to arise from loyalist activities was the formation of the Ladies' Society (for the relief of émigré clergy).

The society was led by the political hostesses, Frances Crewe and the Marchioness (later Duchess) of Buckingham.[27] Hannah More and Frances Burney (d'Arblay) both wrote pamphlets for the cause. Both More's *Remarks on the Speech of M. Dupont* and Burney's *Brief reflections relative to the emigrant French clergy* were specifically addressed to 'the Ladies of Great Britain', though they were careful to disclaim any right to a say in the running of politics.[28] On the publication of *Remarks on the Speech of M. Dupont*, More was approached by a deputation from the society and asked to be their chairwoman. She declined, pleading ill-health, but the real reason, as she told Anne Kennicott, was 'the ostensibleness and publicity attached to such an office'.[29] However, More donated the profits of the pamphlet (about £240) to the society.[30]

The debates surrounding the French Revolution also revived the relationship between More and Edmund Burke. More is often characterised as an unswerving Burkean conservative.[31] However, her relationship with him was complex and varied. During the late 1770s and the 1780s they had grown apart politically. More, a firm loyalist during the American war, found herself in 'a passion' with the 'wicked eloquence' of his parliamentary speeches in favour of the colonists, and thought his peroration at the trial of Warren Hastings 'abusive and vehement beyond all conception'.[32] However, the debate on the French Revolution brought them together again. More's popular loyalist publication, *Village Politics*, remained faithful to Burke's political agenda. In an echo of Burke's assertion of the nature of the 'real rights of man', Jack Anvil, the loyalist protagonist of *Village Politics*, defines his rights in simple, concrete language as 'the use of my limbs, of my liberty, of the laws and of my Bible'.[33] Just as Burke denied that these rights entailed economic equality, so More's contented Spitalfields' weaver asserts that the 'true *Rights of Man*' are 'not equal POSSESSIONS but equal just LAWS'.[34] Even in *Slavery*, written before the French Revolution, her description of the 'unlicens'd monster of the crowd', born of 'rash Sedition' and 'mad Misrule', rejecting the 'rein' of Reason, and outraging Law, anticipated Burke's vision of 'the tumultuous cries of a mixed mob of ferocious men and of women lost to shame'.[35] In a thoroughly Burkean metaphor, in *Village Politics* she associated the feminine with French frivolity and luxury and the masculine with the solid virtues of the British state:

> When Sir John married, my lady, who is a little fantastical, and likes to do every thing like the French, begged him to pull down yonder fine old castle, and build it up in her frippery way. 'No', says Sir John; 'what! shall I pull down this noble building, raised by the wisdom of

my brave ancestors . . . My lady mumpt and grumbled; but the castle was let stand, and a glorious building it is, though there may be a trifling fault or two.[36]

However, though Burke was the political writer who influenced her most, her feelings about him were often ambivalent. She did not dismiss the common people as the 'swinish multitude' and she was more likely to excoriate the aristocracy as the fountain-head of corruption than to praise it as 'the Corinthian capital of polished society'.[37] In unconscious agreement with Mary Wollstonecraft, she was highly critical of his defence of chivalry: 'Our old friend Edmund Burke said, that when vice loses all its grossness, it loses half its evil. I have always ventured to be of a directly contrary opinion. The drunken helots of Sparta were more likely to make youth sober, than the double-gilt vices of Paris'.[38] Most significantly, More deplored what she saw as his extremism. In 1794 she wrote to Wilberforce:

> Horsley [the ultra-loyalist bishop of Rochester] and Burke and the fierce Champions on the government side, by way of plaguing the dissenters have got into a way of making the charge of Popery; and to enhance the horrors of anarchy, they represent Despotism as rather a desirable thing – But why, to prove that Scylla is a destructive rock must it be implied that Charybdis is a safe shore?[39]

At a time when, like many others, she longed for peace with France, she thought his hawkish *Two Letters on a Regicide Peace* 'a wild, malignant rhapsody' that 'kept me in a violent ill-humour the whole time I was reading. We want emollients now, and not inflamers'.[40] After his death, she became deeply distrustful of his political disciple, William Windham.[41] She set out her considered view of Burke, 'this great but often misguided man' in the *Hints Towards Forming the Character of a Young Princess*. The *Reflections on the Revolution in France* was 'the warning voice which first sounded the alarm in the ears of Britain, and which, by rousing to a sense of danger, kindled the spirit to repel it'. But Burke's prejudices 'sometimes blinded his judgment', his vehemence 'often clouded his brightness' and his 'genius' lacked consistency. However, in *Hints Towards Forming the Character of a Young Princess* she argued that in Burke's *Reflections*:

> the violence which had sometimes exhausted itself, unworthily in party, or unkindly on individuals, now found full scope for its exercise,

in the unrestrained atrocities of a nation, hostile not only to Britain but to human nature itself...And happily for his honour, all the successive actors in the revolutionary drama took care to sin up to any intemperance of language which even Mr. Burke could supply.[42]

It is in this context of the Evangelical response to the French Revolution that More's politics have customarily been located. However, it was in the *Hints Towards Forming the Character of a Young Princess* that More's most ambitious disquisition is to be found. Written anonymously, (the *Edinburgh Review* tellingly assumed the author to be male[43]), the *Hints Towards Forming the Character of a Young Princess* formed the most comprehensive account of More's politics.

The origins of the *Hints Towards Forming the Character of a Young Princess* lay not merely in the circumstances of its time but in the humanist genre of advice books to princes from Machiavelli, Erasmus and Rabelais through to Bolingbroke's *Patriot King*.[44] The most direct literary model was Fénelon's *Télémaque*, composed for Louis XIV's grandson, the Duke of Burgundy. More's book was written at a moment of crisis. In the late summer of 1804 the education of Princess Charlotte was the focus of an acrimonious dispute between George III and Charlotte's father, the Prince of Wales.[45] The king was clear that his granddaughter's education 'cannot be alone that of a female, but she being the presumptive heir of the Crown must have one of a more extended nature'.[46] But what did this involve? As it became apparent that the elderly Countess of Elgin was unlikely to keep her post as governess, More picked up an unfounded rumour that caused her much agitation. She told Wilberforce on 24 September:

when you consider the state of things, there is not a month to be lost – The poor child is going on most miserably, and the change talk'd of is likely to be from bad to worse – much worse – the D[uche]ss of Devon[shire] being actually talked of by the unworthy Father as the next Directress – God forbid it shou'd really be so. I have little expectations but that my attempt will be scanted – But it will be a duty done.[47]

The *Hints Towards Forming the Character of a Young Princess* represented More's most determined attempt to invoke the language of patriotism as a royalist celebration of a providentially chosen nation.[48] Providence had been a subversive doctrine in the early seventeenth century, but in the following century it came to legitimate the British state and the

Protestant religion.[49] More's ideology of patriotism was inseparable from her belief in the uniquely providential destiny of the British state:

> It was that goodness which made us an island that laid the foundation of our national happiness. It was by placing us in the midst of the waters, that the Almighty prepared our country for those providential uses to which it has served, and is yet to serve, in the great scheme of his dispensations. Thus … we behold ourselves raised as a nation above all nations of the earth by that very circumstance which made our country be regarded two thousand years ago, only as a receptacle for the refuse of the Roman Empire.[50]

Her aim, as the Whiggish *Monthly Review* stated approvingly, was to create a 'patriot Princess'.[51] As More wrote:

> If we were to enquire what is, even at the present critical period, one of the most momentous concerns which can engage the attention of an Englishman, who feels for his country like a patriot, and for his posterity like a father … what Briton would hesitate to reply, the Education of the Princess Charlotte of Wales?[52]

More placed the education of the princess within the wider philosophical tradition of English rationalists. Referring to Locke as 'the most accurate thinker and the justest reasoner which this … country has produced', she viewed him along with Bacon and Boyle, as the enemies of intellectual despotism and the exponents of 'good sense'.[53] Locke's great educational work, his *Essay on Human Understanding* (1690), had made him something of a hero to the bluestockings. His theory of the *tabula rasa* privileged women's roles as educators and encouraged their own development as rational beings.[54]

However, the central theme of the book was concerned with the unusual situation of an heiress presumptive. She turned to 'the excellent Archbishop of Cambray', and set out to imitate his purpose in 'sketching the character and shadowing out the duties of a patriot King', without, as she pointed out, his need for allegory and coded language.[55] The choice of the Archbishop of Cambrai, who from 1695 was leader of the oppositional, anti-absolutist faction that gathered round the Duke of Burgundy, was intended to remind Charlotte of the limitations of royal power. Far from being over-impressed by the ceremonial trappings of monarchy, which 'are beneath the attachment of a rational, and of no substantial use to a mortal being', she should be made aware that a prince, 'the dignity being hereditary . . . is the more manifestly raised to that elevation, not by his own merit, but by providential destination'.[56] The *Hints Towards Forming the Character of a Young Princess* was a celebration of limited monarchy, the balanced constitution and the rule of law, which 'even female sovereigns' must be taught to reverence.[57] But if the ruler's political power is limited, his influence as 'the maker of manners' is immense.[58] For this reason, 'the supreme concern' of Charlotte's teachers had to be her 'moral and mental cultivation' both 'from a dutiful regard to her own future happiness' and also 'from reasonable attention to the well-being of those millions, whose earthly fate may be at this moment suspended on lessons and habits received by one providentially distinguished female!'[59]

She saw in George III's unyielding Protestantism and domestic virtues the true model of a patriot king.[60] But here she was writing for a princess, and though the book contained some negative comments about women rulers,[61] these were outweighed by her belief that Providence had a special role for the female sovereign. It was here that she made her most original contribution to an otherwise well-worn political discourse. In her claim that the 'just administration' of the monarch's powers of ecclesiastical appointment, 'may be reasonably expected as much, we had almost said even more from a female, than from a monarch of the other sex', More implied that a female ruler is more likely to be devout than a male – and therefore at least as important in the grand design of Providence.[62] She set out this message through the characters of two contrasting pairs of sisters: the wise and tolerant Elizabeth, a great queen in spite of her faults, and her sister, 'the bigot', Mary Tudor; the pious Mary of Orange and her 'less impressive' sister, Anne, whose 'good qualities' were better fitted for private life than for the throne.[63] She paid tribute to Elizabeth's policy of toleration and her shrewd choice of ministers, and took the opportunity to refute a commonly expressed denigration of women rulers. 'Those who wish to derogate from the glories of a female reign, have never failed to urge, that they were owing to the wisdom of the ministers, and not that of the queen [but] is not the choice of sagacious ministers the characteristic mark of a sagacious sovereign?'[64] Even more exemplary was Mary II. Her marriage was appointed by providence 'to protect our liberties' and her character, 'strictly and habitually devout amid all the temptations of a court', was as important as her dynastic role.[65] Here More was drawing on Burnet, who wrote that if Mary had lived she would have helped the nation to 'recover our ancient virtue'.[66] Though she could discern a providence in Anne's dependence on the Duchess of Marlborough, she wanted Charlotte to be a more

independent force for good. Mary II, the reformer of manners and patron of the Church, served her purposes perfectly. She was the ultimate
role model for the young princess, a proof that, in a monarchy that
allowed female succession, providence singled out women as well as men;
a proof, too, that the private virtues of a woman ruler were a public
benefit to her country. More's survey of recent history virtually ignored
the male rulers. She focused instead on the Electress Sophia, providentially chosen from her dispossessed and scattered family to be the
mother of the first Hanoverian king, and on Caroline of Ansbach, the
skilful politician and conscientious ecclesiastical patron, who had turned
down the future Emperor rather than abandon her faith.[67] These royal
women, set apart for a high purpose, were part of the necessary myth of
patriotic Protestantism.

However, More's hopes were crushed by the premature death of Princess Charlotte in 1817, an event which caused an outpouring of national
grief similar to that which had followed the equally unexpected death
of Queen Mary, with women particularly 'devastated by the event'.[68] In
letter after letter More tried to come to terms with the calamity. 'These
blooming and now blasting Royalties' she wrote to Zachary Macaulay,
'had entwined themselves about our hearts and affections so as to excite
an interest altogether new to one's feelings.'[69] She told Wilberforce that
'the departed Princess returns to my mind every minute'.[70] 'The Grief
for the Princess is a feeling one does not get over, it seems like a domestic
bereavement'.[71] She wrote of the 'lovely happy Princess' as if she had
known her.[72] It was, she told Henry Thornton's daughter, Marianne,
'a frowning Providence', and she could almost wish herself a Catholic,
with the privilege of praying for the dead.[73]

By 1820, however, with Queen Caroline's trial obsessing her, she came
to see the tragedy as providentially ordained: 'had her precious life been
spared how dreadfully would it have aggravated the public tumults, she
loved her unhappy Mother, and was not unfriendly to the Opposition.
It must have created a civil war, so much was she the general darling.'[74]
The vision of mother and daughter, the one malevolent, the other
well-intentioned, destroying the state between them appalled her. Certainly she did not share in the widespread female support for Queen
Caroline.[75] An indiscreet letter to Wilberforce reflects the tone of her
correspondence. 'A friend of mine who spoke of his own knowledge
told me that this pernicious woman's chief champion, I had almost
said bully, Lord Carnarvon, has repeatedly call'd the Q[ueen] a d——d
brimstone – *pray burn*.'[76] In other letters she compared Caroline to the
heroine of *The Fair Penitent*, and to Helen of Troy, though without her

beauty.[77] Such comments reflect her abiding belief that the well-being of the state was dependent on the ways in which high-born women exercised their influence.

The death of Princess Charlotte and the trial of Queen Caroline help to account for the pessimistic edge to More's politics in her later years. Another reason lies in her increasing political differences with the Clapham Sect. Wilberforce's vote in favour of Catholic emancipation left her bewildered.[78] In 1823, aged seventy-eight, she joined the Constitutional Association, one of the Ultra groups that sprang up to defend the Protestant constitution; predictably, she claimed that she had only done so because urged by her friend, Lord Radstock.[79] The woman who had once campaigned for the émigré clergy was now firmly in the Protestant 'Orange' camp. By this stage, as Zachary Macaulay told Henry Brougham, her 'feelings and prepossessions are all on the side of toryism', something that was also reflected in her post-war *Cheap Repository Tracts*, in which she railed against 'upstart reformers' and 'new-fangled sages'.[80] Her hostility to political reform was given a personal edge when she cut Thomas Babington Macaulay out of her will following his vote for the Reform Bill in 1832.[81]

In the tense post-war period of economic hardship and political radicalism, many shared More's fears, especially on the Catholic question, on which women were vehemently vocal.[82] But even in this late period of her life, when, on her own admission, she had swung to the right,[83] she went out of her way to praise the Whig, Henry Brougham's 'grand scheme' of education for the poor.[84] She thoroughly disapproved of the type of Anglican loyalism that went out of its way to exclude Dissenters.[85] Indeed, More's views continued to be far more subtle and complex than is usually portrayed. She was, for example, a fervent supporter of Greek independence, writing to her friend Sir William Weller Pepys, 'As to the conflagration between Greece and Turkey, I am a most strenuous champion for the land of Homer.'[86] Above all, she continued to support anti-slavery. At the age of eighty-three, too infirm to give much more than moral support, she joined the committee of the Female Anti-Slavery Society for Clifton.[87] Here she showed herself more liberal than Wilberforce, who believed such activities 'unsuited to the female character as delineated in Scripture'.[88] But the Bible presented women with a greater variety of role models than he allowed, and More was simply the most prominent of the conservative women who interpreted gender codes in a manner that allowed them to show 'the public spirit of a British patriot.'[89] Linda Colley has noted that a number of female patriots in the 1790s were 'staking out a civic role for themselves', demonstrating 'that their domestic virtues possessed a public as well as a private relevance'.[90] In More's most influential conduct book, she had urged her readers to adopt 'a patriotism at once firm and feminine for the general good'.[91] In this, she never wavered, consistently refusing to allow men to monopolise the language of patriotism.

In conclusion, it cannot be denied that Hannah More's politics were instinctively conservative and became more so as she grew older. But hers was a moralistic, activist, Evangelically inspired conservatism rather than a timidly negative reaction to radicalism or feminism. Whether it was sending money to an election campaign, petitioning parliament, dashing off an election ballad, or painstakingly distilling the fruits of her wide reading into an advice book for a princess, she used the ways available to women to enter the great public debates. Indeed, More believed that it was her *duty* to intervene in such issues. At the same time she sought to defend the state from the assaults of the radicals. As a loyalist, she believed that a tried and tested constitution presided over by a monarch with limited powers offered a better guarantee of the liberties of the subject than the speculative 'rights of man' preached by Thomas Paine. She saw the British nation as set apart for a special destiny, and until her untimely death she believed that Princess Charlotte had been providentially chosen to lead this chosen people. Her Evangelically inspired patriotism and her very positive view of a woman ruler's potential for good reveal her to be neither an undiluted Burkean nor the dualistic opposite of Mary Wollstonecraft.

Acknowledgements

The author would like to thank the following libraries for permission to quote from their manuscripts: the William Andrews Clark Memorial Library, University of California, Los Angeles; University College London Library; the Huntington Library, San Marino; the Bodleian Library, University of Oxford; the Syndics of Cambridge University Library; and the Rare Book, Manuscript and Special Collections Library, Duke University, North Carolina.

Notes

1. For More's shared agendas with Wollstonecraft, see Gary Kelly, *Women, Writing and Revolution, 1790–1827* (Oxford: Oxford University Press, 1993), pp. 27–9; Janet Todd (ed.), *Mary Wollstonecraft, Political Writings* (Oxford: Oxford University Press, 1994), p. xxi. For critiques of aristocratic mores, see Donna Andrew, 'The Code of Honour and its Critics: the Opposition to Duelling in England 1780–1850', *Social History*, 5 (1980), pp. 409–34; *idem*, '"Adultery à-la-mode": Privilege, the Law and Attitudes to Adultery 1770–1809', *History*, 82 (1997), pp. 5–23.
2. Mitzi Myers, 'Reform or Ruin: "A Revolution in Female Manners"', *Studies in Eighteenth-Century Culture*, 11 (1982), pp. 199–216; *idem*, 'Hannah More's Tracts for the Times: Social Fiction and Female Ideology', in Mary Anne Schofield and Cecilia Macheski (eds), *Fetter'd or Free? British Women Novelists, 1670–1815* (Athens, OH: Ohio University Press, 1986), pp. 264–84; *idem*, '"A Peculiar Protection": Hannah More and the Cultural Politics of the Blagdon Controversy', in Beth Fowkes Tobin (ed.), *History, Gender and Eighteenth-Century Literature* (Athens, GA, and London: University of Georgia Press, 1994), pp. 227–57; Susan Pedersen, 'Hannah More Meets Simple Simon: Tracts, Chapbooks and Popular Culture in Late Eighteenth-Century England', *Journal of British Studies*, 25 (1986), pp. 84–113; Gerald Newman, *The Rise of English Nationalism: A Cultural History, 1740–1830* (London: Weidenfeld and Nicolson, 1987), pp. 234–5; Beth Fowkes Tobin, *Superintending the Poor: Charitable Ladies and Paternal Landlords in British Fiction, 1770–1860* (New Haven, CT, and London: Yale University Press, 1993), pp. 109–12.
3. Kathryn Sutherland, 'Hannah More's Counter-Revolutionary Feminism', in Kelvin Everest (ed.), *Revolution in Writing: British Literary Responses to the French Revolution* (Milton Keynes and Philadelphia, PA: Open University Press, 1991), pp. 27–63.
4. See, for example, Linda Colley, *Britons: Forging the Nation, 1707–1837* (New Haven, CT, and London: Yale University Press, 1992), pp. 274–6; Mark Philp, 'Vulgar Conservatism 1792–3', *English Historical Review*, 90 (1995), pp. 42–69.
5. The full titles of the works considered in this chapter are: *Village Politics Addressed to all the Mechanics, Journeymen and Day Labourers in Great Britain, by Will Chip a Country Carpenter* (London: Rivington, 1793), *Remarks on the Speech of M. Dupont made in the National Convention of France on the Subjects of Religious and Public Education* (London: Cadell, 1793), *Hints Towards Forming the Character of a Young Princess*, 2 vols (London: Cadell, 1805), her contributions to the shortlived and little known *Anti-Cobbett or the Weekly Patriotic Register* (London: John Knight, 1817), which were reprinted and expanded in *Cheap Repository Tracts suited to the Present Times* (London: Rivington, 1819).
6. See Elaine Chalus, '"That Epidemical Madness": Women and Electoral Politics in the Late Eighteenth Century', in Hannah Barker and Elaine Chalus (eds), *Gender in Eighteenth-Century England: Roles, Representations and Responsibilities* (London: Longman, 1997), pp. 151–78, for a discussion of women's involvement in the electoral process.
7. Henry Thompson, *The Life of Hannah More with Notices of her Sisters* (London: Cadell, 1838), pp. 25–9.

8. For the 'Saints' see Ian Bradley, 'The Politics of Godliness: Evangelicals in Parliament 1784–1832' (unpublished D.Phil. thesis, University of Oxford, 1974); Boyd Hilton, *The Age of Atonement: The Influence of Evangelicalism on Social and Economic Thought, 1785–1865* (Oxford: Clarendon Press, 1991).

9. More to Wilberforce, 15 June 1807, Bodleian Library, Wilberforce Papers c. 3, f. 89 (hereafter Bodleian).

10. For the campaign, see E. A. Smith, 'The Yorkshire Elections of 1806 and 1807', *Northern History*, 2 (1967), pp. 62–80.

11. For Marianne Sykes Thornton's correspondence on the Yorkshire election of 1807 see Thornton MSS, Cambridge University, Add 7674/1/L4, fols 21–3, 30–1 (hereafter Thornton).

12. Thornton Add 7674/1/L4, fol. 31.

13. Clare Midgley, *Women against Slavery: The British Campaigns, 1780–1870* (London and New York: Routledge, 1992), p. 32.

14. R. I. and S. Wilberforce, *The Life of William Wilberforce*, 5 vols (London: John Murray, 1838), vol. iv, pp. 103–4; Bodleian c. 48, fol. 54 [April 1813]. For women's petitions to Parliament, see Colley, *Britons*, p. 355.

15. Not everyone shared this view. In the year of More's death, a pro-slavery pamphlet attacked the Evangelical women who were petitioning for abolition as deviants 'from female retiredness'. *An Address to the Females of Great Britain on the Propriety of their Petitioning Parliament for the Abolition of Negro Slavery, by an Englishwoman* (London: Rivington, 1833), p. 10.

16. More to Wilberforce, 27 August 1795, Duke University, Durham NC, Rare Book, Manuscripts and Special Collections Library (hereafter Duke).

17. More to Marie-Aimée Huber, 28 May 1818, William Andrews Clark Memorial Library, University of California, Los Angeles (uncatalogued) (hereafter Clark).

18. *Cheap Repository Tracts*, pp. 141–2.

19. *The Election: A Quite New Song* (1796).

20. William Roberts, *Memoirs of the Life and Correspondence of Mrs Hannah More*, 4 vols (London: R. B. Seeley and W. Burnside, 2nd edn, 1834), vol. iii, p. 57.

21. More to Ann Kennicott, 20 May [1783], Clark. More was probably referring to Tucker's *Four Letters on Important National Subjects* (London: Cadell, 1783).

22. *British Critic*, 17 (May 1801), p. 528; *Christian Observer*, 4 (August 1805), p. 492.

23. *Dupont*, p. 7. More wrote of her own ambivalent feelings on the storming of the Bastille to Elizabeth Montagu and Horace Walpole (More to Elizabeth Montagu, 10 October 1789, Henry E. Huntington Library, San Marino, MO 3999; hereafter Huntington); W. S. Lewis (ed.), *The Correspondence of Horace Walpole*, vol. 31 (London: Oxford University Press, 1961), p. 321.

24. See, for example, Edward A. Bloom and Lillian D. Bloom (eds), *The Piozzi Letters: Correspondence of Hester Lynch Piozzi, 1784–1821*, 3 vols (Newark, DE: University of Delaware Press, 1989–91), vol. ii, pp. 100–1; Reginald Blunt (ed.), *Mrs. Montagu, 'Queen of the Blues', Her Letters and Friendships from 1762 to 1800*, 2 vols (London: Constable, 1923), vol. ii, pp. 252ff.; Colley, *Britons*, pp. 252–7.

25. [Hester Lynch Piozzi] *Three Warnings to John Bull Before He Dies . . .* (London: R. Faulder, 1798); Philp, 'Vulgar Conservatism', pp. 53–4; 'Fidelia', 4 December 1792, British Library Dept. of Manuscripts, Add MSS 16920, fol. 99; 16923, fols 47–50, recommends loyalist tracts and ballads to counter radical

propaganda. She claims to have written a half-penny ballad of her own and offers to send it and write more if required.

26. Reeves MS: BL Add 16921, fols 121–4; Add 16923, fols 47–50; fol. 76; Add 16920, fol. 115.
27. Joyce Hemlow (ed.), *The Journals and Letters of Fanny Burney (Madame d'Arblay)*, vol. 2 (Oxford: Clarendon Press, 1972), p. 5, n. 3.
28. *Dupont*, Prefatory Address. For Burney's *Brief Reflections Relative to the Emigrant French Clergy* . . . [1793] see Margaret Anne Doody, *Frances Burney: The Life in the Works* (Cambridge: Cambridge University Press, 1998), pp. 203–5.
29. More to Ann Kennicott, 18 November 1793, Clark.
30. Roberts, *Life of More*, vol. ii, p. 359.
31. J. C. D. Clark, *English Society 1688–1832: Ideology, Social Structure and Political Practice during the Ancien Regime* (Cambridge: Cambridge University Press, 1992), pp. 246–7; Robert Hole, *Selected Writings of Hannah More* (London: William Pickering, 1996), p. vii.
32. Roberts, *Life of More*, vol. i, p. 359 and vol. ii, pp. 108–9.
33. Edmund Burke, *Reflections on the Revolution in France, and on the Proceedings in Certain Societies in London Relative to that Event*, ed. Conor Cruise O'Brien (Harmondsworth: Penguin, 1986), pp. 149–50; *Village Politics*, p. 17.
34. *Cheap Repository Tracts*, p. 152.
35. *Reflections*, p. 161; *Slavery: A Poem by Hannah More* (London: Cadell, 1788), ll. 19–36.
36. *Village Politics*, pp. 8–9.
37. *Reflections*, p. 245. For More's critiques of the aristocracy see, for example, *Thoughts on the Importance of the Manners of the Great to General Society* (London: Cadell, 1788).
38. Roberts, *Life of More*, vol. iv, p. 15. Compare Wollstonecraft: 'What a sentiment to come from a moral pen!' (Todd, *Political Writings*, p. 24).
39. More to Wilberforce, 29 November 1794, Duke.
40. More to Elizabeth Bouverie, 3 November 1796, cited in Georgina, Lady Chatterton (ed.), *Memorials, Personal and Historical of Admiral Lord Gambier*, 2 vols (London: Hurst and Blackett, 1861), vol. i, p. 315.
41. James J. Sack, *From Jacobite to Conservative: Reaction and Orthodoxy in Britain, c.1760–1832* (Cambridge: Cambridge University Press, 1993), pp. 92–7, 204–6; Bodleian d. 14, fol. 39; d. 16, fols 34–5.
42. *Hints Towards Forming the Character of a Young Princess*, vol. ii, pp. 203–5.
43. *Edinburgh Review*, 7, no. 13 (October 1805), pp. 91–100.
44. See David Armitage, 'A Patriot for Whom? The Afterlives of Bolingbroke's Patriot King', *Journal of British Studies*, 36 (1997), pp. 397–418.
45. Christopher Hibbert, *George IV* (Harmondsworth: Penguin, 1976), pp. 266–71; Thea Holme, *Prinny's Daughter: A Life of Princess Charlotte of Wales* (London: Hamish Hamilton, 1976), pp. 52–3; Flora Fraser, *The Unruly Queen: A Life of Queen Caroline* (Basingstoke: Macmillan, 1996), pp. 142–6.
46. A. Aspinall (ed.), *The Correspondence of George Prince of Wales, 1770–1812*, 8 vols (London: Cassell, 1968), vol. v, p. 138.
47. More to Wilberforce, 24 September 1804, Bodleian, d. 15, fol. 70.
48. David Eastwood, 'Robert Southey and the Meanings of Patriotism', *Journal of British Studies*, 31 (1992), pp. 265–87; idem, 'E. P. Thompson, Britain and the French Revolution', *History Workshop Journal*, 39 (1995), p. 82; Linda Colley,

'The Apotheosis of George III: Loyalty, Royalty and the British Nation 1760–1820', *Past and Present*, 102 (1984), pp. 94–129; Colley, *Britons*, Chapters 5–7 *passim*.

49. Colley, *Britons*, p. 48; J. Spurr, 'The Church, the Societies and the Moral Revolution of 1688', in John Walsh *et al.* (eds), *The Church of England: From Toleration to Tractarianism, c.1689–c.1833* (Cambridge: Cambridge University Press, 1993), pp. 127–42; Eamon Duffy, 'The Long Reformation: Catholicism, Protestantism and the Multitude', in Nicholas Tyacke (ed.), *England's Long Reformation, 1500–1800* (London: UCL Press, 1998), pp. 58–65.

50. *Hints Towards Forming the Character of a Young Princess*, vol. ii, p. 331.

51. *Monthly Review*, 47 (June 1805), p. 180.

52. *Hints Towards Forming the Character of a Young Princess*, vol. i, pp. ix–x.

53. Ibid., vol. ii, pp. 289, 292–3. By a happy coincidence he had been born in Wrington, the small market town in Somerset where Hannah More lived between 1786 and 1828. There are busts of More and Locke on either side of the door in Wrington church. In acknowledgement of their joint admiration, Elizabeth Montagu presented More with a commemorative urn, which became one of the most admired features of her garden. More to Elizabeth Montagu, 16 August 1791, Huntington MO 4002; *Gentleman's Magazine*, 61 (June 1791), p. 511; More to [?Zachary Macaulay], Tuesday morning, 8 September 1827, Clark.

54. Sheryl O'Donnell, 'Mr. Locke and the Ladies: The Indelible Words on the *Tabula Rasa*', *Studies in Eighteenth-Century Culture*, 8 (1979), pp. 151–64.

55. *Hints Towards Forming the Character of a Young Princess*, vol. i, pp. xiv–xv.

56. Ibid., vol. i, p. 42.

57. Ibid., vol. i, pp. 57, 74–5. More had discussed this theme before. In *Village Politics* (p. 11) she had argued that to demand equality is to 'quarrel with Providence, and not with government. For the woman is below her husband, and the children are below their mother, and the servant is below his master'. However, she did not advocate extreme prerogative in either situation. Jack Anvil declares (p. 6), 'Why the *King* can't send me to prison if I do no harm.' Princess Charlotte was warned that 'a bold oppressor of the people, the people would not endure' (*Hints Towards Forming the Character of a Young Princess*, vol. i, p. 264). In marriage, More argued, a wife's obligation to promote good works in her husband 'restores her to all the dignity of equality' (*Coelebs in Search of a Wife*, 2 vols (London: Cadell, 1808), vol. i, pp. 4–5). In both the state and the family, therefore, government should be limited rather than absolute.

58. *Hints Towards Forming the Character of a Young Princess*, vol. ii, p. 51.

59. Ibid., vol. i, pp. 8–9.

60. See her obituary tribute in *Moral Sketches* (London: Cadell, 1820), pp. iii–xiv, 6th edn.

61. 'The dangers of adulation are doubled, when the female character is combined with the royal . . . All [Elizabeth's] admirable prudence and profound policy could not preserve her from the childish and silly levity with which she greedily invited the compliments of the artful minister of her beautiful rival' (*Hints Towards Forming the Character of a Young Princess*, vol. i, p. 273).

62. Ibid., vol. ii, pp. 319–20.

63. Ibid., vol. i, p. 180; ii, pp. 366–8.

64. Ibid., vol. i, p. 178. She also noted that Blanche of Castile possessed 'talents for government not inferior to most of [the kings of France]'. Ibid., vol. i, p. 177.
65. Ibid., vol. ii, pp. 366–7.
66. Quoted in Lois G. Schwoerer, 'Images of Queen Mary II, 1689–95', *Renaissance Quarterly*, 42 (1989), p. 745.
67. *Hints Towards Forming the Character of a Young Princess*, vol. ii, pp. 368–74. For Caroline see Stephen Taylor, 'Queen Caroline and the Church of England', in Stephen Taylor, Richard Connors and Clyve Jones (eds), *Hanoverian Britain and Empire: Essays in Memory of Philip Lawson* (Woodbridge: The Boydell Press, 1998), pp. 82–101.
68. Compare Schwoerer, 'Images of Queen Mary', p. 742 with Colley, *Britons*, pp. 270–3.
69. More to Macaulay, 2 November 1817, Clark.
70. More to Wilberforce, 12 November 1817, Duke.
71. More to Wilberforce, *c.* 19 November 1817, Duke.
72. More to Ann Kennicott, 3 December 1817, Clark.
73. More to Marianne Thornton, November 1817, Thornton Add 7674/1/E/7.
74. More to François and Marie-Aimée Huber, 9 July 1820, Clark.
75. For women's support of Caroline, see Colley, *Britons*, pp. 265–8.
76. More to Wilberforce [1820], Bodleian, c. 48, fol. 29.
77. Bodleian, c. 48, fol. 26; More to the Hubers, 31 March 1821, Clark.
78. For More and the Catholic question see Anne Stott, 'Hannah More: Evangelicalism, Cultural Reformation and Loyalism' (unpublished Ph.D. thesis, University of London, 1998), pp. 231–6.
79. For the Constitutional Association, see Sack, *From Jacobite to Conservative*, pp. 105–6. For More's membership see More to Macaulay, 12 November 1823, Huntington MO 680.
80. Brougham MSS , University College London, 10,530; *Cheap Repository Tracts*, p. 141.
81. Thomas Pinney (ed.), *The Letters of Thomas Babington Macaulay*, 6 vols (Cambridge: Cambridge University Press, 1974), vol. i, p. 277 [n].
82. Colley, *Britons*, pp. 332–4.
83. For an admission of her change of views, see Roberts, *Life of More*, vol. iv, p. 160.
84. More to Zachary Macaulay, Monday [1820], Clark.
85. More to Zachary Macaulay, [1820], Clark; for earlier criticism of More from a High Church perspective, see the *Anti-Jacobin Review*, 45 (1814), pp. 652–3.
86. Alice C. C. Gaussen, *A Later Pepys: The Correspondence of Sir William Weller Pepys*, 2 vols (London and New York: John Lane, 1904), vol. ii, p. 367.
87. Midgley, *Women against Slavery*, p. 48.
88. Wilberforce and Wilberforce, *Life of Wilberforce*, vol. v, pp. 264–5.
89. *Hints Towards Forming the Character of a Young Princess*, vol. ii, p. 19.
90. Colley, *Britons*, p. 261.
91. *Strictures*, vol. i, p. 5.

3
'Well-neighboured Houses': the Political Networks of Elite Women, 1780–1860

Sarah Richardson

That the opportunities for women's participation in political activity before 1860 were limited has been noted by a range of historians: scrutiny of membership lists of party associations, pressure groups, trade unions and other formal political groupings has shown the extent of the institutional exclusion of women. Adverse conclusions have thus been drawn about women's role in political life and therefore in the public sphere. Comparisons of the decades before 1860 and those that directly followed it have emphasised the limits rather than the opportunities for women and a distinct contrast has been drawn between the extent of men's and women's varying levels of involvement in public life.[1] However, political scientists examining women's activities in contemporary politics have stressed the inadequacy of such crude number-counting exercises when attempting to quantify or assess the penetration of women in the political world, and have argued for the need to construct new models of political behaviour which challenge rather than conform to the accepted wisdom of politics as a male-dominated arena. These models stress that it is in the informal and *ad hoc* arenas where women's participation is most striking. To some extent this is a corollary of women's exclusion from public life but it is also an indication of where women's interests lie. Political activity for women is thus based around the family, the neighbourhood and the local community, dependent on casual and kinship contacts rather than organised meetings, and not in the more visible national public arenas.[2]

This logic can be applied to the political world of the late eighteenth and early nineteenth century: the concentration on 'accepted' or traditional methods of participation in the political sphere perpetuates the notion that the political world was colonised by men and that women were kept to the periphery. There existed alternative political forms to those most commonly examined by historians: women's access to an informal infrastructure was a counter to the formal realm of male-dominated political institutions from which they were largely excluded. Family and community networks were of crucial importance in the political world of Georgian Britain where the central political institutions of the state were linked together and to the wider political nation by a chain of personal and family contacts among the elite. Women's position within these family groups provided the basis for their participation in the political life of the local community and the nation.[3] The examination of women's political and social networks as a method by which they were able to influence political events, to discuss political issues which were of interest to them and to extend their political experiences is a contribution to a reassessment of the arenas, structures and people in politics during this period.[4]

This chapter seeks to relate the structure, extent and operation of elite women's political networks, to uncover some of the issues that fuelled them, and to examine the space which they occupied, physically and intellectually. The importance of family contacts, the neighbourhood and community in shaping the lives and activities of working-class women has long been recognised; however, the social milieu of elite women has generally been viewed as a restricting, rather than an emancipating environment.[5] It has not been the intention to examine the activities of a particular group of women but rather to observe a range of middle- and upper-class women from varying backgrounds with varying experiences. This includes women who may be described as political activists, but also women who eschewed such labels and stressed their conformist, apolitical views. It is clear, though, that many women were active in the 'unofficial' politics of the day, in spite of their protestations to the contrary, and used their informal social and kinship networks to support and sustain their activities.

What should be established first is the extent of these political networks among elite women – in terms of the numbers of people involved, the social range of their contacts and the geographical distance. It was the American essayist and poet Ralph Waldo Emerson who coined the phrase 'a well-neighboured house' to describe Harriet Martineau's cottage in Ambleside in the Lake District, to which she retired in 1845, recognising the importance of Martineau's extensive connections.[6] Although remote from the acknowledged centres of political activity, Martineau functioned as an influential political figure, by the extensive use of these local networks. Those in the vicinity of Ambleside included: the Arnold family, Mr Quillinan, son-in-law to William Wordsworth, the Davys who had been active in political circles in the metropolis during the 1830s, and the campaigning journalist, W. R. Greg. As is made clear by these examples, Martineau's networks were not exclusively female. Contact with both sexes was important to women who wished to exercise political influence.[7] Face-to-face contacts were important to Martineau, who pioneered a number of schemes in Ambleside for the better housing, education and welfare of the 'workies', as she dismissively termed her working-class neighbours.[8] However, her political contacts were constructed, sustained and extended by her comprehensive use of correspondence networks, from her childhood to her death in 1855.[9]

The importance of epistolary exchanges as a dynamic in women's political lives has been recognised by writers such as Dena Goodman, in her work on French salons in the eighteenth century, and Jane Rendall and Kathleen Wilson researching British politics.[10] The numerical extent of these correspondence networks can be illustrated by just a couple of examples: Harriet Martineau, confined to her sickbed, dictated twenty-three letters within a week and personally wrote several more.[11] Amelia Opie, the novelist, commented that 'my maid and I were calculating the other day how many letters I wrote in the year, and it is not less than six in a day, besides notes . . . were writing ever an effort to me I should not now be alive, but must have been *absolument épuisée*; and it might have been inserted in the bills of mortality, – "Dead of letter-writing. A. Opie".'[12]

Writing was a socially accepted activity and thus was a method by which women could penetrate male bastions of power. Many analyses of women's letters (and especially their use in fiction) have emphasised their role as a conduit to female private and domestic spaces and a method of accessing the feminine self, therefore accentuating the introspective, home-based and solitary aspects of letter-writing and reading. However, this interpretation of letters as representing a separate female world has increasingly been challenged. Naomi Tadmor has stressed the communal aspects of family reading in eighteenth-century Britain and Mary Favret has examined women's letters as tools for political action in late eighteenth-century Britain and France.[13] Female correspondence cannot easily be categorised as merely concerned with the trivial details and closeted interiors of women's domestic lives. The letter also provided a space for women (and men) to engage in the public realm and to exercise influence. Correspondence brought women into direct contact with the male politicians they wished to influence. Exchanges were candid and injected (elite) female concerns into the political discourses of the period. This was even when the women concerned shunned a more public role. Thus Sarah Austin actively lobbied Gladstone on the subject of national education and the education of girls in 1839, writing: 'All I *can* do (and that belongs to my sex) is this, to try to persuade some who think different from you . . . to give attentive, respectful, and *grateful* ear to your projects'.[14] However, in a later letter to Gladstone she emphasised the more conventional public image of women, arguing that she: 'shrunk from appearing before the public in my own person or behalf, as the author or champion of any opinions whatever.' Even in this letter, however, she asked Gladstone to read her pamphlet on the subject of national education and asked for his advice in further promotion of the issue.[15] Correspondence gave women effective contact with male politicians and other male public figures whilst shielding them from the social opprobrium that would have accompanied more open campaigning. Favret has argued that the increase in letter-writing and conduct manuals in the eighteenth and nineteenth centuries, such as Samuel Richardson's *Familiar Letters on Important Occasions* (1741), demonstrate the concern of the conservative establishment to check even this method of female interaction with the public sphere.[16]

However, although acknowledged as an acceptable female activity, it is clear that letter-writing could play a subversive, challenging role. It is epistolary exchange in this latter incarnation that led Harriet Martineau and Harriet Grote, among others, to urge friends and correspondents to destroy all surviving letters (a dictate which fortunately many ignored). Martineau called correspondence 'written speech' which should be protected and bound by the same codes of honour as private conversation.[17] Harriet Grote noted that 'no one having important and interesting manuscripts is safe in leaving them behind'.[18] The most powerful counter-argument to these views came from Anna Jameson in a letter to Harriet Martineau, after receiving her instructions to destroy all correspondence between them:

> If you persist in requiring your letters to be destroyed, I must yield to your wishes, but if, instead of a particular case, you make it a general principle and assume it as every lady's right in all cases, then I protest against your reasons and against your right – with all my soul and all my strength . . . It appears to me you are giving the most deadly blow to mutual confidence, to what you call freedom of speech, that ever yet was given . . . I grant you that accidents have happened – and may happen again from our own or others' indiscretion; let such an

experience make us wiser and when we fear treachery or carelessness, let us defend ourselves against it – but rather I would make a law upon the subject, taking away our free will and free spontaneous trust in ourselves and our friends, rather than deliberately set an example to be universally followed, or assert such a principle as you have done, I would suffer every letter I ever wrote in my life to be placarded at Charing Cross and every word I had ever uttered to be blown thro' a speaking trumpet to the four winds of heaven ... [19]

However, even as she passionately defended the freedom of speech and trust between individuals, Anna Jameson was tacitly acknowledging that female correspondence contained within it the potential for abuse. It was the indistinct status of letters – they could be variously interpreted as private, semi-private or public documents – that gave them their subversive character.[20] Correspondence, then was recognised as having a range far beyond that of the sender and receiver. Letters were used as a means of transmitting news, gossip, information and ideas and were often a shared resource for groups of women remote from centres of political action.[21]

The geographical extent of women's political networks can also be demonstrated by employing Ralph Waldo Emerson's depiction of Martineau's Ambleside home. Emerson was part of Martineau's extensive circle of American friends and acquaintances. Martineau's links with America are well documented and Kathryn Kish Sklar, Clare Midgley and Sandra Stanley Holton are among those who have stressed the importance of transatlantic contacts in the evolution of the British and American campaigns against slavery and for the suffrage, for example.[22] However, contacts with the European continent were more common among the elite women of the period. A number of women followed in the footsteps of Mary Wollstonecraft and Helen Maria Williams and travelled to France to observe the effects of successive revolutions at first hand, as well as for the cultural experience.[23] Involvement in European politics offered opportunities to British women that were not available to them in the national arena. The salons of the major European cities were not barred to middle-class women as were many of their counterparts in London.[24] The philosophical discussions that took place in such salons about political economy, democracy and practices of government gave British women the opportunity to influence leading European thinkers and politicians. In European social circles, these women's intellectual prowess was a more than adequate compensation for their lack of noble birth. Contradictory visions of European politics and society abounded amongst British women. Sarah Austin, who was a harsh critic of women overstepping boundaries in Britain, wrote to Guizot of her experiences in Dresden:

> Above all, (you will not laugh), the condition of women, their intellectual and moral station, is so immeasurably lower, that it must take a long time to bring them up to our level. Of course I use 'our' for our two countries. Imagine that here, in this courtly little capital, it is the universal custom in what they call society for the men to go into a separate room, or if there is none, to assemble in a corner, while the women sit round the table or in a circle. No man thinks of talking to a lady. I have told them that I am not accustomed to be insulted in this way, and after such men as M. Guizot have not disdained to speak to me as if I were not quite a fool, I will not take such an assumption of superiority at the hands of little chamberlains, &c. Not that I want to value their conversation, but my English blood boils at seeing myself so degraded. We in England are *oppressed*, but not condemned.[25]

In her view Dresden women were degraded by their treatment. She was accustomed to having access to such men as Guizot, Barthélemy Saint-Hilaire, Cousin, Schlegel and Cucchi and, although cautious in her correspondence about the extent of women's public role, was not in practice circumscribed by her stated views. For example, in Malta, where she lived for a year between 1837 and 1838, whilst her husband was heading a Royal Commission, she acted as a mediator between the 'poor and proud, depressed and insulted' Maltese and the English ruling class, established a system of public education, instituted a procedure for the recording of births, deaths and marriages and introduced other welfare reforms. In a letter to Victor Cousin she wrote: 'As to my little island [Malta]; there it was not a question of writing, but of acting. And I acted.'[26] Again, she appears to have been able to suspend her belief in women's subservient status to men in this foreign clime. Whilst in Malta she 'considered herself an equal member of the Commission' and regarded her time 'the property of the public'.[27] In Paris, in the early 1840s, in spite of her modest means, she established a salon where 'intellect alone was the attraction and the ornament of the house' and, according to the French politician Barthélemy Saint-Hilaire, was:

> a centre where France, England, Germany and Italy met, and learned to know and appreciate each other. Mrs. Austin spoke all four languages, her power of work was wonderful, quite virile ... and to

everything she did she brought an attention and a maturity of judgment which few men possess in so large a measure . . . [28]

Thus, for Sarah Austin many of the European cities were intellectually exciting arenas offering opportunities for direct political action. Both her own and others' descriptions of her betray a vibrancy and virility that she underplayed in her correspondence with English politicians. She participated openly and directly in European affairs, supported by a network of influential women and men, although she would not or could not extent this participation to domestic politics.

In the 1830s, the Austins were prominent among the members of the Benthamite Philosophical Radicals whose circle included Harriet Taylor, John Stuart Mill, George and Harriet Grote, Charles Buller, William Molesworth and John Roebuck. Many of Sarah Austin's political activities stemmed from her progressive Unitarian childhood in Norwich and her immersion in radical Liberalism early in her marriage. She was a competent linguist and a professional translator of intellectual and philosophical studies, for example bringing the work of Leopold von Ranke to the attention of an English audience for the first time. She also translated the work of Victor Cousin, Puckler and François Guizot. As Judith Johnston has recently noted, the importance of female translators and reviewers has been overlooked as work secondary to literary or philosophical writing. Johnston ranks Austin's work in translating the work of German literature and text alongside that of Coleridge and Carlyle.[29] Austin was an 'active' as opposed to a 'passive' translator and thus subtly altered the source texts, allowing them to function in the 'target culture'.[30] Thus her work as a translator reflected her actions in other arenas: she shunned an obviously public role, thus avoiding transgressing conventional boundaries, but played a dynamic and effective part behind the scenes.

Sarah Austin, in part because of her proficiency in languages, was also a prominent supporter of the Italian nationalists exiled in London during this time. The capital city hosted waves of European exiles from the period of the French revolution onwards, including Hungarians, Poles and Italians.[31] Some of these were dispossessed noble émigrés, others leading intellectuals and thinkers seeking political asylum. Elite women were frequently at the forefront of activities connected with these exiles: offering hospitality, organising supportive pressure groups and fundraising. *The Times* in 1824 carried an appeal for subscriptions on behalf of 'not less than 83 Italian gentlemen, expelled from their country for endeavouring to ameliorate its institutions – utterly destitute – actually starving'.[32] To some extent, their motives were romantic, expressing sympathy with these exotic exiles, but women such as Austin and Mary Howitt shared the refugees' political visions.[33] Sarah Austin's activities could not include financial support for the destitute Italians because of her own precarious financial position. However, she attempted to be constructive, dispatching Cucchi and Radice back to her home town of Norwich, persuading her mother and Amelia Opie to find them work as teachers of Italian and (disastrously) encouraging her brother to take a party of Italian refugees to exploit mining opportunities in the Real del Monte region of Mexico.[34] Engagement in European politics whether at home supporting refugees and joining pressure groups to support 'freedom' abroad, or when travelling overseas allowed elite women to be politically dynamic without transgressing the boundaries set by themselves and society between public and private activities.

Sarah Austin's salons in Germany, France, Malta and England illustrated that her sex and lack of wealth were no barriers to establishing effective transnational political networks. These multinational salons often provided the intellectual space where discussions on liberal, conservative and socialist ideology took place, and as such influenced directly developments in this experimental era of European politics in the 1830s and 1840s. Another such salon, headed by an Englishwoman, was that of Madame Sismondi, wife of the Swiss historian and political economist in Geneva from the 1820s to the 1850s. Elizabeth Sismondi had well-established kinship networks in England, being part of the Wedgwood–Darwin–Mackintosh circle whose female members were active in political campaigns as diverse as the abolition of slavery, action to prevent cruelty to animals, parliamentary and electoral reform and support for Mazzini's Italian nationalists.[35] Via her husband she also had links with the intellectuals who had formed the influential Coppet circle, based round the salon of Madame de Stäel in Geneva from 1804 to 1810 and comprised such distinguished ideologues as Constant, Schlegel and Barante as well as Sismondi.[36] From the extensive correspondence that passed between Elizabeth Sismondi and her female relations it is evident that she was an important conduit of information, relaying her opinions and those of other European intellectuals to her family back in England. For example, she describes the revolution of 1848 in France as 'the most sublime political movement that has ever taken place in any country' but cautions against Fanny Wedgwood's participation in the London Committee supporting Mazzini, distrusting the latter's motives.[37] Knowledge from women on the ground in Europe was important, not merely to convey news in an era of primitive international communications but also to gather information and opinion on the practice of politics abroad.[38]

Elizabeth Sismondi was keen to encourage female participation in the intellectual debates which took place at her salon. She wrote to her sister:

> My Thursday evenings are in great repute, so that I even receive solicita-
> tions of admittance, but this more embarrasses than pleases me,
> because it is ill-natured, pedantic and a thousand evil things to refuse,
> yet their convenience and agreeableness is completely destroyed by
> admitting numbers. It is a great fashion and a great pride to admit as
> many men as possible in the soirées and I am the only one who exclude
> or rather limit them, and it is one of the great reasons that my soirées
> are more agreeable, because the conversation being general, the
> women take a part.[39]

Again, it is British women who viewed women rather than men as the central participants in the arena of salon politics. In a similar way to female letters, salons straddled the private, semi-private and public realms. They were not exclusively female arenas but were female-*managed* spaces where women could not only participate in politics but exercise varying degrees of influence on the female and male guests. A wide variety of salons, 'at homes', dinners and parties existed, ranging from the exclus-ive 'pink' parties of the leading aristocratic hostesses such as Lady Cork and the Countess of Jersey; the intellectual and literary 'blue' gatherings which were descended from the bluestocking salons of Elizabeth Mon-tagu, Hannah More, Elizabeth Carter and Hester Piozzi in the 1760s to the more modest, provincial, social evenings which nevertheless were important in shaping civic political culture.[40] The original bluestocking parties had eschewed any political debate or discussion of public affairs. However, the 'blue' parties of the late eighteenth and early nineteenth centuries were frequented by men and women who met on equal terms. Discussions on these occasions ranged from current affairs to art, philo-sophy, religion and literature.[41] Harriet Martineau wrote of her 'blue' parties:

> ...some people may be disposed to turn round upon me with the
> charge of giving blue-stocking parties. I believe that to blue-stocking
> people my soirées might have that appearance, because they looked
> through blue spectacles: but I can confidently say that, not only were
> my parties as diverse in quality as I could make them, – always
> including many who were not literary; but I took particular care that

no one was in any way shown off, but all treated with equal respect
as guests . . .[42]

Thus though contemporaries may have made distinctions between literary and political parties, in practice it is difficult to distinguish between
them. Debates on literature, philosophy and religion were frequently
entwined with more overtly political discussions. It was common to
attend two or more parties in one evening and thus discussions were
often carried over from one establishment to the next. The numerous
salons, dinners and parties that took place in the major cities of Europe
were undoubtedly of immense political importance. However, the extent
of women's political influence within the arena of the salon is more difficult, if not impossible to quantify. The female rather than the male
guests were often what made one gathering more attractive than another
and women's opinions and advice were eagerly sought and discussed.

The range of political issues discussed mostly between women, but also
between men and women, in the political networks discussed in this
chapter are extensive and encourage us to expand our assessment of
women's political activities into areas hitherto largely neglected. The
larger (male-initiated) issues of the day, of course are prominent fields
of action and debate. Issues such as the repeal of the Corn Laws, the anti-
slavery movement, and political reform loomed large on their agenda.
But equally important were questions such as the rights of oppressed
minorities: the Hungarians, Poles and Italians in Europe but also groups
such as the Aborigines further afield; education, especially the education
of women and girls; and a host of activities relating to fields such as
vivisection, cruelty to animals, vegetarianism and homeopathy.[43] This
is not to suggest that men and women had mutually exclusive spheres
of interest and action, merely that we should widen our perspective to
include those more marginal areas where a large number of women's
interests lay and where women had taken the lead in initiating political action. These have been characterised as 'soft' political issues as
opposed to the 'hard' mainstream topics such as electoral reform or economic policy, where women's scope for engagement was more limited.[44]
However, it is involvement in these 'soft' areas which gave women
a taste of political combat and encouraged the next generation of 'political women' to organise campaigns on more 'mainstream' issues. It is
also clear that the women concerned did not discriminate between the
issues that concerned them in this manner. Thus, Harriet Martineau
used the same techniques, energy and attention in her informal crusade
to convince her friends and the wider public of the health benefits,

especially to women, of hypnotherapy (or magnetism, as it was called in the 1850s) as she employed when campaigning on issues such as anti-slavery and women's rights.[45]

The 'well-neighboured' houses of the elite women discussed in this chapter were at the centre of their efforts to establish and extend their political networks. Household and kinship networks were of primary importance in social and political relations (this was equally true for men engaged in political activities). These kinship networks were pivotal to women's engagement in electoral politics, for example.[46] The women of important political families such as the Stuarts, who controlled seats in Scotland, England and Wales, used their extensive kinship networks to organise electoral campaigns and bring influence to bear in favour of their family's political interests.[47] They acted both in con-cert with and independently from their male kin.

Correspondence networks were crucial to the successful operation of the electoral machine. The number of letters passing between women increased markedly as the election approached and letters were used not only for the exchange of accurate information (often letters beg for up-to-date and accurate news from the women 'on the ground') but carry instructions to be actioned and advice on the best means to apply pressure. William Smith, the Member of Parliament for Norwich between 1802 and 1818, depended on his wife, Frances, to organise campaigns among the crucial out-voters living in London whilst he was at Nor-wich. Influential dissenting Norwich women, such as Amelia Opie and the daughters of the Gurney family, also kept Frances Smith and her daughters supplied with up-to-date information on the city's politics.[48]

The next level up from the household and family were the neigh-bourhood and local community links which were vital in providing the contacts necessary for political campaigning. Anne Lister, the Halifax landowner and businesswoman, used her daily contacts with women in the neighbourhood, not only her tenants but also casual acquaintances such as the woman organising the local Sunday School, in order to extend her political and electoral influence.[49] Fanny Wedgwood wrote to her cousin that: 'we have established a Ladies' Society at Newcastle [to campaign against slavery], but we don't meet with much success among the higher gentry. The set below them (our *Rue Basse*) is much more impressible...'.[50] The streets and market-places, as well as the domestic environment, remained important areas for female, even elite female, sociability and activity. Amelia Opie participated in a number of pressure groups in Norwich, including the Ladies Negroes' Friends which passed a resolution that its 'efforts should not cease until every negro mother in the British dominions should press a free-born child to her bosom'. Women went from house to house to dissuade use of 'slave-grown' sugar and to encourage wearing of worsted or silk instead of 'slave-grown' cotton. Opie was also secretary of the Norwich Ladies Association for Prison Discipline and spent one day a week visiting prisons, reading scriptures to female prisoners.[51]

A third important political and intellectual space where elite female networks were established and sustained were the salons which proliferated not only in London but in provincial towns and, as we have seen, in continental cities. The fact that women continued to control and dominate these important social and political institutions was crucial in order that women could express and extend their political interests. There was obviously a tremendous variety of political salons and parties in existence but their enduring popularity showed that they were important arenas to air political issues and encourage female political ambition, often by providing an informal mentoring process. An analysis of the physical and intellectual 'space' occupied by women therefore illustrates the need to avoid the dichotomy of public versus private sphere: in fact much of elite women's political activity took place in semi-public areas, not necessarily in separate female domains but usually in female-dominated areas. There was also much cross-fertilisation between these public, semi-public and private spaces.

It has been noted of seventeenth-century England that, 'female sociability found little place in the conduct-books, but it was central to the female experience'.[52] This remained true for the decades before 1860 and these female networks could be closely linked to political action. For elite women, whose conduct manuals accentuated the propriety of home-based, domestic activities, informal networks offered a method of participating in political affairs, an alternative to the clubs and coffee houses of their male partners. Rather than being socialised out of active politics, elite women were socialised into engagement with public affairs. Thus we should not see elite women as inevitably excluded from politics during this period – although they may have had limited contact with the public sphere they developed mechanisms and techniques in order that they could engage with the issues that concerned them. The most important of these was undoubtedly face-to-face contacts with other influential women and men. These ranged from casual encounters on the street, meetings in 'acceptable' public places such as the theatre or church, to the array of formal visits, soirées and parties in the drawing-rooms of elite society. The problem for the historian is that many of the experiences of women's informal contacts were not recorded and thus cannot be captured or quantified. Female correspondence networks, unlike their conversations, can, however be recreated in many cases and illustrate the importance of the written word in transmitting political news, gossip and information among women, from women to men and from men to women. The contents of women's letters demonstrate an engagement in a variety of political affairs including elections, party politics, local government and pressure groups but these issues are intermingled with interests in a wide range of 'alternative' political issues including animal rights, dress, diet and health. Women were not necessarily the more 'natural' letter-writers nor were their correspondence networks more extensive than those of their male relatives; however, exploring female epistolary exchanges gives historians access to the semi-private world of the political woman.[53] The formal letter from elite intellectual women to male politicians (and vice versa) was an acceptable technique of influencing public policy. Familiar letters exchanged with kinfolk and close friends served many political purposes: a source of news, gossip and information; discussion, debate and opinion-forming; the management of political events including elections; and contact with international affairs.

The women discussed in this chapter used an array of strategies to engage with current affairs and to participate in political events. Perhaps what is most striking is not the limited nature of these women's activities but the breadth of their political experiences. The early experiments in democracy and national self-determination in late eighteenth- and early nineteenth-century Europe made the continent a stimulating political arena and as such attracted a range of intellectual women (and men) who wished to be part of the exciting developments. By searching for the contexts in which women exercised political influence, exploring the extensive issues which concerned them, and examining the resources and strategies employed, it is possible to look afresh at the public realm in the decades before 1860.

Notes

1. A range of texts expound these views. See, for example, Leonore Davidoff and Catherine Hall, *Family Fortunes: Men and Women of the English Middle Class, 1780–1850* (London: Hutchinson, 1987) and Catherine Hall, 'Private Persons versus Public Someones: Class, Gender and Politics in England, 1780–1850', in Catherine Hall, *White, Male and Middle Class: Explorations in Feminism and*

History (Cambridge: Polity, 1992), pp. 151–71, for the argument that women began to be excluded from the public sphere as growing affluence among the middle class led to the dominance of the ideology of domesticity. The argument is taken further by James Vernon, *Politics and the People: A Study in English Political Culture, c. 1815–1867* (Cambridge: Cambridge University Press, 1992), who emphasises the 'closure' of politics to the working class and women, especially after 1832. Recent work has challenged this interpretation, however. See, for example: Linda Colley, *Britons: Forging the Nation, 1707–1807* (New Haven, CT, and London: Yale University Press, 1992), especially Chapter 6; Sarah Richardson, 'The Role of Women in Electoral Politics in the West Riding of Yorkshire During the 1830s', *Northern History*, 32 (1996), pp. 133–51; and Elaine Chalus, '"That Epidemical Madness": Women and Electoral Politics in the Late Eighteenth Century', in Hannah Barker and Elaine Chalus (eds), *Gender in Eighteenth-Century Britain: Roles, Representations and Responsibilities* (London: Longman, 1997), pp. 151–78.

2. See, for example: Vicky Randall, *Women in Politics: An International Perspective* (Basingstoke: Macmillan, 1987); Janet Siltanen and Michelle Stanworth (eds), *Women and the Public Sphere: A Critique of Sociology and Politics* (London: Hutchinson, 1984); Judith Evans 'Women in Politics: a Reappraisal', *Political Studies*, 28 (1980), pp. 210–21; and Liz Sperling and Charlotte Bretherton, 'Women's Policy Networks and the European Union', *Women's Studies International Forum*, 19 (1996), pp. 303–13.

3. Chalus 'An Epidemical Madness', and Richardson, 'The Role of Women in Electoral Politics' discuss the importance of kinship contacts in the electoral politics of the period. Jane Rendall, 'Friendship and Politics: Barbara Leigh Smith Bodichon (1827–91) and Bessie Rayner Parkes (1829–1925)', in Susan Mendus and Jane Rendall (eds), *Sexuality and Subordination* (London: Routledge, 1989), pp. 136–70 discusses the significance of female friendship to the development of women's political activities.

4. The suggestion that women may use their informal networks as a method of participating in politics was suggested by Jane Rendall (ed.), *Equal or Different: Women's Politics, 1800–1914* (Oxford: Blackwell, 1987), p. 13.

5. For a later period, see for example: Melanie Tebutt, *Women's Talk? A Social History of 'Gossip' in Working-Class Neighbourhoods, 1880–1960* (Aldershot: Scolar Press, 1995).

6. Harriet Martineau, *Autobiography: With Memorials by Maria Weston Chapman*, 3 vols (London: Virago, 1983, first published 1877), vol. iii, p. 265. Martineau's wide circle of friends provided her with material comforts as well as supporting her political activities (ibid., vol. iii, pp. 265–9).

7. This argument contrasts with some of the research undertaken on exclusively female networks in American politics, for example: Mary P. Ryan, 'The Power of Female Networks: a Case Study of Female Moral Reform in Antebellum America', *Feminist Studies*, 5 (1979), pp. 66–85, and Blanche Weisen Cook, 'Female Support Networks and Political Activism: Lillian Wald, Crystal Eastman, Emma Goldman', *Chrysalis*, 3 (1977), pp. 43–61. For a contrary view see Barbara Caine, *Victorian Feminists* (Oxford: Oxford University Press, 1992).

8. See, for example, a letter from Martineau to Henry Reeve in March 1859 where she writes: 'Come – what we shall do, – about the "Workies"', in Valerie

Sanders (ed.), *Harriet Martineau: Selected Letters* (Oxford: Clarendon Press, 1990), pp. 176–7.

9. There are numerous examples of the extent of Martineau's epistolary networks both in her autobiography and the large number of her letters that survive in defiance of her instructions to her friends to destroy all copies. The centrality of correspondence to her life and her work is neatly summed up by the following description of her writing-desk by Maria Weston Chapman: 'These are the labels on each great package of papers:'
   1. Accounts and correspondence with booksellers.
   2. Letters of pecuniary business.
   3. Letters of moral business.
   4. Letters from strangers or otherwise curious.
   5. Letters from deceased persons.
   6. Letters to be returned unopened.
   7. Correspondence with reviews and newspapers.
   8. Letters of literary business.
   9. Letters of family business.
   10. Letters of Testimony and American intercourses.
                                          (Martineau, *Autobiography*, vol. iii, p. 270).

10. Dena Goodman, *The Republic of Letters: A Cultural History of the French Enlightenment* (Ithaca, NY: Cornell University Press, 1994), especially Chapter 4; Rendall, 'Friendship and Politics', and Kathleen Wilson, *The Sense of the People: Politics, Culture and Imperialism in England, 1715–1785* (Cambridge: Cambridge University Press, 1995), especially p. 50. Wilson makes the point that these female correspondence networks were central in the exchange of political news and gossip among women *and* men.

11. *Harriet Martineau's Letters to Fanny Wedgwood*, ed. Elisabeth Sanders Arbuckle (Stanford, CA: Stanford University Press, 1983), p. xxiv.

12. Cited in Celia Lucy Brightwell, *Memoir of Amelia Opie* (London: R. T. S., 1855), p. 166.

13. Naomi Tadmor, '"In the Even My Wife Read to Me": Women, Reading and Household Life in the Eighteenth Century', in James Raven, Helen Small and Naomi Tadmor (eds), *The Practice and Representation of Reading in England* (Cambridge: Cambridge University Press, 1996); Mary A. Favret, *Romantic Correspondence: Women, Politics and the Fiction of Letters* (Cambridge: Cambridge University Press, 1993) and Rebecca Earle (ed.), *Epistolary Selves: Letters and Letter-writers, 1600–1945* (London: Ashgate, 1999), especially the introduction. I am grateful to Rebecca Earle for discussions and references on this topic and for pre-publication access to this edited collection of essays on correspondence and the self.

14. Sarah Austin to W. E. Gladstone, 18 February 1839, cited in Janet Ann Ross, *Three Generations of Englishwomen: Memoirs and Correspondence of Mrs. John Taylor, Mrs. Sarah Austin and Lady Duff Gordon,* 2 vols (London: T. Fisher Unwin, 1892), vol. i, p. 143.

15. Sarah Austin to W. E. Gladstone, 27 May 1839, ibid., p. 150.

16. Samuel Richardson, *Familiar Letters on Important Occasions* (reprinted London: George Routledge and Sons, 1928). Richardson states that 'Nature, propriety of character, plain sense, and general use' have been his guidelines in the construction of model letters. See also Favret, *Romantic Correspondence*, p. 37.

17. Martineau, *Autobiography*, vol. i, p. 3.
18. Elizabeth Eastlake, *Mrs. Grote: A Sketch* (London, 1880), p. 143.
19. Anna Jameson to Harriet Martineau, 17 January 1843, cited in Mrs. Steuart Erskine, *Anna Jameson: Letters and Friendships, 1812–60* (London: T. Fisher Unwin, 1915), pp. 222–4.
20. Earle, *Epistolary Selves*, introduction.
21. This point has been noted by Amanda Vickery, who reconstructed the social networks of Eliza Shackleton, a member of the Lancashire gentry, from her correspondence. She observed the importance of contact with London for Shackleton and her kin. Amanda Vickery, *The Gentleman's Daughter: Women's Lives in Georgian England* (New Haven, CT, and London: Yale University Press, 1998), especially pp. 29–30 and appendix 2. It is also clear that correspondence served this role for Martineau, who, despite remaining in the Lake District for long periods, maintained her engagement with political life.
22. Clare Midgley, 'Anti-Slavery and Feminism in Nineteenth-Century Britain', *Gender and History*, 5 (1993), pp. 343–62; Kathryn Kish Sklar, '"Women Who Speak for an Entire Nation": American and British Women Compared at the World Anti-Slavery Convention, London, 1840', *Pacific Historical Review*, 59 (1990), pp. 453–99; Sandra Stanley Holton, '"To Educate Women into Rebellion": Elizabeth Cady Stanton and the Creation of a Transatlantic Network of Radical Suffragism', *American Historical Review*, 99 (1994), pp. 1112–36, and Lee Virginia Chambers-Schiller, 'The CAB: A Trans-Atlantic Community. Aspects of Nineteenth-Century Reform' (unpublished PhD thesis, University of Michigan, 1977).
23. Examples include: Anne Lister, who was a travelling companion to Vere Stuart, a relation of Lord Stuart de Rothesay, the British Ambassador to Paris in 1830; Amelia Opie, who visited Paris twice in 1802 and 1829; Harriet Grote, who first visited France in 1830, and Sarah Austin who travelled extensively round Europe in the 1830s accompanying her husband, the lawyer John Austin.
24. The role of aristocratic women in the more exclusive English political salons is described in K. D. Reynolds, *Aristocratic Women and Political Society in Victorian Britain* (Oxford: Clarendon Press, 1998), esp. Chapter 5.
25. Ross, *Three Generations of Englishwomen*, vol. 1, pp. 172–3.
26. Ibid., pp. 142–3.
27. Cited in Lotte and Joseph Hamburger, *Troubled Lives: John and Sarah Austin* (Toronto: University of Toronto Press, 1985), p. 96.
28. Ibid., pp. v–viii.
29. Judith Johnston, *Anna Jameson: Victorian, Feminist, Woman of Letters* (Aldershot: Scolar Press, 1997), especially Chapter 5.
30. Ibid., p. 153.
31. For further examples of women's involvement in the Italian nationalist campaigns, see Chapter 7.
32. *Times*, 28 August 1824. Cited in 'Italian Exiles in Mexican Mining', *Journal of the West*, XXXII (1975), pp. 93–103.
33. Rumours abounded of 'wicked' aristocratic Polish and Hungarian counts eloping with the daughters of British aristocrats who were transfixed by their exotic characters. See, for example, the account given by Mary Lucy of Count Teleki's wooing of Lord Langdale's daughter: Alice Fairfax-Lucy (ed.),

Mistress of Charlecote: The Memoirs of Mary Elizabeth Lucy (London: Gollancz, 1987), pp. 100–1. Mary Howitt's support for Francis and Theresa Pulszky and other Hungarian supporters of Kossuth is given in Margaret Howitt (ed.), *Mary Howitt: An Autobiography*, 2 vols (London: W. Isbister, 1889), vol. ii, p. 85.

34. Sarah Austin was acclaimed as the 'protecting saint of refugees' by the Italians and the Chevalier de Santa Rosa wrote: 'Dear Madam, I like you because you are most affectionate in the world to your fireside ... ' (Ross, *Three Generations of Englishwomen*, vol. i, p. 63). Austin's role in finding work for the Italians in Mexican silver mines is described in 'Italian Exiles in Mexican Mining'.

35. For more information see Henrietta Emma Litchfield (ed.), *Emma Darwin: A Century of Family Letters*, 2 vols (London: John Murray, 1915).

36. For more information on the Coppet circle see: Susan Tennenbaum, 'The Coppet Circle: Literary Criticism as Political Discourse', *History of Political Thought*, 1 (1980), pp. 453–73.

37. Mme Sismondi to Elizabeth Wedgwood, 4 March 1848 and Mme Sismondi to Elizabeth Wedgwood, 4 August 1851: 'Mazzini for these twenty years, has been living on what he has duped from the poor Italian exiles, whom he has sent without number to death and dungeon, taking care to keep himself safe; and now that they begin to understand him and their funds fail, he begins to gull the English. Lift your voice with mine, dear Elizabeth, only do it calmer, wiser, better, but above all do not be betrayed into giving your money tho but in half-crowns, or even in pence ... ', cited in Litchfield, *Emma Darwin*, vol. ii, pp. 115 and 143.

38. Thus Sarah Austin's work on education was influenced by the information she gathered from her extensive European visits. See also Reynolds, *Aristocratic Women and Political Society*, pp. 183–5.

39. Mme Sismondi to Mrs Josiah Wedgwood 28 January 1824, cited in Litchfield, *Emma Darwin*, vol. i, p. 153.

40. An example of a provincial salon is that of Susannah Taylor (the mother of Sarah Austin) at Norwich in the late eighteenth and early nineteenth centuries. The biographer of Sir James Mackintosh wrote that: 'our chief delight was in the society of Mrs. John Taylor, a most intelligent and excellent woman, mild and unassuming, quiet and meek, sitting amidst her large family, occupied with her needles and domestic occupations, but always assisting, by her great knowledge, the advancement of kind and dignified sentiment and conduct. Manly wisdom and feminine gentleness were in her united.' Cited in Celia Lucy Brightwell, *Memorials of the Life of Amelia Opie, Selected and Arranged from her Letters, Diaries and Other Manuscripts* (Norwich: Fletcher and Alexander, 1854), p. 32. Although Mackintosh emphasises Susannah Taylor's domestic and feminine qualities, from other descriptions of her conduct and her surviving correspondence, it is clear that she held firm political views and was an important influence on other leading Norwich women, including her daughter Sarah Austin, Amelia Opie and the Martineau family.

41. An indication of the merging of the boundaries between blue and pink parties is given by Amelia Opie. She wrote of a party at Elizabeth Inchbald's house: ' ... I found myself *tête à tête* with an Edinburgh reviewer, and a lecturer on moral philosophy [Dr Brown]. However, I did not *die* of it, as I offered to take him to Lady C[ork].'s *pink* party to-night. And her *blue* one on the 11th, and

42. Martineau, *Autobiography*, vol. iii, pp. 373–4.
43. These issues are beginning to be discussed in relation to women and politics. See, for example, Ruth Watts, *Gender, Power, and the Unitarians in England, 1760–1860* (London: Longman, 1998); Hilda Kean, *Animal Rights: Political and Social Change in Britain since 1800* (London: Reaktion books, 1998) and Leah Leneman, 'The Awakened Instinct: Vegetarianism and the Women's Suffrage Movement in Britain', *Women's History Review*, 6 (1997), pp. 271–88.
44. For a discussion of 'hard' and 'soft' political issues in a contemporary context see Sperling and Bretherton, 'Women's Policy Networks and the European Union'.
45. After Martineau's treatment by mesmerists she publicised her recovery in a controversial series of articles in the *Athenaeum*, later published as *Letters on Mesmerism* (London: E. Moxon, 1845). Her description of the public debate that arose after the publication of this pamphlet can be found in Martineau, *Autobiography*, vol. ii, pp. 194–202.
46. These points are developed in Chalus, 'That Epidemical Madness' and Richardson, 'The Role of Women in Electoral Politics'.
47. The political interests of the Stuart family (which included descendants of the Earl of Bute and the Stuart-Wortleys) for example, included constituencies in Scotland, England and Wales. The female members of the family were pivotal in the information network which sustained the family's various political campaigns. See Richardson, 'The Role of Women in Electoral Politics', and Caroline Susan Theodore Grosvenor and Charles Beilby Stuart Wortley (eds), *The First Lady Wharncliffe and her Family, 1779–1856*, 2 vols (London: William Heinemann, 1927).
48. R. W. Davis, *Dissent in Politics, 1780–1830: The Political Life of William Smith, MP* (London: Epworth Press, 1971), esp. Chapter 8, and Smith MSS, Cambridge University Library. See, for example, 305, Amelia Opie to Patty Smith, 29 October 1812.
49. Richardson, 'The Role of Women in Electoral Politics'.
50. Litchfield, *Emma Darwin*, vol. i, pp. 181–2.
51. Jacobine Menzies-Wilson and Helen Lloyd, *Amelia, the Tale of a Plain Friend* (London and New York: Oxford University Press, 1937), pp. 225–6.
52. Bernard Capp, 'Separate Domains? Women and Authority in Early Modern England', in Paul Griffiths, Adam Fox and Steve Hindle (eds), *The Experience of Authority in Early Modern England* (Basingstoke: Macmillan, 1996), p. 128.
53. These points are further explored in Earle, *Epistolary Selves*, introduction. Some women's correspondence networks did, however, rival those of their male counterparts. Note, for example, the extent of Elizabeth Montagu's correspondence at the Huntington Library, San Marino which contains 6,923 pieces.

4
From Supporting Missions to Petitioning Parliament: British Women and the Evangelical Campaign against *Sati* in India, 1813–30

Clare Midgley

Between 13 February 1829 and 29 March 1830 a total of fourteen separate groups of women from around England sent petitions to Parliament calling on it to abolish *sati*, or rather what they described as 'the practice in India of burning widows on the funeral piles of their husbands'.[1] Amongst the earliest examples of female petitioning, and directly preceding women's more extensive petitioning for the abolition of colonial slavery, this intervention in the political process was taken not by women who identified themselves as radicals or supporters of the 'rights of women' but rather by women associated with the evangelical missionary movement. The petitions formed the climax of a broader campaign against *sati* linked to women's support for missionary activity in India and to the first coordinated attempt to provide Christian education for Indian girls and women.

All this took place some forty years prior to the emergence of an organised women's movement in England.[2] At this later period, as Antoinette Burton has shown, feminist interventions on the behalf of Indian women became a way of promoting their own claim to a place in the national body politic.[3] This chapter shows how women's interventions in the *sati* debate perhaps fulfilled a rather similar function during the early nineteenth century, helping to extend 'women's sphere' beyond the purely private and domestic.[4] Previous research on anti-slavery has suggested that it was where charitable philanthropy shaded over into movements for humanitarian social and moral reform that there was most scope for women to extend the boundaries of feminine activity and promote expanded visions of women's sphere.[5] This study of the contemporaneous campaign against *sati* confirms this. In exploring women's support for the foreign mission movement it also offers new insights into the complex and ambivalent relationship of evangelicalism to the origins of modern feminism.[6]

In exploring British women's developing involvement in the missionary campaign against *sati*, this chapter begins by outlining their organisation in general support of missionary activity in India from 1813. It then moves on to look at women's specific promotion of Indian female education as a means of eradicating *sati* in the 1820s. Finally, it focuses on women's petitioning of Parliament in 1829–30 as part of the campaign to abolish *sati* by legislative means.

The roots of the British campaign against *sati* lay in the beginnings of missionary activity in India by the new missionary societies set up by evangelical Christians in the 1790s.[7] This 'foreign mission' movement was concerned with the conversion of the heathen abroad, particularly within the British Empire, but it had close links with the 'home mission' movement, which focused on the propagation of 'active' Christianity to the working class within England.[8] The missionary movement as a whole was informed by the evangelical conviction that the key to the eradication of vice and sin lay in combating both religious infidelity at home and 'heathen' idolatry in the Empire.[9] Missionary societies were supported by local auxiliary societies, and from the 1800s they also began to develop networks of ladies' associations which drew in thousands of middle-class women to raise funds by door-to-door visiting to collect penny-a-week subscriptions from the poor.[10] The societies became increasingly reliant on such female support: the official historian of the Church Missionary Society (CMS), for example, commented that the ladies' associations 'were a great power' on which the CMS 'largely depended' for the collection of funds. Female subscribers to the Society increased from 12 per cent in 1801 to 29 per cent in 1823.[11] The missionary movement was thus crucial to the development of a new pattern of organised female philanthropy. This was characterised by local ladies' associations which were linked to male-run national organisations. In other words, evangelical initiatives in the imperial field were intimately linked to new arenas of activity for middle-class women in Britain.

One of the first battles which evangelicals fought in Parliament was to get the Charter of the East India Company modified so that India would be opened up to missionary activity. Their first attempt in 1793 failed, but in 1813 a concerted campaign conducted both within Parliament and by pressure from without proved successful.[12] As well as achieving its immediate objective, the campaign gave wide public exposure to missionary propaganda and drew a large section of the public into active support for missions. Evangelical Anglicans who were members of the influential Clapham Sect spearheaded the missionary campaign in Parliament. In their propaganda the position of Indian women, and in particular the practice of *sati*, played a crucial role in arguments that Britain had a duty to bring Christianity and civilisation to its Indian subjects. A practice, which was confined to a minority of Hindus, came to stand for the depravity of the culture of the Indian subcontinent as a whole. Thus Charles Grant, who had spent over twenty years in India and who was elected to the Board of the East India Company in 1794, sought to combat positive views about India promoted by eighteenth-century British Orientalist scholars such as William Jones by stressing the suffering of women 'doomed to joyless confinement through life, and a violent premature death'.[13] His colleague William Wilberforce, who led the successful Parliamentary campaign to open India to missions in 1813, gave a powerful speech in the House of Commons in which he described 'the evils of Hindostan' as 'family, fireside evils', paying particular attention to the ill-treatment of women, as evidenced by polygamy and *sati*, and contrasting this with the equality to which women were entitled in all Christian countries.[14]

Wilberforce's rhetoric of 'fireside evils' would have had great resonance for evangelicals. It set up an implicit contrast between the fireside as the scene of the horrible spectacle of the Hindu widow burning on the funeral pyre, and evangelicals' idealised view of 'fireside enjoyments, homeborn happiness' as the hub of the Christian family.[15] Indeed, inter-linking the domestic and the political in characteristic evangelical fashion, Wilberforce would read out at the dinner table a list of women who had recently committed *sati*.[16] Evangelical women were expected to exert an important influence over moral and religious matters from such a domestic base and, while the public campaign of 1813 was an exclusively male preserve, the leading female member of the Clapham Sect, Hannah More, worked energetically behind the scenes to encourage signatories to petitions in favour of the opening up of India to missionaries.[17]

Sati became the focus of appeals designed to draw British women into active support for missions. In June 1813, for example, the *Missionary Register* based their appeal to British women on an item 'On the burning of women in India' which they had selected from the influential *Account of the Writings, Religion, and Manners of the Hindoos* by the Revd William Ward, one of the early group of British Baptist missionaries at

the Danish enclave of Seramapore.[18] The appeal, in contrasting the lot
of British women living in a Christian land with that of Indian women
living in a land of superstition, set a pattern for future calls for English
women's help:

> Let every Christain woman, who reads the following statement, pity
> the wretched thousands of her sex who are sacrificed every year in
> India to a cruel superstition, and thank God for her own light and
> privileges, and pray and labour earnestly for the salvation of these
> her miserable fellow subjects.[19]

Soon members of the new ladies' associations themselves began to shape
missionary discourse on *sati*, drawing on missionary accounts but presenting them in ways which they felt would most appeal to an audience of English women. An early example is the 1814 Address of the
Southwark Ladies' Association. One of the first female auxiliaries of the
Church Missionary Society, the Association had as its patroness Mrs Henry
Thornton, wife of one of the Clapham Sect leaders of the CMS. The
women's Address described *sati* as 'one picture of misery . . . which
appeals to their own sex'. Breaking with the usual pattern of a lurid
account accompanied by general expressions of horror at the barbarous
practice, the Address instead set out to draw women into sympathy for,
and empathy with, Indian women. Defining a characteristic of the female
sex as being 'to commiserate with suffering humanity', the Address
opened with an attempt to get women to identify as mothers with the
sufferings of Indian widows, taking it for granted that Indian and
British women shared the same loving feelings for their children:

> Let the anxiously fond mother, who trembles lest her tender off-
> spring should, by a wise but inscrutable Providence, be deprived of
> either of the guardians of their early years, for a moment endeavour
> to realize the poignant anguish which must rend the breast of that
> other, who in the decease of her children's best support, hears the
> summons for her to forsake them, at a time, too, when they most need
> her fostering care; and to immolate herself on her husband's funeral
> pile! – The affecting representation excites our sympathy: let it stimu-
> late our exertions.[20]

British women supporters of missions thus couched their opposition
to *sati* in terms of an Indian widow's duty as a mother. This accorded
with the evangelical idealisation of motherhood. It also linked women's

support for missions in the Empire to their preoccupations in the domestic philanthropic arena with work among working-class women and children.[21] Here we see middle-class 'women's mission to women' taking on an imperial dimension at a very early stage.[22] Here, too, we see the evangelical ideology of domesticity being deployed to promote a pro-imperial message. Readers were encouraged to evoke the following scene of family prayer along the ideal evangelical model:

> Enter the dwelling where your messenger has proclaimed the glad tidings of salvation. Behold a father, a mother, a family, forming an assembly of humble, grateful worshippers, who, while they adore the Fountain of their mercies, are fervently craving Heaven's richest blessings on the British Isles, the medium through which those blessings flowed.

The building block of the ambitious missionary project of the conversion and moral reform of India is represented not as the individual convert but rather as the Christianised family. This was in accordance with the centrality of the household to the evangelical project.[23] The reward for British women's exertions would be the gratitude of Indian families towards both Christian missionaries and the British nation. In these ways evangelical British women were encouraged to imagine that they had the power, under the auspices of the British Empire, to extend their own 'privileges' to other women, and so to mitigate what Wilberforce had labelled the 'family, fireside evils' of 'Hindostan', epitomised in the horror of *sati*. 'Women's sphere' of domestic responsibility was given a truly global reach.

From the outset, a central element of missionary activity in India was the spread of education. The setting up of mission schools was motivated by the belief that intellectual enlightenment would lead to the rejection of Hindu idolatry, conversion to Christianity, and moral reform of society.[24] Since missionaries identified many of the evils of Hindu society as involving the ill-treatment of women, promoting Indian female education was potentially crucial to their success. Progress in this area was initially slow, however, partly because of the reluctance of missionary societies to employ single women as teachers.[25] Convinced that the education of women was vital if *sati* was to be eradicated, William Ward, one of the leading Baptist missionaries active in India, issued a series of appeals to English women between 1817 and 1821 in which he urged them to take the initiative in this field.[26] British imperial rule had, he claimed, come about so that 'one of the smallest portions of the civilized world' would have the opportunity to 'accomplish some very important moral change' in the 'long-degraded state' of India.[27] British women were themselves privileged – 'raised by gracious Providence to the enjoyment of so many comforts' and British society was 'much improved by their virtues'.[28] It was thus their duty to help the seventy-five millions of less fortunate Indian women. As Brian Stanley has concluded, in his study of the relationship between missions and empire, the 'Christian belief in divine providence led by logical steps to the concept of Britain's imperial role as a sacred trust to be used in the interests of the gospel'.[29] Here we see articulated British women's duty to help fulfil this sacred trust.

To meet this duty Ward urged both British and American women to organise themselves into societies to rescue Indian women 'from ignorance, and by that means from these funeral piles'.[30] Implicit in this appeal was a recognition that it was not enough for women to simply raise funds for missionary societies in the hope that their male leaders would take initiatives in Indian women's education: women needed to organise independently in order to achieve this specific objective. The importance of taking steps which lay outside the realm of official government action was also recognised: government action against *sati* would fail, Ward believed, without educational initiatives to back it up: 'government may do much to put an end to these immolations; but without the communication of knowledge, the fires can never be wholly quenched'.[31] Ward stressed the power of British women to bring about social improvements: 'There can hardly be a misery, connected with human existence, which the pity and the zeal of British females, under the blessing of Providence, is not able to remove'.[32] This was truly a women's cause, one only they could successfully carry out: 'Other triumphs of humanity may have been gained by our Howards, our Clarksons, our Wilberforces; but this emancipation of the females and widows of British India must be the work of the British fair';[33] this was 'the cause of woman – but especially of every christian widow – of every christian mother – of every christian female'.[34]

Ward's appeals to women were translated into a specific plan of action in 1820 by the British and Foreign School Society which set up a women's committee to coordinate developments.[35] The Society's 'Appeal in behalf of Native Females' urged British women to contribute to a special fund set up to fund the sending out of one of their countrywomen to train Indian women as teachers. Given that 'The state of Indian Manners forbids females to be placed under the tuition of men':

Is it not manifest that the Ladies in Britain are the natural guardians of these unhappy Widows and Orphans in British India? Is it possible that our fair countrywomen ... can ... continue unmoved by the cries issuing from these fires, and from the thousands of orphans which surround them. . . . This appeal cannot be made in vain: such a tale of woe was never before addressed to the hearts of British Mothers. Let every Lady of rank and influence in the United Empire do her duty, and these fires cannot burn another twenty years.[36]

British women were now being urged to take on an active, guiding 'maternal' role as tutors and guardians of suffering Indian women. By 1820 the issue of *sati* was just beginning to attract parliamentary attention and the *Missionary Register*, urging support for women's initiative, suggested, 'If the Females of the United Empire will act on the appeal now made to them, the Voice of the Country will be so decisive in behalf of just and efficient measures on this subject, that the wishes of humane Senators will be fully accomplished'.[37] In other words, widespread female support for the educational initiatives would in itself act as strong public pressure on Parliament to take action against *sati*.

By May 1821 a total of £521:9s had been collected by the Ladies' Committee of the British and Foreign School Society to fund sending a woman teacher to Calcutta.[38] A former governess, Mary Anne Cooke, was selected.[39] She succeeded in setting up a network of schools in the Calcutta district, which taught more than 800 pupils over a three-year period to 1825.[40] In 1828 she became head of the new Central School for Girls in Calcutta, an impressive stone building, providing education for some 150–200 scholars with the aim of training them to be teachers.[41]

In developing girls' education, Cooke attempted to gain support from several sources. First, there were prominent local Hindu reformers who were supportive of girls' education.[42] Secondly, there were English women resident in Calcutta, who in 1824 set up a Ladies' Society for Native-Female Education and brought Cooke's schools under female management.[43] Thirdly, there were women in England itself. Voluntary financial support from Britain was particularly important because it was against imperial policy to give official financial support to schools in India, which had an explicitly Christian curriculum.[44] An 'Indian Female Education Fund' in aid of the Ladies' Society was opened in England in 1825, under the auspices of the CMS, and it issued an 'Appeal to the Ladies of the United Kingdom'.[45] In 1829 the fund-raising passed into the hands of a separate women's organisation, the Ladies' East India Female Education Society. This was set up in London by Amelia Heber, widow of the former Bishop of Calcutta, and drew support from a number of aristocratic ladies and Evangelicals associated with the Clapham Sect.[46] It was the first society in Britain to focus specifically on Indian female education and marked the beginning of independent organisation by women, who were excluded from the all-male management of the missionary societies. As such, it formed part of the broader move towards female-run philanthropic societies, which began in England at this period.[47]

Alongside attempts to undermine Hindu support for *sati* through Christian education, missionaries and their supporters increasingly put pressure on the British authorities to take legal steps to eradicate the practice. This pressure was stepped up when official statistics suggested that the regulation of *sati* introduced from 1813 onwards had actually led to an increase, rather than a decline, in widow immolation. At the same time, a growing campaign against *sati* was developing within indigenous Indian society itself, led by the influential Bengali Hindu reformer, Rammohun Roy. He not only gained the support of a section of the Bengali elite but his tracts on *sati* also heavily influenced missionary discourse against the practice. English editions of his tracts were published and his evidence that Hindu scriptures did not sanction *sati* was deployed by British campaigners.[48]

Within the British Parliament missionaries gained vital support from Thomas Fowell Buxton, Wilberforce's successor as leader of the Evangelical Anglican group of reformers. In 1820 the first Blue Book on *sati* was published, and the following year Buxton initiated the first parliamentary debate on the issue.[49] In 1823 public pressure for the prohibition of *sati* began to mount, with the presentation of the first anti-*sati* petition to Parliament.[50] The campaign gained renewed momentum in 1827, following the publication of the first edition of what became the most widely circulated and extensively reviewed anti-*sati* tract, the Reverend James Peggs's *The Suttees' Cry to Britain*.[51] Peggs urged that petitions be sent to Parliament from the inhabitants of Great Britain and Ireland, suggesting that the government, having abolished the slave trade, must surely now act against *sati*.

Peggs promoted his anti-*sati* campaign by a tour around England, addressing local missionary meetings and raising funds. At the end of 1828 he founded in Coventry the Society for the Abolition of Human Sacrifices in India.[52] The Society's remit was broader than *sati* alone: it also aimed to campaign for the passage of British laws to abolish a range of other 'heathen' practices which Peggs had drawn to public notice: infanticide, the exposure of the sick on the banks of the Ganges, and deaths on pilgrimages to holy places. By the beginning of 1830 the Society had circulated 104 books and 5,264 pamphlets, had arranged a public

meeting in Coventry to petition Parliament against *sati*; and had stimu-
lated the formation of similar committees in both London and Birmingham. The Society had close links with the Anti-Slavery Society, which
acted as the London distributor of its pamphlets.[53]

Altogether, between 1823 and 1830 a total of 107 petitions against
sati were presented to the House of Commons, the majority from 1827
onwards, with petitioning reaching a peak in the first half of 1830.[54]
Despite this substantial expression of public opinion, historians have
largely ignored the extra-parliamentary campaign against *sati*, which took
place in Britain. This is largely because it was completely overshadowed
in scale by the contemporary anti-slavery campaign with its influential
central committee, impressive nationwide network of local auxiliaries,
massive propaganda drive and its success in presenting thousands of
petitions between 1823 and 1833.[55]

Amidst this general neglect, the participation of women in the anti-
sati campaign has gone unrecognised. There is no evidence for the formation of related ladies' associations, in contrast to the missionary and
anti-slavery societies. Female financial support was certainly solicited
and welcomed: after Peggs preached in the Particular Baptist Chapel at
St. Ives in Cornwall, the Misses Barnes donated a sovereign to fund the
sending of copies of *The Suttees' Cry* to 'the principal European func-
tionaries in India', while a Miss Witchurch of Salisbury donated £5 'for
expenses of publications before the [Coventry] Society was formed'.[56]
Peggs and other activists, however, were cautious about urging women
to undertake public action against *sati*. At this period, although there
was no explicit rule prohibiting women from signing petitions to Parliament, it was generally felt to be inappropriate and it was feared that the
presence of their signatures would bring discredit and ridicule to the
causes they supported.[57]

In the first edition of *The Suttees' Cry* (1827), Peggs concluded with a
tentative call for public action by women against *sati*. He urged the
British inhabitants of Calcutta to petition against *sati* and suggested
that the ladies of Calcutta should petition, to 'impress on their husbands
the importance of rescuing a degraded part of the female sex'.[58] Here
female petitioning was safely removed to a distant colonial setting and
presented as nothing more than a way of exerting private, wifely, moral
influence on husbands. Peggs made a bolder suggestion in March 1828
when he produced a second, updated edition of *The Suttees' Cry*. In this
he suggested 'petitions to the British Parliament, signed by females
from the principal Cities and Towns in Britain and Ireland'. He justified
his call in these terms: 'should it be objected – this is an unprecedented

method of expressing public opinion: it may be replied, "Is not the destruction of so many hundred unhappy widows annually in British India, a sufficient justification of it?"'[59] Peggs's suggestion was cautiously tucked away in a footnote, though he did support the inclusion of women in the campaign. For example, he closed this edition with the text of a poem by Ellen of Matlock, Bath, entitled 'A Voice from India; or the Horrors of a Suttee'. In this, following a lurid description of the burning of a widow, the poet made a gender-inclusive appeal to 'British matrons, husbands, sires' to 'haste to quench the horrid fires' by urging government to end the practice as well as by supporting the spread of Christianity.[60] As in the anti-slavery movement, poetry was used by women as campaigning propaganda.

Despite Peggs's own suggestions, the Coventry society never publicly called for female petitions. The London committee formed to combat *sati* was initially equally cautious: when it was set up in June 1829 it signalled its desire for women to take up the anti-*sati* cause, but confined this to a melodramatic and sentimental appeal for women to unite in using their informal influence: 'Were each British female to shed one honest tear on these flames, they would go out for ever; for such an influence would then be employed, as would secure the glorious object'.[61] In January 1830, however, the London committee took the plunge, suggesting that ladies unite in petitioning Parliament for the abolition of *sati*. Even now, their approach remained cautious: they settled on a separate female petition, and delayed the adoption of this until after the public meeting.[62]

This hesitant approach by the committee was echoed by the stance of the denominational journals, which only endorsed female petitions retrospectively. The *Baptist Magazine* made no mention of female petitions until March 1830, when it gave the full text of the anti-*sati* petition of the females of the congregation of Protestant Dissenters meeting in Eagle Street, London. It prefaced this by a statement, which sought to establish its acceptability by emphasising that it was a response to exceptional circumstances, and by stressing the respectability and lack of stridency of the petitioners:

> Among the petitions now presenting to parliament for this purpose, we are happy to find some from that sex whose sympathies must be supposed to be peculiarly alive on this subject, and who, touched by the urgency of the case, are coming forth from their accustomed retirement, clad in the veil of modesty, and in a tone of amiable commiseration to express their feelings, to solicit on behalf of these

daughters of oppression the protective shield of a British and a Christian government.[63]

Despite the cautious approach by the male evangelical missionary leadership, between February 1829 and April 1830 a total of fourteen separate groups of women from around England sent anti-*sati* petitions to Parliament, comprising around one-fifth of the anti-*sati* petitions presented over this particular period and around one-eighth of total anti-*sati* petitions.[64] Anti-*sati* petitions were presented to the House of Commons from the female inhabitants of the towns of Castle Donnington and Loughborough in Leicestershire; from Melbourne, Heanor and Ilkestone in Derbyshire; from Stroud in Gloucestershire; from Alcester in Warwickshire; and from Blackburn in Lancashire. Petitions were also presented from the female members of the following nonconformist congregations: Protestant Dissenters of the Independent denomination meeting at Bassingbourn in Cambridgeshire; Protestant Dissenters of Old Gravel Pit Meeting in Hackney in Middlesex; Protestant Dissenters meeting in Eagle-Street, London; Protestant Dissenters of the Calvinistic Meeting-House in Kettering, Northamptonshire; and Baptists of Cockspur-Street Chapel in Liverpool, Lancashire. In addition, a mixed petition was sent from the male and female inhabitants of Falmouth in Cornwall. Five of the groups also presented petitions to the House of Lords.[65]

Female petitions thus came from a wide range of English counties, encompassing the Northwest, the Midlands, the West Country and the capital. They originated from dissenting congregations and town inhabitants, and from communities ranging from small rural towns to large industrial cities. Their distribution mirrors the overall spread of petitions against *sati*, all but one of which (from Belfast) came from England. This spread reflects the English base of the missionary societies and religious denominations active in the campaign against *sati*, the wide diffusion of missionary propaganda at the period, and James Peggs's own tours of the country to address missionary meetings.[66] Peggs was based in Derby in 1827 and in Coventry in 1828, and he may well have encouraged the female petitions from Derbyshire and the Midlands. Many female petitions came from the same towns as men's petitions, and may have been promoted by local male activists or their female relatives: from Liverpool and Blackburn, where there was a concentrated flurry of petitioning in 1830; from the same dissenting congregations in London and Kettering; and from the towns of Melbourne, Heanor and Loughborough, from where the inhabitants had already sent petitions a year or two before. Unfortunately, however, definite information about the organisation of the petitions is lacking; in particular, we know nothing about the extent of women's own initiatives.

Interestingly, there is no evidence that female petitions against *sati* excited the disapproval or ribald dismissal that greeted women petitioners against Roman Catholic emancipation at this period.[67] Perhaps this was because *sati* had long been presented in evangelical and missionary circles as an appropriate area of female concern – a part of women's philanthropic mission to women. Certainly the women's petitions presented the issue as one within women's sphere.

One way the women petitioners did this was to stress their identification with the sufferings of their own sex. They urged Parliament to take action 'on a subject in which, as females, they are deeply interested' and which demanded their 'peculiar sympathy'. They described *sati* as 'degrading to the character, and disgusting to the moral feelings, of every *British* female', and they expressed 'heartfelt commiseration with Indian widows'. Presenting their public action as an extension of their private familial roles, they stated that 'as Wives, as Mothers, as Daughters, or as Sisters' they could not contemplate practices such as *sati* and infanticide 'but with emotions of the most painful Nature'. Women also presented the issue as one of humanity – and thus within their sphere as philanthropists and guardians of morality – rather than one of politics. Acknowledging that they were 'aware that it is unusual for persons of their sex to express opinions on matters of legislation', they attempted to disarm criticism by stating that they would not 'have done so on the present occasion, had they not been impelled by the convictions of conscience and the claims of benevolence'. Nor would they have acted 'on any other subject than humanity'. Finally, women petitioners diffused the potential interpretation of their action as usurping men's role by presenting themselves as pleading for Christian paternal protection for women. Thus the women of Eagle-Street congregation described Indian women as 'their fellow-subjects' who 'had an equal right to the paternal protection of the British Government'. One group of petitioners even appended the following lines of verse to their appeal:

> Say but a single word and save
> Ten thousand mothers from a flaming grave,
> And tens of thousands from that source of woe,
> That ever must to orphan'd children flow.[68]

By 1830 the British campaign against *sati* had achieved its objective. In contrast to the campaigns against slavery, it did not result in direct legislation by Parliament. However, it did create a sense of widespread public outrage about the practice and this helped to motivate and enable action by the new Governor-General of India, Lord William Bentinck, who was himself an Evangelical Anglican supporter of missionary activity.[69] After canvassing opinion in India, on 4 December 1829 Bentinck issued his regulation on *sati*, which forbade widow-burning in the Bengal Presidency. The Governors of Madras and Bombay followed suit in February and April 1830 and as news of these developments filtered back to Britain petitioning came to a halt.[70]

The successful conclusion of the missionary campaign against *sati* marked the beginnings of a shift to a more culturally interventionist imperial policy by the British in India during the 'Age of Reform' associated with Bentinck's governorship.[71] British women's organised support for missionary activity in India, initiatives in promoting the development of Christian education for Indian women, and petitioning of Parliament to legislate against *sati* had played a part in bringing about this shift. Expressions of concern about the oppression of women by unchristian and uncivilised men became, from this period onwards, crucial to the moral justification of Empire.

When British women's attempts to intervene in Indian women's lives are viewed alongside their participation in the anti-slavery movement, in which they focused on the sufferings of women under slavery, we can see that during the period between 1813 and 1838 there emerged an important imperial dimension to women's philanthropic work. From an early stage middle-class 'women's mission to women' encompassed not only working-class women within Britain but also black and Indian women in distant parts of the British Empire. They asserted themselves as the group best able to speak on behalf of and offer help to women within an imperial frame. Their mission was based both on notions of cultural superiority and on a sense of identification and empathy with non-Western women; on the grounds of women's common experiences as wives, as mothers and as widows. This helped to shape women philanthropists' sense of their own identity as not simply middle-class but also as civilised, Christian and British; it also encouraged them to feel that they had the power to bring about change in women's lives worldwide.

It was to challenge women's social position in a colonial rather than a metropolitan context that British women first felt impelled to intervene directly in the political process through petitioning Parliament, and it was the women campaigners against *sati* who initiated this process, closely followed by much larger numbers of women anti-slavery campaigners.

The emergence of British women into public life and politics in the 1820s and 1830s was thus intimately linked to the development of missionary evangelicalism and its associated projects of imperial social and moral reform.

The implications of this for the origins of modern Western feminism need to be considered. In petitioning, women were establishing their right to intervene directly in the political process on issues which combined questions of religion and morality with humanitarian concern for colonial 'fellow-subjects' of their own sex. They were also becoming publicly involved in defining the limits of acceptable male behaviour on the global stage, asserting the value of a woman's life and the unacceptability of male violence. However, in favourably contrasting their own position with that of Indian women, and in stressing their own privileges in a civilised and Christian country, British women campaigners against *sati*, like women anti-slavery campaigners of the following decade, were signalling acceptance of their own subordination.[72] In anti-*sati* literature problems of male dominance were projected away from British women's own menfolk and on to Indian men. Christian British men's patriarchy was associated with paternal protection of women, whereas Hindu Indian men's patriarchy was associated with male violence and the ill-treatment of women.

While women campaigners against *sati*, together with their sisters in the anti-slavery movement, thus expanded the bounds of 'women's mission to women' in the early nineteenth century, even to the extent of direct interventions in the political sphere on behalf of women in the British Empire, they did not explicitly challenge the ideology of 'separate spheres' or directly address their own social subordination. It was not until the emergence of an organised feminist movement in the second half of the nineteenth century that British women found a way of combining action on behalf of women in the Empire with action against their own subordination in the metropolis.

Acknowledgements

This is a heavily revised and refocused version of a paper published as 'Female Emancipation in an Imperial Frame: English Women and the Campaign against *Sati* (Widow-Burning) in India, 1813–1830' in *Women's History Review*, 9 (2000). I would like to acknowledge the financial assistance of the Leverhulme Trust for a Research Fellowship, which facilitated the research and writing of this chapter.

Notes

1. See, for example, text of the petition of the female inhabitants of Melbourne, *Journal of the House of Commons*, 84 (1829) entry for 2 April 1829, p. 192. The term 'suttee' rather than *sati* was used in British nineteenth-century texts. Definitions of *sati* vary in English and Indian languages: see John Stratton Hawley (ed.), *Sati, the Blessing and the Curse: The Burning of Wives in India* (New York: Oxford University Press, 1994), pp. 11–15. In this article the term *sati* is used to refer to the practice of widow-burning (rather than to the woman herself).
2. The focus in the chapter is on British women although, to date, I have not found any evidence of the active involvement of Scottish, Welsh or Irish women in the campaign against *sati*. This may reflect the predominantly English support base of the missionary societies that were most involved in the campaign (although the campaign as a whole should be described as 'British' since it concerned Britain's relationship with India).
3. Antoinette Burton, *Burdens of History: British Feminists, Indian Women, and Imperial Culture, 1865–1915* (Chapel Hill, NC: University of North Carolina Press, 1994).
4. For a description of the dominant middle-class ideology of 'separate spheres' and the vital part played by evangelicals in developing it, see Catherine Hall, 'The Early Formation of Victorian Domestic Ideology', in *White, Male and Middle Class: Explorations in Feminism and History* (Cambridge: Polity Press, 1992), pp. 74–92. There has been a lively debate over the extent to which 'separate spheres' actually characterised gender roles in the early nineteenth century.
5. Clare Midgley, *Women against Slavery: The British Campaigns, 1780–1870* (London: Routledge, 1992).
6. Jane Rendall, *The Origins of Modern Feminism: Women in Britain, France and the United States, 1780–1860* (Basingstoke: Macmillan, 1985), Chapter 3.
7. The Baptist Missionary Society was formed by the Particular Baptists in 1792; the non-denominational, but predominantly Congregational, London Missionary Society was founded in 1795; and the Evangelical Anglicans founded the Church Missionary Society in 1799.
8. For the close link between 'home' and 'foreign' missions see Susan Thorne, '"The Conversion of Englishmen and the Conversion of the World Inseparable": Missionary Imperialism and the Language of Class in Early Industrial Britain', in Frederick Cooper and Laura Stoler (eds), *Tensions of Empire: Colonial Cultures in a Bourgeois World* (Berkeley, CA: University of California Press, 1997), pp. 238–62.
9. Brian Stanley, *The Bible and the Flag: Protestant Missions and British Imperialism in the Nineteenth and Twentieth Centuries* (Leicester: Apollos, 1990), Chapter 3.

10. F. K. Prochaska, *Women and Philanthropy in Nineteenth-Century England* (Oxford: Clarendon Press, 1980), pp. 23–9.

11. Eugene Stock, *The History of the Church Missionary Society*, 3 vols (London: Church Missionary Society, 1899), vol. i, p. 243, vol. iii, p. 321; Prochaska, *Women and Philanthropy*, appendix 1, p. 231.

12. Stanley, *The Bible and the Flag*, p. 98; Ernest Marshall Howse, *Saints in Politics: The 'Clapham Sect' and the Growth of Freedom* (London: George Allen and Unwin, 1953), p. 92.

13. Charles Grant, *Observations on the State of Society among the Asiatic Subjects of Great Britain, Particularly with Respect to Morals; and on the Means of Improving it – Written Chiefly in the Year 1792* (London: House of Commons, 1813), pp. 30, 56.

14. William Wilberforce, 'Substance of the speech of William Wilberforce, Esq. on the clause of the East India Bill for promoting the religious instruction and moral improvement of the natives of the British dominions in India, on the 22nd of June, and the 1st and 12th of July, 1813', *The Pamphleteer* (London), 3, no. 5 (March 1814), pp. 43–113: quote from p. 70.

15. The quotation is from the leading evangelical poet William Cowper's 'The Task', as quoted in Leonore Davidoff and Catherine Hall, *Family Fortunes: Men and Women of the English Middle Class, 1780–1850* (London: Hutchinson, 1987), p. 165.

16. John Pollock, *Wilberforce* (Tring: Lion Publishing, 1986), p. 236.

17. Letter from H. More to W. Wilberforce, Barley Wood, 12 April 1813, as quoted in Robert Isaac Wilberforce and Samuel Wilberforce (eds), *The Correspondence of William Wilberforce*, 2 vols (London: John Murray, 1840), vol. ii, pp. 240–1; Howse, *Saints in Politics*, p. 86. See Chapter 2 of this volume for further discussion of More's political activities.

18. Ward's text became a key source of information on Hindu religion and society in Britain at this period – see Lata Mani, *Contentious Traditions: The Debate on Sati in Colonial India* (Berkeley, CA: California University Press, 1998), Chapter 4.

19. *Missionary Register*, June 1813, p. 215.

20. *Missionary Register*, April 1814, pp. 136–40.

21. Prochaska, *Women and Philanthropy*, p. 30.

22. For pioneering examinations of the links which women made between metropolitan and imperial philanthropic missions to women and children at this period, see Alison Twells, '"Let us Begin Well at Home": Class, Ethnicity and Christian Motherhood in the Writing of Hannah Kilham, 1774–1832', in Eileen Janes Yeo (ed.), *Radical Femininity: Women's Self-Representation in the Public Sphere* (Manchester: Manchester University Press, 1998), pp. 25–51; Alison Twells, '"Happy English Children": Class, Ethnicity and the Making of Missionary Women, 1800–40', *Women's Studies International Forum*, 21, no. 3 (1998), pp. 235–46.

23. For the similar centrality of family and household to the British missionary project in the West Indies, see Catherine Hall, 'Missionary Stories: Gender and Ethnicity in England in the 1830s and 1840s', in *White, Male and Middle Class*, pp. 205–54.

24. M. A. Laird, *Missionaries and Education in Bengal, 1793–1837* (Oxford: Clarendon Press, 1972), p. xii; Kenneth Ingham, *Reformers in India, 1793–1833:*

An Account of the Work of Christian Missionaries on Behalf of Social Reform (Cambridge: Cambridge University Press, 1956), p. 55; Kanti Prasanna Sen Gupta, *The Christian Missionaries in Bengal, 1793–1833* (Calcutta: Firma K. L. Mukhopadhyay, 1971), p. 97.

25. In 1815, for example, the Church Missionary Society decided not to send unmarried women abroad (see Stock, *History of the Church Missionary Society*, vol. i, pp. 124–5). A number of schools were set up by missionaries' wives prior to 1820 but these only taught very small numbers of girls.

26. William Ward, *A View of the History, Literature and Religion of the Hindoos*, 3rd edn, 3 vols (London: Baptist Missionary Society, 1817), vol. i, preface; William Ward, 'Letter to the Ladies of Liverpool, and of the United Kingdom', *The Times*, 3 January 1821, p. 3; William Ward, *Farewell Letters to a Few Friends in Britain and America, on Returning to Bengal in 1821* (London: Black, Kingsbury, Oarbury and Allen, 1821), letter to Miss Hope of Liverpool, pp. 62–85. For information on Ward's visit to Britain see John Clark Marshman, *The Life and Times of Carey, Marshman, and Ward*, 2 vols (London: Longman, Brown, Green, Longmans and Roberts, 1859), vol. ii, pp. 199, 242.

27. Ward, *A View*, vol. i, preface, p. xvii.

28. Ibid., vol. i, preface, p. 1.

29. Stanley, *The Bible and the Flag*, p. 68.

30. Ward, *A View*, vol. i, preface, p. 1.

31. Ward, 'Letter to the Ladies'.

32. Ibid.

33. Ibid.

34. Ward, *Farewell Letters*, p. 82.

35. The British and Foreign School Society was a society set up by nonconformists in England in 1814 to organise non-denominational schools in Britain and abroad along the lines of the monitorial system developed by Joseph Lancaster, as a way of providing basic education within a Christian framework to large numbers of working-class children.

36. *Missionary Register*, October 1820, p. 434.

37. Ibid., p. 435.

38. Ibid., May 1821, p. 197–8.

39. Ibid., November 1822, p. 481.

40. Ibid., June 1825, p. 245.

41. Church Missionary Society, *Missionary Papers*, no. 49 (1828).

42. Sen Gupta, *The Christian Missionaries*, p. 120; Ingham, *Reformers in India*, p. 93.

43. *Missionary Register*, November 1822, pp. 509–10; June 1826, pp. 346–50. Cooke's activities had initially been placed by the British and Foreign School Society under the direction of the Calcutta School Society (set up in 1818 mainly to improve indigenous elementary schools for boys), but Hindu members of the society were unhappy about the Christian curriculum in her schools, and control was soon shifted to the Church Missionary Society.

44. It was on these grounds that the Governor-General Lord Amherst in 1825 overruled his council and refused a government grant to the Ladies' Society for Native-Female Education – see Bengal General Letter, 30 September 1825, paragraphs 54–57, India Office Records E/4/116.

45. *Missionary Register*, March 1825, pp. 124–5; April 1825, pp. 192–3; June 1825, pp. 244–6.

46. *Missionary Register*, September 1829, p. 392.
47. Prochaska, *Women and Philanthropy*, pp. 31–2. Prochaska points out that it was not until 1891 that the London Missionary Society became the first of the great missionary societies to permit women to join its management committee.
48. There is an extensive literature on Roy: a useful starting point is V. C. Joshi (ed.), *Rammohun Roy and the Process of Modernization in India* (Delhi: Vikas, 1975). For the English text of Roy's tracts on *sati* see 'Translation of a Conference between an Advocate for and an Opponent of the Practice of Burning Widows Alive, Calcutta, 1818', and 'A Second Conference between an Advocate for and an Opponent of the Practice of Burning Widows Alive, Calcutta, 1820', in J. C. Ghose (ed.), *The English Works of Raja Rammohun Roy*, 2 vols (New Delhi: Cosmo, 1982), vol. ii.
49. *The Parliamentary Debates* (London: Hansard, 1822), new series, 5, entry for 20 June 1821, col. 1217.
50. 'A Petition of the Gentry, Clergy and other Inhabitants of the County of Bedford', *Journal of the House of Commons*, 78 (1823), p. 404, entry for 18 June.
51. Joseph Peggs, *The Suttees' Cry to Britain* (London: Seeley, 1827).
52. For reports of the Society's formation see *General Baptist Repository and Missionary Observer*, 1829, p. 37; *Baptist Magazine*, 21 (January 1829), p. 33; *Missionary Register*, March 1829, p. 146; *Monthly Repository*, new series, 3 (January 1829), p. 71.
53. First report of the Coventry Society for the Abolition of Human Sacrifices in India, 1 February 1830, *The General Baptist Repository and Missionary Observer*, 1830, pp. 113–8.
54. *Journal of the House of Commons*, 78 (1823), p. 404; 79 (1824–5), p. 144; 82 (1826–7), pp. 234, 334, 340, 462, 472, 478, 486, 491, 505, 511, 567, 571, 575; 83 (1828), pp. 6, 313, 409, 443, 467, 477, 491, 494, 525, 555; 84 (1829), pp. 28, 192, 370, 384, 406; 85 (1830), pp. 69, 148, 160, 184, 190, 214, 235, 242, 255, 282, 402, 590, 603.
55. David Turley, *The Culture of English Antislavery, 1780–1860* (London: Routledge, 1991), p. 63.
56. *General Baptist Repository and Missionary Observer*, 1828, p. 80; 1830, p. 115.
57. For debate about female petitioning among anti-slavery campaigners in the 1790s and again in 1830, see Midgley, *Women against Slavery*, pp. 23–4, 62–4; for debate in 1829 over female signatures to petitions against Roman Catholic Emancipation, see Linda Colley, *Britons: Forging the Nation, 1707–1837* (New Haven, CT, and London: Yale University Press, 1992), pp. 278–9.
58. Peggs, *The Suttees' Cry*, p. 81.
59. Joseph Peggs, *The Suttees' Cry to Britain*, 2nd edn (London: Seeley, 1828), p. 91, footnote.
60. Ibid., p. 97.
61. *Baptist Magazine*, 21 (November 1829), p. 475.
62. Ibid., 22 (February 1830), pp. 74–5.
63. Ibid., 22 (March 1830), p. 116.
64. Unfortunately, as with the men's petitions, there is no surviving record of the number of signatories to each petition or of the names of signatories.
65. *Journal of the House of Commons*, 84 (1829), pp. 28, 192, 370, 375, 406; 85 (1830), pp. 69, 148, 184, 235; *Journal of the House of Lords*, 61 (1829), p. 591; 62 (1830), pp. 45, 74, 136, 183.

66. For the widespread distribution of missionary propaganda at this period, see Thorne, 'The Conversion of Englishmen'.

67. Colley, *Britons*, pp. 278–9; for parliamentary reception of these petitions in 1829 see *Parliamentary Debates* (London: Hansard, 1829), new series, 20, pp. 570–2, 372–3; 1322–7.

68. For texts of petitions from which these quotes are taken, see: *Appendix to the Votes and Proceedings of the House of Commons*, 1830, pp. 148, 285; *Baptist Magazine*, 22 (March 1830), p. 116; *Journal of the House of Lords*, 62 (1830), p. 183; *Appendix to the Votes and Proceedings of the House of Commons*, 1829, p. 1515.

69. John Rosselli, *Lord William Bentinck: The Making of a Liberal Imperialist, 1774–1839* (Delhi: Thompson Press, 1974). Rosselli describes Bentinck as a supporter of anti-slavery, a friend of Charles Grant, an active member of the British and Foreign Bible Society and an associate of the Clapham Sect.

70. C. H. Philips (ed.), *The Correspondence of Lord William Cavendish Bentinck* (Oxford: Oxford University Press, 1977), pp. xxvi–xxviii, 94, 191–5, 335–45, 360–2 (text of the regulation). For Bombay and Madras see Kenneth Ballhatchet, *Social Policy and Social Change in Western India* (London: Oxford University Press, 1957), pp. 304–5.

71. C. A. Bayly, *Indian Society and the Making of the British Empire: The New Cambridge History of India*, 2, no. 1 (Cambridge: Cambridge University Press, 1988), Chapter 4.

72. For women anti-slavery campaigners' perspectives see Midgley, *Women against Slavery*, Chapter 5.

5
Women Writers and the Campaign for Jewish Civil Rights in Early Victorian England

Nadia Valman

In the parliamentary debate of December 1847 on the admission of Jews to Parliament Lord Ashley, later Earl of Shaftesbury, articulated what was at stake in the question of Jewish emancipation. *Hansard* reports his speech:

> Some years ago they stood out for a Protestant Parliament. They were perfectly right in doing so, but they were beaten. They now stood out for a Christian Parliament; and perhaps they would have a final struggle for a male Parliament. His noble Friend [Lord John Russell, who had proposed the motion to remove Jewish disabilities] was too candid to conceal his ultimate intentions; but he would just ask him, before he proceeded much further, to consider that, according to the principle laid down by him, not only Jews would be admitted to Parliament, but Mussulmans, Hindoos, and men of every form of faith under the sun in the British dominions. [*Cheers*].[1]

Ashley, evidently supported by a good number of MPs, considered opposition to the principle of Jewish emancipation as crucial to the preservation of a white, male, Christian Parliament. In opposing constitutional reform in these terms he was also constructing a particular version of English national identity. Indeed, the public debates on Jewish civil rights in mid-nineteenth century England were an occasion for the contestation of the future relationship between religion and the state, during which a number of models for understanding the place of the Jews in the polity were articulated by both Jews and non-Jews, politicians, clergymen and novelists. This article explores the ways in which the debate about Jewish citizenship was disseminated and extended by women – in the novels, romances and periodicals which proliferated in this period, sometimes reflecting and sometimes eschewing the terms of the public campaign, and sometimes, but not always, linking the political, legal and social status of the Jews with that of women.

The struggle for Jewish emancipation began after 1829, when the Roman Catholic Emancipation Act granted the right to sit in Parliament to the last Christian denomination to be denied it. In view of the apparent tendency towards religious liberalisation evidenced by Catholic Emancipation and by the repeal of the Test and Corporation Acts relating to Protestant Dissenters in 1828, a group of prominent British Jews, including Moses Montefiore, Isaac Lyon Goldsmid and members of the Rothschild family, decided that the climate was right to launch their own campaign. Jews had been effectually, although not formally, barred from parliamentary office because on taking office all Members of Parliament had to swear to abjure Jacobite claims to the throne 'upon the true faith of a Christian'.[2] Quakers too were prevented from taking parliamentary office by this requirement, although in 1833 they were granted the right to affirm rather than swear their oath of allegiance.

Between 1830 and 1858 there were fourteen attempts to remove the disabilities preventing Jews from taking parliamentary office, and emancipation was in fact finally granted eleven years after the first Jew had been elected to a seat. During these decades the question was widely debated in Parliament, pamphlets and periodical reviews, and a range of positions emerged. On the grounds of a suspicion that the Jews were loyal firstly to other Jews, the high Tory Sir Robert Inglis asserted in the House of Commons in 1833 'that a Jew could never be made an Englishman, even though he be born here'.[3] The Tory *Quarterly Review* argued that the law should not encode 'prejudice' against 'these domesticated strangers', but 'to give all the rights and privileges of citizens to them whilst holding to Judaism would be to bind ourselves wholly to those who cannot so bind themselves to us; to confer on them strength which might be turned against ourselves'.[4] Some Tories like Inglis and Finch questioned more closely the elision of rights and privileges and argued that eligibility to sit in Parliament was a privilege rather than a civil right.[5] Thomas Macaulay, on the other hand, turned Inglis's argument on its head. 'As long as they are not Englishmen,' he contended, 'they are nothing but Jews.'[6] Whigs like Macaulay and Lord John Russell favoured the principle of Jewish emancipation on the grounds that British political tradition had always affirmed the right of every free-born citizen to be treated equally before the law in all matters which did not threaten the security of the state, and that any restriction of their liberties constituted 'persecution'.[7] Thus, the debates were about more than the theoretical rights of a small minority of Jewish Englishmen; in fact they turned on competing ideological definitions of the nation. Was Britain above all a Christian nation, no longer legislated for exclusively by Anglicans, but nevertheless a nation whose legislature was deeply bound up with Christian morality – or was the British constitution, as Whigs contended, primarily characterised by its ongoing adaptation to protect the liberties of every individual citizen, regardless of religious creed?[8] As David Feldman has argued, 'the defence of established institutions or their reform in the face of new conditions meant that Jewish disabilities – whether to maintain, reform or abolish them – were inserted within the decisive conflicts of mid-nineteenth century British politics'.[9]

Although women, even Anglican women, had neither the franchise nor the right to sit in Parliament, they were nevertheless vocal in responding to these public questions of representation, and in some cases influential in constituting them. Yet despite the striking number of religious, domestic and historical novels about Jews produced by women writers for a female audience during this period, these texts have rarely been connected with the political context of their production. Historians of the campaign for Jewish emancipation in Victorian England have never looked for political argument in women's literature, which was often produced for a popular or youthful readership. Furthermore, literary critics such as Linda Gertner Zatlin have suggested that the work of Jewish romance writers is limited as literature by an underlying propagandist purpose, a 'reliance on stereotypes, didacticism, and heavy-handed direct addresses', while Bryan Cheyette has labelled these writers 'apologetic' as they 'were called on to represent their nascent community in the best possible light'.[10] It is only recently that mid-nineteenth-century Jewish women writers have been rediscovered for their particular contributions to contemporary debates about the status of Jews and of women, and that fiction about Jews in popular genres has been reconsidered in the light of the political and religious debates that underlie and inform it.[11]

It is to Evangelical discourse that we must look in order to re-insert the role of women in defining and contesting the place of the Jews in nineteenth-century society. For the ideology and theology of Evangelicalism conferred a special status on both Jews and women as both, in different ways, were crucial agents of millennial transformation. The Jews, Evangelicals believed, were in need of urgent conversion in order to precipitate the Second Coming of Christ, and English Protestants had a special role to play in their conversion. The mission to convert the Jews, supported by vast funds and thousands of subscribers, was largely unsuccessful.[12] But through the numerous periodicals, tracts and novels which arose from their efforts the literary imagining of Jews became an important way of articulating what it meant to be a British Christian.

From the outset a particular emphasis was placed on the conversion of the Jews as a specifically female concern.[13] As Jane Rendall and others have argued, Evangelical ideology and theology had a significant impact on the conception of femininity in early Victorian England. Women were increasingly assumed to be not only morally but spiritually superior to men, and thus more fully to embody the Evangelical appeal. A new emphasis on the humility and sacrificial character of Christ made him a personal saviour, with whose sufferings women especially could identify and whose redemptive powers they could emulate.[14] In particular, Protestant women, according to the London Society for Promoting Christianity amongst the Jews [LSPCJ], the century's most important conversionist organisation, had an urgent redemptive responsibility towards their Jewish sisters. Indeed, the LSPCJ had one of the highest percentages of women subscribers among nineteenth-century voluntary societies.[15] One of its early tracts demanded: 'does not every female in happier circumstances feel herself called upon to attend to her perishing sister, when she says, "Oh! pity me, for the hand of God hath touched me"?'[16]

Sympathetic pity was certainly the keynote of the rhetoric of Evangelical philosemitism. The Revd John Wilson considered that the correct attitude to the Jews should be one of 'compassion, condescension, and long-suffering patience', qualities gendered as feminine, and Charlotte Elizabeth Tonna, a widely-read Evangelical novelist and editor, wrote that she hoped for the Jews' conversion 'from the innermost core of a heart filled with love for Israel'.[17] Although conversionists mostly opposed political interference on behalf of the Jews, by the 1830s some Evangelical politicians like Lord Bexley and Robert Grant saw the campaign for Jewish emancipation as an opportunity to demonstrate precisely this feminised version of Christian identity in the public sphere. In contrast to those who argued that the best way to preserve the Protestant character of the state would be to 'rally round the Cross' and fight to exclude unbelievers from Parliament, Evangelical supporters insisted that a Christian state should show 'love and charity' towards the Jews and offer them the chance to join the Protestant nation as political subjects, which might lead to their incorporation as religious subjects.[18] Thus the language of the emancipation debate in Parliament was itself gendered – divided between the images of violently defending Christianity and gracefully extending its privileges.

The representation of the Jews within the debates also had an implicitly gendered dimension. Supporters of the Jewish cause frequently figured Jews as passive, suffering and humble. Unlike Roman Catholics, Macaulay claimed, 'the Jews have borne their deprivations long in silence, and are now complaining with mildness and decency'.[19] Many advocates of emancipation emphasised the 'peaceful' nature of the Jews, who, far from presenting a political or religious threat to the state, were exemplary in their homely virtues. John Poulter asserted that

> this peculiar people were distinguished by their veneration for the domestic and social relations of life. Instances of the violation of the duties of husband and wife – of parent and child – were rare amongst them ... From drunkenness which, beyond any other vice called for the most anxious and urgent correction of the Legislature, and which was more and more infecting and demoralizing the whole of the lower classes, and had become a great national calamity, they were happily, and beyond others, exempted.[20]

The figuring of the English Jew as a paradigm of domestic virtue was one aspect of the feminisation of the Jews in political debate and writing in this period which this chapter will examine. Another aspect, the maternalism of conversionist discourse, is apparent in the first text under discussion here, 'The Jewess', a story published in 1843 by Elizabeth Rigby, a middle-class Tory Anglican, at the beginning of her career as a periodical journalist.

Set on the shores of the Baltic sea, Rigby's romance begins with the arrival of a Jewish peddler and his young wife and baby at the house of an aristocratic Englishwoman married to a Russian. Only the lady treats the strangers with respect and sympathy, defending them against the intolerant accusations of her Russian servants. The English lady opposes reason to the remarks of the Russians, whose prejudices are marked as peasant and primitive.[21] When, later, her home is invaded by Cossack soldiers searching for the Jews, she helps them escape, pluckily defending her domestic sanctuary against all forms of tyranny (65–76). In this text, Rigby demands sympathy for the Jews through the links she establishes between the two women, the exiled English aristocrat and Rose, the poor Jewess, who is introduced to the narrative as an emblem of her people: 'in the mixture of loftiness and gentleness which her countenance expressed, seemed equally united the sense of her people's wrongs and their habits of passive endurance' (15–16). The Jewess's sufferings, as the wife of a wandering, persecuted peddler, are a source of admiration and empathy for the homesick Englishwoman, who identifies with Rose's humble piety.

The fugitive couple escape the Cossacks, but encounter new troubles as they are stranded at sea on an ice floe. The significant differences between the Jew and the Jewess are revealed by their respective responses to this catastrophe: 'the knit brow, the fever gathered on the cheek of the Jew, showed the anxiety that was preying within; while Rose was pale, gentle and quiet, like one accustomed to take and bear whatever necessity imposed upon her, equally without inquiring or even understanding its object' (99–100). The Jew's anger and frustration suggest his inability to submit to his destiny, while trusting passivity marks the Jewess's habitual response to suffering. Rose's gentleness indicates that her true affinity lies not with her Jewish husband but with the Christian Englishwoman who had protected her and who exhibits a similar, if more imperious, form of serenity, an 'acquired control over warm feelings often tried, and the submission of a lofty spirit to loftier convictions' (19). This identification is understood by the lady herself, who describes her experience of marriage as similar to that of the poor Jewess: 'I did like yourself. I married young, and now I am older I must be wise enough to make the best of it. Women must follow their husbands, you know' (34). Here the Englishwoman suggests that her alienation as an unhappy wife and an exile is analogous to the deracination of the Jewess. The Jewess is allegorised: the text invites the female reader to identify with Rose's 'people's wrongs and their habits of passive endurance' as with a woman constrained socially and politically by an unhappy or restrictive marriage.[22]

But Rose's affinity with the Englishwoman is also linked to an identification with Christianity. When she is trapped on the drifting ice, Rose pleads the cause of a helpless dog that the men want to kill for food, on the grounds that 'the animal has not, like us, a life beyond'. When one of the Russian peasants abuses her for, as a Jew, knowing nothing of the life beyond,

> Rose was not to be daunted, and identifying the cause of the poor dog with her own, she replied with more fire than any would have attributed to her, – 'And what do you know of the Hebrews? There are as many Hebrews as little like what you call Jews, as there are Christians who act not up to the creed they profess, and if you Christians think your religion the better of the two, more's the

shame. I have ever found those the best Christians who were kind-est to the Israelite. No, – touch him not; you shall strike me sooner.'
(113–14)

In defending her own capability for compassion, Rose unconsciously mimics the Englishwoman's sense of the responsibility of the strong to defend the weak. One of her Russian companions sees this as an example to Christians: 'For shame, Tomas! let her alone, and the dog also. The woman is right; no Christian could have spoken better ... I wish all Christians were as patient in times of affliction as she' (114).

It is only logical, then, that Rose should learn the lesson of her own true character when she survives the winter, returns to the home of the Englishwoman, and has her child baptised into Christianity. The story indicates that, as conversionists hoped, compassion for the Jews would lead to their voluntary conversion. Even one of the Russian peasants, initially hostile towards Rose, comes to admire her for her exemplary patience. The reconciliation between the Jewess and the prejudiced peasantry through the mediation of the Englishwoman points to the implicit politics of Rigby's tale. While Rose's Christ-like 'passive endurance' is the attribute that most qualifies her for tolerance by Christians, it is also a spiritualised form of political acquiescence. Rose's passivity denotes an unquestioning acceptance of history, a political disengagement and implicit forgiveness of the perpetrators of persecution: the Jewess is one 'accustomed to take and bear whatever necessity imposed upon her, equally without inquiring or even under-standing its object' (99). While Rose's patience is compared with that of the virtuous Englishwoman, it also enhances the authority of her 'benefactress' (129).

The Jewess's deference to social hierarchy in this text had particular resonance in the 1840s, and was clearly of importance to Rigby. Her essay on *Jane Eyre* in the *Quarterly Review* of December 1848 contended that Brontë's novel was 'pre-eminently an anti-Christian composition ... The tone of mind and thought which has fostered Chartism and rebellion is the same which has also written *Jane Eyre*.' Here, Rigby closely associ-ated Christianity with the established social order, and her interpretation of the novel clearly identified the political connotations of Jane Eyre's anger. In particular, she was outraged that Jane was 'ungrateful'.[23] In contrast, Rigby's Jewess cannot be grateful enough. She accepts the social order and her place in it uncomplainingly, whilst providing the opportunity for a benevolent demonstration of aristocratic mater-nalism. Rigby's text suggests, by extension, that Jews can *merit* tolerance in a Christian nation, but this is not a matter of rights. Tolerance must be granted as a privilege from above, and accepted gratefully below.

Defending Jews, and in particular Jewish women, from the culture of conversionism was the explicit aim of the earliest works published by the Anglo-Jewish writer Grace Aguilar.[24] Most of Aguilar's books were published after her death in 1847, but were actually written in the 1830s when the social influence and literary productivity of the Evangelical movement was at its height. Aguilar's earliest publications were on Jewish historical and theological themes, but her most successful books, the domestic novels *Home Influence: A Tale for Mothers and Daughters* (1847) and its sequel *The Mother's Recompense* (1851), became bestsellers and continued to be reprinted throughout the century. Although by her mid-twenties Aguilar herself was the family breadwinner through a school she ran with her mother in Hackney, London, her novels depicted the lives of the leisured middle classes. They celebrated home life and expounded the dominant ideology of femininity, according to which women's central role in directing the morality of the nation was enacted in the home through her spiritual influence over husband and children. As such her work appealed widely to Evangelical readers and writers. Charlotte Elizabeth Tonna, the editor of the *Christian Lady's Magazine*, saw Aguilar as an ally in the wider battle against religious indifference, praising Aguilar's 'lofty tone of spirituality' and her efforts to turn Jews 'from the words of men to the Word of the Living God'.[25] Indeed, Aguilar was anxious to insist that her own religious persuasion would have no effect on the domestic principles which her novels were designed to illustrate. In the preface to *Home Influence* she wrote:

> having been brought before the public principally as the author of Jewish works, and as an explainer of the Hebrew Faith, some Christian mothers might fear that the present Work has the same tendency, and hesitate to place it in the hands of their children. [The author], therefore, begs to assure them, that as a simple domestic story, the characters in which are all Christians, believing in and practising that religion, all *doctrinal* points have been most carefully avoided, the author seeking only to illustrate the spirit of true piety, and the virtues always designated as the Christian virtues thence proceeding.[26]

In this, her first foray into the wider market of Gentile domestic fiction, Aguilar expressed anxiety about the lasting effect of her previous publications, whose declared intention was to counter charges against Judaism by Evangelical conversionists.

But Aguilar had an ambivalent relationship with Evangelicalism: while she saw conversionists as a threat to her co-religionists, she was nevertheless deeply influenced by their terms of reference and by their favoured literary forms. Thus, for example, Aguilar's Jewish works focused in particular on the history of the Jews of Spain and Portugal, contrasting their heroism and willing martyrdom at the time of the Inquisition with Catholic cruelty – a favourite subject for Protestant Evangelicals. But Aguilar also reproduces a Christian analysis of Jewish persecution. 'The Edict', one of her Inquisition tales, tells of a community of Spanish Jews who are shocked and devastated by Ferdinand and Isabella's proclamation of expulsion from the country to which they are devoted. Yet the community patriarch urges submission to the will of God:

> ... as to His decree, let us bow without a murmur. Have we forgotten that on earth the exiles of Jerusalem have no resting; that for the sins of our fathers the God of Justice is not yet appeased? Oh! if we have, this fearful sentence may be promulgated to recall us to Himself, ere prosperity be to us, as to our misguided ancestors, the curse, hurling us into eternal misery. We bow not to man; it is the God of Israel we obey! ... There are some among ye who speak of weakness and timidity, in thus yielding to our foes without one blow in defence of our rights. Rights! unhappy men, ye have no rights! Sons of Judah, have ye yet to learn, we are wanderers on the face of the earth, without a country, a king, a judge, in Israel?[27]

While this speech does take its theme from the Hebrew scriptures, it also echoes the arguments of those in contemporary England who opposed emancipation on the ground that 'strangers and sojourners the Jews must be until the restoration of their own Jeruasalem – their ultimate home'.[28] The patriarch's conviction that diaspora Jews 'have no rights' comes very close to a Christian interpretation of Jewish suffering which would emphasise Jews' own responsibility for rejecting salvation in Christ, rather than states' culpability for persecution. Many Evangelicals, like Lord Shaftesbury, also argued that it would be wrong to lend support to the Jews' campaign for civil rights as it was spiritual rather than temporal freedom that mattered.[29] Aguilar's writing here suggests the author's own indifference to the question of contemporary Jewish civil rights, on similarly theological grounds.

However, her other romance and domestic fiction on Jewish themes draws differently on Evangelical principles to produce an argument more sympathetic to Jewish grievances. In *The Vale of Cedars* (1850), another Spanish Inquisition tale, the heroine Marie is a secret Jew whose religion is eventually exposed, and who becomes a victim and martyr to the tortures of the Inquisition. Like Rose in Rigby's tale, the heroine is protected by a maternal figure, Queen Isabella, who pleads Marie's cause with her husband: '...Unbeliever though she be, off-spring of a race which every true Catholic must hold in abhorrence, she is yet a *woman*, Ferdinand, and, as such, demands and shall receive the protection of her Queen'.[30] Similarly, Isabella reproaches her court-iers for their horror at Marie by invoking the redemptive figure of fem-ininity: 'Has every spark of woman's nature faded from your hearts, that ye can speak thus?...Detest, abhor, avoid her *faith* – for that we command thee; but her sex, her sorrow, have a claim to sympathy and aid, which not even her race can remove'.[31] Aguilar suggests, like the author of the LSPCJ tract, that Christian women's responsibility to their Jewish sisters, and Jewish women's feminine virtue, urge a differ-ent response to Jewishness, one of pity, sympathy and tolerance. So when Aguilar argued, in the preface to *Home Influence*, that her Judaism would not be a barrier to illustrating 'the spirit of true piety', she was not only trying to calm the potential fears of a zealous Protestant reader. She was also suggesting that the domestic novel was an arena in which it could be proved that there was no substantive difference between Jewish and Protestant moral principles, a crucial question in the public debate about the Jews' capacity to legislate in the British parliament.[32]

This argument is most explicit in Aguilar's 'History of the Jews in Eng-land', the first history of Anglo-Jewry written by a Jew, which was pub-lished in 1847. This was the year both of Aguilar's own death and of the election to Parliament of the first Jewish MP, Lionel de Rothschild, and the consequent intensification of the emancipation campaign.[33] In her history, Aguilar argues that the Jews' status in England has progressively improved since the Reformation, and the Readmission of the Jews to England in the seventeenth century. England was on the way to recog-nising that Jews were

> Jews only in their religion – Englishmen in everything else...In externals, and in all secular thoughts and actions, the English natur-alised Jew is...an Englishman, and his family is reared with the edu-cation and accomplishments of other members of the community. Only in some private and personal characteristics, and in religious belief, does the Jew differ from his neighbours.[34]

She considers that 'the disabilities under which the Jews of Great Britain labour are the last relic of religious intolerance ... Is it not discreditable to the common sense of the age that such anomalies should exist in reference to this well-disposed and, in every respect, naturalised portion of the community?'[35] Her argument thus rests less on the notion of the unconditional rights of the citizen than on the idea of the Jews being 'well-disposed' and 'in every respect naturalised', that is to say, worthy of equal political status. But how does Aguilar demonstrate the Jews' worthiness? Her argument for Jewish emancipation turns on a domestic definition of identity:

> The domestic manners of both the German and the Spanish Jews in Great Britain, are so exactly similar to those of their British brethren, that were it not for the observance of the seventh day instead of the first [as the Sabbath], the prohibition of certain meats, and the celebration of certain solemn festivals and rites, it would be difficult to distinguish a Jewish from a native household ... The virtues of the Jews are essentially of the domestic and social kind. The English are noted for the comfort and happiness of their firesides, and in this loveliest school of virtue, the Hebrews not only equal, but in some instances surpass, their neighbours.[36]

Here the trope of domesticity is put to political purposes. If Rigby feminised the Jews to cast them as pleasingly passive, Aguilar finds a different use for the rhetoric of femininity.[37] In Aguilar's account, Jews qualify for citizenship with Protestants because their home life so closely resembles that of English Protestants. The connection between Aguilar's work in domestic fiction and the political debate about the status of the Jews was recognised only a few years after her death, when the very existence of didactic novels for women by an Anglo-Jewish writer was hailed by the *Jewish Chronicle* as an important contribution to what it called the 'onward struggle' for Jewish public recognition: 'whilst we can, in reply to the false accusation of the charge of the Bishop of Oxford that "the Jews have no literature" direct his attention to our writers of ancient days, we can call on him with pride to read, among other modern Jewish writers, the moral and religious works of the virtuous and pious Grace Aguilar'.[38]

The final section of this chapter will consider some of the work of Celia and Marion Moss, two sisters from the provincial Jewish community of Portsea, Hampshire who published poetry and biblical romance based on Jewish history aimed, like Grace Aguilar's work, to dispel misconceptions about Jews. Unlike the widely-read Aguilar, the Moss sisters published their first books by private subscription, and rather than invoking the Evangelical novels, conduct books and tracts of writers like Mrs Ellis, they refer constantly instead to the oriental nationalism of Byron and the Irish patriotic poet Tom Moore. These Romantic influences also predominate in the volume of poetry they published, aged sixteen and eighteen, in the late 1830s. In the poems, the sisters link radical causes and contemporary national liberation struggles such as those in Poland and Spain in the 1830s with the question of the status of the Jews. Enforced expatriation is a significant preoccupation, for example, Marion's 'Polander's Song' which laments that 'the land of the noble and free / Should be conquered by tyrants and slaves':

> Our hearth-stones with blood are defiled,
> Not even our religion remains;
> Our warriors are dead or exiled,
> And our little ones weeping in chains.[39]

The imagery of exile and slavery links the eulogies to national struggle with the poems on biblical subjects. Celia's 'Lament for Jersualem' adopts the same vocabulary as the poems of modern patriotism:

> How long shall pagan foot profane
> Jehovah's hallow'd shrine;
> And memory's [*sic*] alone remain
> Of all that once was thine:
> How long shall we thy children roam
> As exiles from our ancient home.
>
> To weep o'er Salem's blighted fame,
> To gaze upon her strand,
> 'Tis all the heritage we claim
> Within our father land;
> To mourn o'er our free parents' graves
> That we their children are but slaves
>
> When will that glorious hour come,
> When shall we once more see
> Thy temple rear its stately dome,
> Thy children with the free:
> And thou, our fair, ill-fated land
> Amongst the nations take thy stand?
> (125–6)

Celia's 'The Massacre of the Jews at York', a long narrative poem about another tragic example of patriotic devotion, relates the story of the mass suicide of Jews in medieval York, besieged in York Castle by 'the zealots of a barb'rous age' (130). The poem also contains a strong indictment of British prejudice:

> We asked these Britons for a home,
> A shelter from the inclement skies:
> Have we despoil'd a Christian dome,
> Or sought a Christian sacrifice?
> We did but ask a dwelling place,
> And in return our wealth we gave;
> They spurn'd us as an outcast race,
> And brand us with the name of slave:
> They hate us, for we seek to tread
> The peaceful path our fathers trod,
> They hate us, for we bow our heads
> Before the shrine of Israel's God;
>
> (131)

However, in the later tales, which are based on the post-biblical history of the Jews, the spirit of Byron is combined with the female genre of historical romance.[40] The authors provide 'Historical Summaries' of political and military developments as a preface to each chapter. Meanwhile, against the background of the doomed Jewish struggles for national unity and, later, national liberation, stories of women's suffering and heroism on the margins of this heroic history are imagined. The theme of sexual oppression pervades the Moss sisters' romances; it is their means of gendering a Jewish history of resistance and martyrdom. While men refuse to submit to military invasion, women enact a similar battle in resisting sexual coercion. But the recurrent references to captivity, physical torture and scourging create intertextual resonances not only with Old Testament lamentations of the Jews' enslavement in Egypt and Babylon, but also with abolitionist literature of the previous few decades. The Moss sisters brought to the discussion of Jewish emancipation the language and associations of an older emancipation controversy, the debate on African–Caribbean slavery, in which, as Moira Ferguson and Clare Midgley have shown, women had played a crucial role.[41]

One of the sisters' tales, Marion's 'The Twin Brothers of Nearda', explicitly links the liberties of Jews and slaves, concerns which are not present in the narrative of Milman's *History of the Jews* which is its source text.

Moira Ferguson has argued that between the seventeenth and nineteenth centuries 'anti-slavery protest in prose and poetry by Anglo-Saxon female authors ... displaced anxieties about their own assumed powerlessness and inferiority onto their representations of slaves', whom they often represented as silenced and in need of protection and pity.[42] The image of a grieving African mother was famously deployed by Anna Laetitia Barbauld in a volume of hymns for children in 1781, and again by the Evangelical writer Hannah More in 1788, in order to criticise slavery for disrupting the institution of the family. Invoking the immorality of slavery had also become a strategy used by dissenters arguing for the abolition of discrimination against them. For the Moss sisters, stereotyping the suffering Jewish woman had a similar purpose. As Vron Ware has commented on the rhetorical use of slavery by Victorian feminist polemicists, 'appropriating the language of slavery was a way of claiming that theirs was a moral cause, not a revolutionary demand that threatened the whole of society'.[43]

Marion Moss's tale is set during the Jews' exile in Babylon and Parthia and concerns the fortunes of Anilai and Asinai, twins of noble birth who are left without family and sold as slaves to a cruel merchant, Moses Ben Yussuf. After they have finally fled their master's house, Asinai returns for a short time to reveal to Ben Yussuf's daughter Paula that he has loved her for many years. Paula has been reading the lamentations of Jeremiah, and thinking of the famous psalm of exile, the source for Barbauld's and More's anti-slavery poems, and one of Byron's *Hebrew Melodies* (1815), 'By the Rivers of Babylon'. She reflects on the diasporic condition of the Jews, who are now voluntarily living in exile from Judea:

A ray of exalted enthusiasm lighted up her large black eyes, as these thoughts filled her mind, and yielding to the spell, she arose, and forgetful of the lateness of the hour, wandered down to the side of that river, upon whose banks her captive people had hung their harps upon the willows, and sat down and wept.

'How, indeed, could they sing the songs of Zion in a strange land!' exclaimed the fair enthusiast, clasping her hands together, and raising her eyes to heaven: 'the tender and sublimely beautiful anthems of David, the warrior minstrel, and King of Israel, were not made to be chanted in captivity, at the bidding of the idolatrous heathen. It would have been profanity to sing the songs composed in honour of the true God, to the worshippers of images. Bitter, indeed, must be the bread of servitude, and the earth must be watered with the tears of the slave, who toileth upon it for another's gain alone, and knoweth though its graceful bosom yieldeth abundance, he hath no portion therein.'[44]

Paula sees the life of the diaspora Jew as a continued 'captivity', analogous to slavery because 'he hath no portion therein'. Her thoughts are suddenly interrupted by the appearance of Asinai, who affirms her sentiments with an account of his own bid for freedom. Asinai justifies his decision to break the bond of slavery in terms of a belief in divinely sanctioned human equality, reiterating an argument which had become particularly associated with women abolitionists:

> When God made this bright world, filling it with all that is good and beautiful, he created man to be its lord, and reign king over all his works. But he found there was a void in the fair creation of his hand; a something wanting, and he called woman into being, and, lo, it was perfect. But when he gave it to man, to rule over all the other works of his hand, he said not that he should tyrannise over his weaker brother, and make him the bond slave of his will. When our first parents were driven from the blessed home they had defiled with the first sin, and God said, 'Thou shalt eat the bread of toil, and earn it with the sweat of thy brow,' he said not, 'Thou shalt take another, and make him toil for thee, giving him bread that is made of bitters and mixed with tears for his portion, whilst thou livest on the fat of the land;' neither did He who is all benevolence say, 'Thou shalt reward the bondsman with stripes.'   (I:119–20)[45]

Asinai's impassioned argument insists that slavery usurps God's authority which decreed that all men should work.

Moss's use of ideas circulating in the public debate on the ethics of slavery implicitly addresses the question of Jewish emancipation, a link which is made through the rhetorical identification between the exiled Jewess and the slave. While male campaigners for emancipation in the 1830s and 1840s were arguing for Jewish rights on the rational grounds of 'consistency', given that since the Catholic Emancipation Act other non-Anglicans no longer suffered political disabilites, the Moss sisters here approach the issue through the Christian abolitionist language of biblically sanctioned equality.[46]

But the Mosses' engagement with the emancipation question through the metaphor of slavery is in fact more controversial. When Paula thinks of the Jewish diaspora as slavery, she mourns because it is a subjection that has become voluntary:

Why, when the yoke of the captive had been taken from their necks,
and the fetters of their bondage which had pressed so heavily upon
them for threescore years and ten were unriveted, had they lingered
by the waters of Babylon . . . ?   (I:117)

Paula is repelled by her father's insistence on remaining in exile because
his material profits are greater in Babylon. She identifies more with her
uncle, Simon, who 'deems himself only as a sojourner in the land of the
stranger' (I:233). In another story, 'The Promise', the narrator herself
expresses similar sentiments. As the heroine listens to the hero singing
'the songs of Zion in a strange land', the narrator interjects:

O that beautiful word! whose every letter is poetry. Even as I write, I
could weep and turn with the passionate yearning of the expatriated
to the far-off home, beyond the blue Mediterranean. Vain yearning!
futile dreams! – the inheritance of Israel is again in the hand of the
stranger, and the time has not arrived for the wandering exiles to
return.[47]

The contemporary narrator shares the patriotic sorrow of the ancient
Hebrew heroine; she is living in the same epoch, the same exile. Moss's
reference to the 'yearning of the expatriated' distinctly recalls the nationalist language of the sisters' earlier political poetry. While Evangelicals
looked forward to a spiritual restoration of the Jews as part of the
Second Coming of the Messiah, the Moss sisters, like the Poles or the
Scots in their poetry, anticipate a redemption that is material.

    The narrator's patriotic pronouncements, what she calls elsewhere
her 'national enthusiasm', and her description of herself as 'expatriated'
were potentially explosive at this time, when Jews were mostly trying to
demonstrate their rootedness in Britain (I:233). Even though she claims
to be resigned to a time of indefinite waiting before national restoration, this does not dispel Moss's controversial implication of disloyalty
to Britain – a scepticism which contrasts strikingly with Aguilar's optim-
ism about the Jews' future in Britain. In fact, Moss seems to hold little
faith in the capacity of British democracy to liberate the Jews: in the
story of the slaves the narrator asserts 'that the people of every nation
whither we have been driven to this refuge, England not excepted, hath
treated us as a haughty mother-in-law does her step-children' (I:232).
This metaphor, an allusion to Macaulay's famous essay 'Civil Disabilities of the Jews' (1831), ironically inverts Macaulay's reasoning for removing Jewish disabilities. By arguing that Jews' primary loyalty is never to

the country in which they live but to an imagined homeland based on 'national' memory, Marion Moss's writing runs counter to the mainstream of Jewish argument about emancipation at this time.

Such scepticism about the limits of liberal democracy for those who remain socially underprivileged is also evident in *Character; or, Jew and Gentile*, published in 1833 near the beginning of the Jewish emancipation campaign by the radical unitarian and feminist novelist Mary Leman Grimstone. Unlike the writers discussed above, Grimstone explicitly links religious prejudice with gender inequality. Her heroine, Agnes Lennox, rails against female complicity with legal subordination, 'the timidity that acquiesces in receiving wrongs – the supineness that shrinks from asserting rights. How has any particle of human liberty been gained? By resistance. When endurance has been goaded to the last gasp, it has wrenched power from the reluctant hand of oppression.'[48] But Lennox invests more hope for the future welfare of women in education than in legal reform, since 'Laws . . . are everywhere made for the strong against the weak', whereas through education 'Bad laws will be abrogated by disuse before they are repealed by Parliament.'[49] Grimstone's polemic against both the ignorance of women in the present state of society and the religious prejudices between Jews and Gentiles which precipitate the novel's tragic plot is part of a wider argument to the effect that 'We are the creatures of education, receiving the word in its most extended sense'.[50] Reaching beyond the scope of law in the direction of more comprehensive cultural change, and casting the question of Jewish rights in terms of Enlightenment thinking about the social construction of character, Grimstone locates as much responsibility for the progress of humanity in domestic education as in institutional reform.

Significantly, despite their political differences, it is the non-Jewish authors, Grimstone and Rigby, whose writing attempts to develop links between Jewish political disabilities and the legal subordination of women. At the same time, I have argued, there are important resonances between the work of both Jewish and non-Jewish writers who use the rhetoric of femininity and forms of women's fiction to articulate responses to the question of religious tolerance, even though each of the writers under discussion here constructs a different and complex relationship between gender and Jewish rights. For Celia and Marion Moss, adapting Evangelical arguments about abolition, using the female genre of the national romance and alluding to the poetry of Romantic nationalism made possible both an appeal for Jewish 'freedom' and a scepticism about its efficacy. Their work thus allowed the articulation of controversial ideas about Jewish citizenship and nationality which were all but absent from the public debate. Marginalised by geographical location and by access to the commercial market-place, the Moss sisters attempted to construct a literature of Jewish romantic nationalism, in striking contrast to Grace Aguilar, whose use of the popular domestic novel was linked to an identification with Anglican bourgeois values and a faith in liberal democracy. Both their approaches, and indeed those of the Tory conversionist Elizabeth Rigby and the radical unitarian feminist Mary Leman Grimstone, derive as much from the terms and forms of the female literary genres in which they were working as from the language of contemporary parliamentary debate.

Notes

1. *Hansard*, third series 95 (18 November–20 December 1847), p. 1278.
2. M. C. N. Salbstein, *The Emancipation of the Jews in Britain: The Question of the Admission of the Jews to Parliament, 1828–1860* (Rutherford: Fairleigh Dickinson University Press; London and Toronto: Associated University Presses, 1982), p. 50.
3. *Hansard*, third series 18 (30 May–1 July 1833), p. 50.
4. 'On the Present State of the Jews', *Quarterly Review*, 38 (1828), pp. 114–15.
5. *Hansard*, third series 35 (8 July–20 August 1836), p. 872; 17 (2 April–20 May 1833), p. 225.
6. *Hansard*, second series 24 (8 April–4 June 1830), p. 1311.
7. See, for example, Macaulay's reply to Inglis in the 1833 debate, *Hansard*, third series 17 (2 April–20 May 1833), p. 229, suggesting that those who would maintain Jewish disabilities were no different in principle from the Spanish Inquisitors.
8. For the most detailed and nuanced discussion of the debates and their relationship to contested ideas of British political tradition, see David Feldman, *Englishmen and Jews: Social Relations and Political Culture, 1840–1914* (New Haven, CT, and London: Yale University Press, 1994), Chapters 1–2.
9. Ibid., p. 28.
10. Linda Gertner Zatlin, *The Nineteenth-Century Anglo-Jewish Novel* (Boston, MA: Twayne, 1981), p. 40; Bryan Cheyette, *Contemporary Jewish Writing in Britain and Ireland: An Anthology* (London: Peter Halban, 1998), Introduction, p. xiv.
11. See Michael Galchinsky, *The Origin of the Modern Jewish Woman Writer: Romance and Reform in Victorian England* (Detroit, MI: Wayne State University Press, 1996) and Michael Ragussis, *Figures of Conversion: 'The Jewish Question' and English National Identity* (Durham, NC: Duke University Press, 1995). In her brief account of Victorian Jewish women's redefinition of their role in the British Jewish community through philanthropy and writing, Linda Gordon Kuzmack does not consider the ways in which they also participated indirectly in political campaigning through writing. See Linda Gordon

Kuzmack, *Woman's Cause: The Jewish Woman's Movement in England and the United States, 1881–1933* (Columbus, OH: Ohio State University Press, 1990), pp. 7–17.

12. For the history of British missions to the Jews, see Mel Scult, *Millennial Expectations and Jewish Liberties: A Study of the Efforts to Convert the Jews in Britain, up to the Mid Nineteenth Century* (Leiden: E. J. Brill, 1978) and Robert Michael Smith, 'The London Jews' Society and Patterns of Jewish Conversion in England, 1801–1859', *Jewish Social Studies*, 43 (1981), pp. 275–90. For the importance of book production to the evangelical effort see Leslie Howsam, *Cheap Bibles: Nineteenth-Century Publishing and the British and Foreign Bible Society* (Cambridge: Cambridge University Press, 1991) and Joseph L. Altholtz, *The Religious Press in Britain, 1760–1900* (Westport, CT: Greenwood Press, 1981), pp. 45–56.

13. See Nadia Valman, 'Jews and Gender in British Literature 1815–1865' (unpublished Ph.D. thesis, University of London, 1996), Chapter 3.

14. Jane Rendall, *The Origins of Modern Feminism: Women in Britain, France and the United States, 1780–1860* (Basingstoke: Macmillan, 1985), pp. 74–7.

15. See F. K. Prochaska, *Women and Philanthropy in Nineteenth-Century England* (Oxford: Clarendon Press, 1980), pp. 29, 38.

16. A Lady, *An Appeal to the Females of the United Kingdom, on behalf of the London Society for Promoting Christianity amongst the Jews, more especially with reference to the degraded situation of the Poor Jewesses, 'That through your mercy, they also may obtain mercy'* (London: B. R. Goakman, n. d. [1812?]), p. 4.

17. Charlotte Elizabeth, 'The Jewish Press', *Christian Lady's Magazine*, 18 (October 1842), p. 367.

18. *Hansard*, third series 16 (1 March–1 April 1833), pp. 16; 17 (2 April–20 May 1833), p. 242.

19. *Hansard*, second series 24 (8 April–4 June 1830), p. 1309.

20. *Hansard*, third series 17 (2 April–20 May 1833), p. 241.

21. *The Jewess: A Tale from the Shores of the Baltic*. By the author of 'Letters from the Baltic' [Elizabeth Rigby, later Lady Eastlake], (London: John Murray, 1843), pp. 25–6. Further references to this edition are given after quotations. The story was also reprinted in Rigby's collection *Livonian Tales* (1846).

22. See bell hooks, *Ain't I a Woman: Black Women and Feminism* (London: Pluto Press, 1981), pp. 140–3 for a critique of the way that white women campaigners of the nineteenth and twentieth centuries identified their social and political disabilities with enslaved black people. See also Vron Ware, *Beyond the Pale: White Women, Racism and History* (London: Verso, 1992), pp. 104, 107. Rigby's text is a similar example of the universalisation of an historically specific instance of political inequality through an association with the grievances of upper-class Englishwomen.

23. *Quarterly Review*, 84 (December 1848), pp. 173–4, quoted in Sandra M. Gilbert and Susan Gubar, *The Madwoman in the Attic: The Woman Writer and the Nineteenth-Century Literary Imagination* (New Haven, CT, and London: Yale University Press, 1979), pp. 337–8.

24. For a detailed account of Aguilar's work, see Galchinsky, *Origin of the Modern Jewish Woman Writer*, pp. 135–89.

25. [Charlotte Elizabeth], 'Jewish Literature', *Christian Lady's Magazine*, 20 (September 1843), pp. 223, 226.

26. Grace Aguilar, *Home Influence: A Tale for Mothers and Daughters*, 2 vols (London: Groombridge & Sons, 1847), vol. i, p. v (original emphasis).

27. Grace Aguilar, *Records of Israel* (London: John Mortimer, 1844), pp. 46–7. In the preface to the same volume, Aguilar complains that 'The awful sufferings and martyrdoms of the Hebrews . . . are passed over, with scarcely a notice, as the justly ordained punishment for our awful sin of rejection, when eternal salvation and temporal happiness were so mercifully proffered' (pp. v–vi). But the object of her book, she argues, is to present a Jewish history of martyrdom 'in the same glorious light' as Christian marytrdom, not, in other words, to protest at its injustice (p. vi).

28. Sir Robert Inglis, *Hansard*, third series 17 (2 April–20 May 1833), p. 224. See also, for example, Earl of Winchilsea in *Hansard*, third series 118 (1 July–8 Aug 1851), p. 892.

29. For Evangelical leaders' discouragement of involvement in the political sphere see D. W. Bebbington, *Evangelicalism in Modern Britain: A History from the 1730s to the 1980s* (London: Unwin Hyman, 1989), pp. 72–4. Evangelicals were nevertheless very active in some of the most important social reform campaigns of the period, such as the anti-slavery and 'Ten Hours' campaigns. Yet, as Bebbington argues, their motives were conservative rather than liberal, focusing on the obstacles which slavery and long working hours presented to missionary activity and regular worship. See Bebbington, pp. 132–7. Similarly, Evangelicals generally opposed the campaign for Jewish civil rights, and although the Philo-Judean Society was established in 1826 to express the views of those Evangelicals who did support the campaign, their support was premised not on liberal principles but because it might provide a more effective means of achieving Jewish conversion. See Scult, *Millennial Expectations and Jewish Liberties*, pp. 88–134.

30. Grace Aguilar, *The Vale of Cedars; or, The Martyr: A Story of Spain in the Fifteenth Century* (London: Groombridge and Sons, 1850), p. 172.

31. Ibid., p. 174.

32. For example, the Archbishop of Canterbury argued in 1834 that 'Every act of the Legislature of this country ought to be regulated by Christian principles. Whatever might be said in favour of the Jews in other respects, it was impossible that they could understand the Christian faith' (*Hansard*, third series 24 (2 June–9 July 1834), p. 725). Lord Ashley asked: 'How was it possible that Christianity could be in the ascendant in the Legislature – how was it possible it could predominate and infuse its spirit into the Legislature, when there were parties in that House who rejoiced in the avowal that they would do all they could to resist its influence?' (*Hansard*, Third Series 95 (18 November–20 December 1847), p. 1276).

33. Although elected, Rothschild was unable to take up his seat due to the Christian oaths required – unlike Benjamin Disraeli, elected to Parliament in 1837, who, though Jewish-born, had been baptised at the age of thirteen and was a professing Christian.

34. [Grace Aguilar], 'History of the Jews in England', *Chamber's Miscellany of Useful and Entertaining Tracts*, 18 (Edinburgh: William and Robert Chambers, 1847), p. 16.

35. Ibid.

36. Ibid., pp. 17–18.

37. See also Michael Ragussis's discussion of the *amor patriae* of Aguilar's Jewish heroines in *Figures of Conversion*, pp. 147–52.

38. Unsigned review of 'The Mother's Recompense' by Grace Aguilar, *Jewish Chronicle*, 31 January 1851, p. 33.

39. *Early Efforts: A Volume of Poems, by the Misses Moss, of the Hebrew Nation, aged 18 and 16* (London: Whittaker, 1839), p. 52. Further references to this edition will appear in parentheses.

40. For a longer account of the national romances and historical romances of Sydney Owenson, Jane Porter and Anna Porter see Gary Kelly, *English Fiction of the Romantic Period, 1789–1830* (London and New York: Longman, 1989), pp. 92–8. The Moss sisters' romances provided for an Anglo-Jewish readership a literature similar to that of the Porter sisters, whose recasting of medieval and renaissance history in terms of modern bourgeois ideals 'expropriated the "national" past for the professional middle classes' vision of present and future' (p. 95).

41. Moira Ferguson, *Subject to Others: British Women Writers and Colonial Slavery, 1670–1834* (New York and London: Routledge, 1992); Clare Midgley, *Women against Slavery: The British Campaigns, 1780–1870* (London and New York: Routledge, 1992). There was a significant overlap between supporters of abolition and supporters of Jewish emancipation. Isaac Lyon Goldsmid, who was in the forefront of the campaign for Jewish emancipation in the early 1830s, was a member of the Anti-Slavery Society and greatly encouraged by their successful public agitation. He canvassed support for the Jewish cause from other abolitionists, particularly Dissenters. Prominent abolitionists like Stephen Lushington and Zachary Macaulay were also supporters of Jewish emancipation. See Salbstein, *The Emancipation of the Jews in Britain*, pp. 62–7 and A. Gilam, *The Emancipation of the Jews in England, 1830–1860* (New York: Garland, 1982), p. 78.

42. Ferguson, *Subject to Others*, pp. 3–4.

43. Ware, *Beyond the Pale*, pp. 104–8.

44. The Misses C[elia] and M[arion] Moss, *Tales of Jewish History*, 2 vols (London: Miller & Field, 1843), vol. i, pp. 117–18. Further references to this edition will appear in parentheses.

45. In particular, this argument recalls the widely read pamphlet published in 1824 by the Jacobin sympathiser and Quaker abolitionist Elizabeth Heyrick, who opposed slavery from the perspective of both natural rights philosophy and religion. She asserted that liberty is a 'sacred inalienable right' and demanded immediate rather than gradual abolition of slavery because slavery was a sin against God. This principle was taken up by many women's auxiliaries and only later adopted by the national organisation, the Anti-Slavery Society. See Midgley, *Women against Slavery*, pp. 103–9, 112–3.

46. For Parliamentary and public debate on the 'inconsistency' of Jewish disabilities see Salbstein, *The Emancipation of the Jews in Britain*, especially pp. 64–5.

47. The Misses C[elia] and M[arion] Moss, *The Romance of Jewish History*, 2 vols (London: Saunders and Otley, 1840), vol. ii, p. 88.

48. Mrs Leman Grimstone, *Character; or, Jew and Gentile: a Tale*, 2 vols (London: Charles Fox, 1833), vol. i, p. 91. For a full account of the work of Grimstone, see Kathryn Gleadle, *The Early Feminists: Radical Unitarians and the Emergence of the Women's Rights Movement, 1831–51* (Basingstoke: Macmillan, 1995).

For Unitarian support of Jewish emancipation, see Gilam, *The Emancipation of the Jews in England, 1830–1860*, pp. 18–19.
49. Grimstone, *Character*, pp. 146–7.
50. Ibid., i, p. 17.

6
Domestic Economy and Political Agitation: Women and the Anti-Corn Law League, 1839–46

Simon Morgan

The important role that women played in the agitation against the collection of protectionist legislation known as the Corn Laws has been a neglected area in the historiography of nineteenth-century women's politics. This is despite the views of those early women's rights campaigners who agreed with Helen Blackburn that 'the Anti-Corn Law agitation was the nursery in which many a girl of that generation learned to know how closely public questions concerned her'.[1] Moreover, the sheer scale of women's participation marks out the Anti-Corn Law campaign as an important historical subject in its own right. At the height of the agitation tens of thousands of women signed petitions to the Queen on the subject, while thousands of others attended political meetings in Manchester, London and elsewhere. Hundreds more supported tea parties and bazaars, whose profits helped to fund the Anti-Corn Law League's huge propaganda effort and paid for the expenses of registering voters and fighting elections.

The only historian to examine these activities in any detail has been Alex Tyrrell, in his article '"Woman's Mission" and Pressure Group Politics (1825–1860)'.[2] Tyrrell argues that the discourse of 'Woman's Mission' allowed respectable women to participate in political movements with demonstrably humanitarian aims, by representing their actions as pious acts of philanthropy for the greater good – so distancing them from the 'masculine' sphere of political debate. By the time of the Corn Law agitation, this discourse had already been successfully adopted by the anti-slavery movement. However, by applying the same arguments to encourage female support of a campaign to change laws that were seen by many as an essential bulwark of the landed constitution, the League went a step further.[3] This not only allowed women to expand their public roles; it also bolstered the League's claim to occupy a moral standpoint far above the petty squabbles of mere party interest. Tyrrell also emphasises the way that the League maximised the financial and propaganda potential of female support through the use of peculiarly feminine modes of fundraising – particularly charity bazaars. In addition to being very lucrative, these bazaars were vital components of the League's efforts to re-invent itself as a charitable campaign to provide cheap bread for the poor, and to escape from the popular perception that it was merely an economic pressure group acting in the narrow interests of manufacturing industry.[4]

The aim of this paper is not to refute Tyrrell's analysis, but to provide a more variegated account of the role that women played in this movement. Firstly, closer examination of the printed literature produced by the League suggests that 'Woman's Mission' was not the only discourse used to attract women to the campaign. Arguments from political economy which politicised women's role in the household, as well as appeals to women's duties as wives and mothers, were also important and had equally good pedigrees in previous political agitations involving women.[5] Moreover Tyrrell's emphasis on the role of men, such as the League's secretary, George Wilson, in orchestrating women's involvement in the campaign from 1841 onwards has obscured the degree to which such activities could be self-generating or even independent. This chapter will therefore provide a reassessment of female involvement in the League by looking at its origin in essentially local activities, which were then mobilised on a wider scale by the national leadership of the League. The development of the League from a provincial agitation with its roots in the Lancashire cotton districts, to being a major political campaign drawing support from across the country, provides an important context here.[6] It will be argued that women's participation was vital in helping to establish the League as a national movement. The final part of the chapter will examine the importance of the Great Bazaar at Covent Garden, and will draw attention to the significance of charity bazaars more generally as sites where women could develop and express feelings of civic pride and public virtue.

Before proceeding further, it would be beneficial to establish a chronology of women's involvement. For convenience this may be divided into three main phases. The first, from the inception of the League in February 1839 to October 1840, saw women attending lectures and meetings in relatively small numbers with sporadic attempts at organisation on a local basis. The League welcomed these demonstrations of support and even delayed its great banquet in January 1840 so that a ladies' gallery could be added to the pavilion on St. Peter's Fields in Manchester. However, there were as yet no concerted attempts to organise women for active campaigning.

The second phase began with the Manchester Tea Party of October 1840, attended by a mixed audience of 850, which heralded a more determined effort to enlist female opinion.[7] From April 1841 similar parties were held in a number of towns. To make the cause more palatable to female audiences the League engaged the services of the popular anti-slavery lecturer, George Thompson, who traversed the manufacturing districts addressing meetings and organising women's committees to send petitions to the Queen. During the summer of 1841 it was decided to hold a bazaar in Manchester to raise funds for the League. This helped to maintain the momentum of the petitioning campaign and was the first major event to bring women together from across the country to work actively for repeal. Held in February 1842, the bazaar was a great success and raised nearly £10,000 for the League's funds.[8] In May of that year the petitioning reached a climax with the presentation of memorials from Leicester, Edinburgh and the Lancashire towns bearing well over a quarter of a million signatures. When the League launched its £50,000 fund in November, women were called upon to canvass from door to door for subscriptions.[9]

Thereafter the more public aspect of women's contribution to the campaign declined in intensity, although there was a steady stream of petitions, soirées and tea parties throughout the following year.[10] In November 1843, *The Times* famously announced that the League had become a 'Great Fact', claiming that 'A NEW POWER HAS ARISEN IN THE STATE: and maids and matrons flock to theatres, as though it were but a new translation from the French'.[11] The presence of ladies in such numbers demonstrated just how respectable involvement in the League's activities had become. Taking advantage of its new-found popularity, the League was able to launch its most ambitious project yet – the Covent Garden Bazaar of 1845. The preparation for this, which included many smaller bazaars, canvasses and petitions, represents the third phase in our scheme. Women's activities were at the centre of attention for a number of months and thousands became involved in organising and preparing work for sale. Female effort, formerly diffuse and localised, became centred on one event of national significance. This Bazaar, which lasted for seventeen days and raised £25,000, was unquestionably the crowning moment of women's involvement in the Corn Law agitation.[12]

As the above chronology suggests, women's interest in the League was not conjured out of thin air by a clever propaganda campaign. Often it began with female initiatives, which took place at the local level and were grounded in essentially local ties of religion, kinship and political sympathy. In particular, the League benefited from the central role that women played in the social and religious life of nonconformist chapels, which often brought them into contact with the political dimensions of dissent. For instance, when free-trade lecturer Sydney Smith began to give lectures in dissenting chapels, he noted that women formed a significant proportion of the audience. In November 1839 he gave two Anti-Corn Law lectures at Haslingden Baptist chapel, which he claimed to be the first in an English church. One was 'graced by a fair proportion of ladies', whilst at the other 'a considerably greater proportion of the audience consisted of ladies', who contributed generously to the subscription at the end of the meeting.[13] These lectures were followed by meetings at other chapels in the area. In the first week of January 1840 Smith lectured to an audience of around 2000, including 500 ladies, at the Wesleyan Chapel in Hebden Bridge.[14]

The potential of this new constituency was enormous. Dissenting communities could provide an important basis for the political activity of both men and women, with many petitions against the Corn Laws emanating from religious congregations. In January 1842 the *Leeds Mercury* reported that congregational petitions against the Corn Laws had been sent in by Wortley Wesleyan Methodists and the Armley Wesleyan Association Methodists, 'and also memorials to her majesty on the same subject, signed by the females of their congregations'.[15] In February the same paper noted that 'The ladies attending the Westgate chapel, Bradford, have originated a petition to her majesty, in favour of a repeal of the Corn Laws, which has received a great number of signatures.'[16] Ryland Wallace's work on the Anti-Corn Law League in Wales supports this impression. Of eleven petitions submitted to Parliament from Caernarfon in 1842, for instance, nine of them were from dissenting congregations. The existence of congregational support meant that it was often deemed unnecessary to create separate Anti-Corn Law Associations.[17] Such local community actions, in conjunction with the great conferences of ministers in Manchester, Caernarfon and Edinburgh, helped to strengthen the League's connections with the traditions of radical dissent; although they also maintained a significant degree of independence from the League itself.

Sydney Smith had been one of the first to recognise the political significance of female endorsement, particularly if the women concerned belonged to influential families. Writing from Hanley in 1839 he told Wilson excitedly: 'I drive to the lecture with the ladies of Mr R's family in their *carriage* – this will show you the powerful interest which supports our cause here.'[18] Such support became vital as the focus of the agitation shifted from lobbying and propaganda to the application of direct political pressure at the polls. As the League became embroiled in by-election campaigns around the country, women with an independent interest in a particular constituency quickly became part of the political equation. For instance, while on the stump for the League in Wenlock, James Acland reported that Lady Lawson's interest in Ironbridge and Bridgenorth was said to be sufficient to turn the scale in the coming by-election.[19]

However, it was during the Walsall by-election of February 1841, the League's first significant foray into electoral politics, that the potential for the group mobilisation of women became apparent. On this occasion the League's President, J. B. Smith, was narrowly beaten by the Tory candidate, Captain Gladstone, in a contest which caused great controversy and split the liberal interest in the town. After the declaration of the poll Smith was met by a deputation of women in the town hall, who informed him of their intention to form a female Anti-Corn Law Association and their resolution 'to go from house to house to solicit subscriptions, in the same manner as for missionary societies'.[20] The women were serious in their designs and on 11 February David Stanley wrote to Smith concerning recent attempts to form an Anti-Corn Law Registration Society in the town. He declared that 'the Ladies are determined to organise themselves and to have theirs as a separate fund. I believe they are *Heartier* in the cause if possible than the gents.'[21] It was claimed that during the general election later in the year the ladies had blockaded shopkeepers who had supported Gladstone in February until they declared their votes.[22] On this occasion the League made great propaganda from the claim that 'the wives and daughters of the electors and non-electors read anti-corn law tracts and discussed free-trade principles by their firesides', as well as aiding the work of the registration committee.[23] The episode was symbolic of the League's campaign to rouse the whole nation against the Corn Laws.

In attempting to forge these sporadic and local displays of interest into a coherent national movement, the League faced a number of difficulties. It was imperative to convince people of the rightness of the cause and to make the issue one of principle, in order to avoid identification with any particular party.[24] This was particularly the case if women were to be encouraged to support the campaign. From at least 1841 the idea that the League campaign was part of 'Woman's Mission' was being widely disseminated in tracts and speeches, most notably those of George Thompson. By the time of the Covent Garden Bazaar, it had reached its apotheosis in the 'Letters from a Norwich Weaver Boy', which were published in *The League* in 1844–5. These letters were specifically aimed at women who wanted to participate in the Bazaar. As Tyrrell has rightly noted, this discourse was full of potential and provided a convenient umbrella for women's political activities. Unfortunately, it was also inherently limiting, as it reaffirmed the basically apolitical nature of 'woman' – an idea which Catherine Hall has claimed became increasingly prevalent after the Great Reform Act had explicitly excluded women from the parliamentary franchise for the first time.[25] A closer examination of the League's periodical literature, however, reveals that by no means all appeals to women were based solely or even primarily on this ideal. By exploring the inconsistencies of League propaganda it is hoped that some of the difficulties facing those who wanted to develop inclusive political identities for the 'Women of England' will become apparent. Moreover, it will become clear that 'Woman's Mission' was not the only possible form that such an identity could take.

The scale of the task that the League faced in bringing women to the fore may be demonstrated by considering some of the more hostile reactions from the national press. Among the most virulent was an article by J. W. Croker in the *Quarterly Review* of December 1842, which portrayed female work in the Anti-Corn Law League as at best debasing and unfeminine; at worst a threat to the social order itself. The basis of this article was an attempt to explain the 'Plug Plot' disturbances of August that year as a direct result of the inflammatory language of class conflict employed by the League. In painting the Anti-Corn Law campaign as an insurrectionary movement, the author adverted to the pointed references made by a few of its representatives to the precedent of the French Revolution, and their claims that a failure to end agricultural protection would goad the populous into similar excesses during the economic slump of the early 1840s. Having thus characterised the League's leaders as radical demagogues, Croker then turned his attention to the organisation's female supporters:

> We are warned in prose and verse to 'remember France,' and in short they all appear to have had the *French* Revolution constantly floating in their minds – rather, however, in their *view* than in their *memory*, for it is quite clear to anyone who knows the facts alluded to that the learned Mr Massie had *not* 'read the page of history,' and knew nothing of the scenes he talked about: but he had heard, and that was enough for his purpose, that *women* had been made useful agents in

the earlier stages of the French revolution; and it is probable that some idea of that sort suggested the frequent exhibition which these Anti-Corn Law Associations make of *female* countenance and co-operation – a practice in our opinion equally offensive to good taste and good feeling, and destructive of the most amiable and valuable qualities of the female character.[26]

The images provoked by such a comparison, of hungry women marching on Versailles and female Jacobins debating politics in Parisian clubs, were in complete contrast to the vision of the 'sister of charity, bearing a message of mercy to the oppressed, and an indignant rebuke to the guilty oppressor', as the *Anti-Bread Tax Circular* had described the women who organised the 1842 bazaar.[27] However, between these two extremes of the demonised and the idealised woman, there lay a real constituency capable of forming opinions on the country's ills and the best way of dealing with them. These women had to be persuaded that repeal of the Corn Laws was in their best interests and those of the nation as a whole. One of the ways in which the League sought to achieve this was through direct appeals to women's domestic experiences in their roles as housekeepers, wives and mothers. Such arguments first made their appearance in League publications before the Anti-Corn Law Banquet of January 1840. The idea of making an effort to attract women to this event seems to have been something of an afterthought. The *Anti-Corn Law Circular* announced as late as December 1839 that a soirée for the ladies would precede the event, while the banquet itself was postponed so that a gallery could be added to the pavilion. Significantly, the *Circular* made no mention of any supposed mission to the poor. Instead it argued, 'our fair friends...have as deep an interest in getting cheap flour for their puddings, as the weaver has for the starching of his calicoes';[28] and that 'our fair countrywomen ... as wives and mothers, are as much interested in cheap bread as any of us.'[29]

Similar attempts to politicise domestic economy may be traced back at least as far as the boycotts of slave-grown sugar by anti-slavery campaigners from the 1790s onwards.[30] The League was extremely conscious of the impact of female participation in this particular campaign, and tried to promote parallels between African slavery and the 'white slavery' of the Corn Laws wherever possible. As a result, arguments from American anti-slavery literature were sometimes pressed into service, which carried far-reaching and radical implications. For instance, on 14 January 1841 the *Circular* printed an extract from the anti-slavery publication *New York Emancipator*, which argued that 'when a female calculates how to cut the cloth to make her a garment, that is politics. The management of culinary affairs is political economy. The government of the family is politics.' As well as pointing to philanthropic considerations, the editorial comment urged female readers,

> to bear in mind the above excellent definition of the word politics, and to recollect that to exert their all powerful influence in abolishing the food monopoly is merely performing, on a larger scale, the duty which they everyday perform, as good housekeepers, in obtaining at the cheapest possible rate, their domestic supply of provisions.[31]

It was in such attempts to establish a political link between the household economy and economic policy that the truly radical significance of the League lay for women.

Although these examples pre-date the concerted efforts at mobilising women which took place from the spring of 1841, the increasingly elaborate construction of women as ministering angels to the oppressed failed to submerge these more radical discourses. Throughout the campaign, appeals to women as pious philanthropists coexisted with hard economic arguments and claims for women's political prerogatives. Take, for example, this article from the *Morning Chronicle*, reprinted in *The League* of 12 April 1845:

> That, on the one hand, the active participation of women in political agitation and debate is, generally speaking, decidedly undesirable; that, on the other hand, there are, from time to time, certain public questions of a *quasi*-political character on which the expression of female opinion and feeling is both natural and graceful – are safe truisms.

However, instead of reiterating the arguments for women's charitable and improving role as one might expect, the article goes on to argue for a recognition of the capacity of women for understanding technical questions of political economy – citing the strong tradition of female writing on the subject, particularly by Harriet Martineau, Margracia Loudon and Jane Marcet – before advocating women's right to agitate for reasons of class and family interest:

> None are more interested ... than the women of the middle classes of Great Britain in the removal of obstructions to trade and industry, which ... make husbands anxious and careworn, drive sons and

brothers to Australia or Canada, compel daughters to go out as governesses or dressmakers, and charge them with the burden of carrying out those painful and pinching economies which so grievously interfere with the comfort of everyday domestic life.[32]

This piece plays on the fears of middle-class women about the threat of poverty, family breakdown and the loss of respectability. A similar message may be found in an address from the Sunderland Anti-Corn Law Committee to the ladies of Sunderland in 1843, which urged women to remember, alongside their responsibilities to the poor, their duty as wives, daughters and sisters to uphold the interests of their menfolk, which depended on the prosperity of the shipping industry.[33] Of course women were in this context being politicised through their accepted roles as wives and mothers; nevertheless there are striking implications here regarding the areas of public policy which could legitimately be defined as 'women's questions'.

The League pursued this female constituency because its intention was nothing less than the politicisation of the whole nation in the cause of repeal. This was the rationale behind its operative branches, its rural lecture campaigns, and ultimately the Great Bazaar itself. The aim was to turn what had initially been a provincial agitation in the industrial districts into a national campaign. In this respect it expanded the political horizons of men and women from all classes of the community.[34] However, before we can fully appreciate the wider implications this mobilisation had for women, we must first look at some of their responses to the League and the political identities with which it provided them.

Some women were quick to grasp the opportunities for an expanded sphere of involvement which the Corn Law agitation offered, while others still felt constrained by the limits of their own particular connections as much as by their sex. The problems faced by the League are neatly illustrated by the Manchester Bazaar of 1842. Increasingly anxious to obtain an influential list of patronesses for the undertaking, the League's secretary, George Wilson, sent out circulars in September and October 1841 to the wives of known liberals and radicals, as well as to sympathetic members of the aristocracy. The range of responses to these circulars provides a great insight into the issues involved in mobilising women on anything other than a local scale. Of course, the sample of eighty-seven replies is too small to draw firm conclusions and many women did not feel it necessary to elaborate on their reasons for declining to take part. Others gave reasons such as illness which could have simply been excuses, although some of these professed their sympathy for the

League and promised to help in other ways. However, some of the responses suggest that the League had a long way to go before it could persuade women that political agitation was a respectable business. Lady Kinnaird complained, 'I hardly think it right that ladies should take a prominent part in politics, and unfortunately the Corn Laws have now become a purely party question'.[35] Some women cited their own or their husbands' objections to their appearing on a committee or patronage list for such a cause. At the other extreme were those who declined because their political views were not in harmony with the objectives of the League. At least one woman declined to take part because 'my opinions, tho' friendly to an alteration of the Corn Laws, would not be satisfactory to the committee'.[36]

For the remainder, however, family ties, especially the care of children or infirm relatives, and the practical difficulties involved in travelling to Manchester (particularly for single women), were great limitations. This reminds us that for the majority of women – indeed for many men – the 'public' sphere did not extend much beyond their own localities. In all, fourteen women declined to participate in the work of the bazaar committee because distance and other commitments prevented them from attending to its business. A few of these, such as Mrs Seville and Sarah Brown, consented to their names being publicised as supporters of the League.[37] However, there seemed to be a certain amount of confusion amongst many women as to what the League actually required of women who were not part of Manchester society. Some, such as Mrs Gaskell and Hannah Day, promised to promote the cause in their own localities.[38] Others wanted clarification as to what Wilson required from committee members who resided at a distance.[39] At least one woman, a Mrs Beardsall, declined to take part in the bazaar not just because she had young children to look after, but also because she feared that her name was unknown in Manchester and therefore could not possibly do any good.[40] This suggests a misunderstanding of the League's intentions. The bazaar was not *meant* to be a Manchester affair – as Prentice later wrote, one of its main purposes was 'to bring to friendly communication, and daily social intercourse, the friends of free trade, and especially the ladies who had taken a deep interest in the question as affecting the welfare of suffering millions'.[41] Hence the desire to involve women not directly connected with the town. Many of the women contacted were known to Wilson purely through the reputation of their husbands as supporters of liberal politics. It seems that he often had little or no personal knowledge of these men, as demonstrated by the replies he received from bachelors such as Robert Stewart, who complained, 'I am not a married man, so you can scarcely expect me to comply with the request of your circular of the 18th'.[42] Clearly there was a long way to go before a real sense of national community could be established between the supporters of Corn Law repeal, and the Manchester Bazaar was merely one of the first faltering steps along that road.

Despite this, enough women were persuaded to back the bazaar to make it a success.[43] It is difficult to say with any precision how much this owed to the kinds of female political identities which were discussed earlier in this chapter. It is certain, however, that many of the men and women involved in the enterprise were motivated by the distress that they saw around them and were convinced by the League's argument that it had been exacerbated, if not caused, by the operation of the Corn Laws. The continuing economic difficulties of the manufacturing districts and the poor harvest of 1841 promised a difficult winter for the urban poor; to hold a charity bazaar in the depths of winter for a *political* objective, unless one was firmly convinced of its social and economic benefits, could have been seen as tantamount to fiddling while Rome burned. Unfortunately the women who answered Wilson's call for support positively were even less likely to state their reasons for doing so. However, many surely agreed with Mrs Clure's claim that her support for the League stemmed from a sense of duty to the urban poor on account of the prevailing distress in the town.[44]

Mrs Clure, for one, was still acting on what was essentially her own local stage. For some women, though, the League offered possibilities for wider association and greater access to a national public stage. For example, in August 1841 Richard Cobden received a letter from Juliana Gifford of Hampstead concerning a pamphlet she had written on the Corn Laws. This letter reveals much about the psychological barriers facing women who attempted to write on such subjects and the way in which the League enabled them to be overcome:

My brother Captain Gifford has sent you a little pamphlet of which I am the authoress and as it is I believe the first female attempt on this subject I have been quite ashamed of it and too shy to advertise it but since you advise the ladies to assist, you have taken that chain from my mind. Still I confess I do not think you will like it or me . . . [45]

The same sense of expanded opportunities can be detected in a letter from a woman reader to the *Manchester Times* of February 1845, which compliments the 'Letters of a Norwich Weaver Boy' and the League itself for providing women with a way in which to 'aid them in an enterprise which claims our sympathies by its intimate alliance with justice and humanity'. However, the letter also demonstrates the potential complexity of reactions to the League's categorisation of female support:

> I leave to others the task of exposing the folly of the Corn Law as a matter of policy, its gross violation of the principles of political economy, its utter inefficiency to serve its avowed purpose; points these though on which I would never resign the right of exercising and expressing my opinions.[46]

This suggests a consciousness that by accepting the mantle of the 'sister of charity' too uncritically, women risked their right to an opinion on anything that savoured of political controversy.

Other women remained unconvinced about the League's claim to have raised itself above the taint of party and continued to see its message as divisive. In December 1844 *The League* carried a letter from 'Some of the Women of England' to the Norwich Weaver Boy, in which they claimed that many women who agreed with the object of the agitation held aloof because of the language of class hatred which it frequently employed.[47] Although these charges were rejected in the strongest terms, the following year appeals could still be found in *The League* calling for women to liberate 'industry from the landlord yoke, and . . . bread from the landlord tax'.[48] Such inconsistencies demonstrate clearly the tension between the need to appeal to the political understandings and loyalties of women whilst maintaining the fiction of 'Woman' as above party and politics – a tension which underlay much of the League's propaganda.

Despite all of these qualifications, the League became increasingly successful in attracting female support, as demonstrated by a meeting of 2000 women at the Hanover Square rooms, London, in April 1845.[49] By this time the League's efforts to recast itself as a national movement had progressed tremendously since the Manchester Bazaar of 1842. The *Anti-Bread Tax Circular* had been relaunched as *The League* in 1843 and was now printed and edited in the capital. The League also began to hold huge weekly meetings at Covent Garden theatre, which were well attended by both sexes. Tickets to these events were eagerly sought after, as may be inferred from Mary Howitt's obvious excitement on the prospect of obtaining some in 1845.[50] In addition, the ties of the central office of the League to the various local Anti-Corn Law associations had been strengthened and rationalised and the country divided up into districts for the purpose of fundraising from the end of 1841.[51] This strategy allowed the League to raise enormous sums of money through its great annual funds – which paid for election expenses and a concerted campaign of voter registration.

In 1844 the League launched its £100,000 fund and felt confident enough to mount its most ambitious project – a Grand Bazaar at Covent Garden theatre, which was to incorporate an exhibition of industrial goods, methods and machinery from across the kingdom. The aim was to demonstrate the unity of popular opinion of all classes behind the repeal campaign. Large numbers of women were mobilised around the country, and the excitement that it generated is captured in the following eye-witness account of the scene at the theatre the night before the bazaar opened in May 1845:

> On entering, I was bewildered. There were persons just arrived from all parts of England, running this way and that ... I then regretted not having enrolled myself. The scene was so exciting, that I felt inclined to run from the pit to the gallery, or to dive to the lowest depths beneath the stage; but in so doing I should only have fatigued myself and been in everybody's way.[52]

As a public relations and fundraising exercise the bazaar surpassed all expectations. It had also allowed women to take centre stage in a national political agitation. The importance of this cannot be overemphasised. The Great Bazaar was an innovation in a number of respects – not least in the fact that it combined a traditional ladies' sale of fancy goods with an exhibition of local trades and manufactures from around Britain. Such exhibitions had been an increasingly important feature in the development of civic pride in the industrial regions of south Lancashire and the West Riding since the 1830s, and were often linked to those great symbols of the middle-class 'civilising mission' – the Mechanics' Institutes.[53] At the Covent Garden Bazaar each participating town had its own stalls, thus encouraging competition to produce the best one. The *Leeds Mercury* chided local manufacturers who had not matched the example of their womenfolk in providing material; they were also compared unfavourably to the manufacturers of Bradford, who had 'quite taken the lead of their fair co-adjutators'.[54] The bazaar was therefore an outlet for local pride, as well as being the symbol of national cooperation. At the same time it was a high-profile and successful fundraising event, which could not have taken place without the hard work and dedication of women willing to risk their public reputations in support of the cause.

As a way of involving women in the work of the League, the bazaars were therefore invaluable. There is also evidence to suggest that such bazaars provided sites where women could develop and express public identities based around ideals of civic pride and service. However, men were often suspicious of bazaars in that they did not conform to the model of the 'subscriber democracies' which R. J. Morris has argued were the foundation of middle-class culture in the nineteenth century.[55] These middle-class voluntary societies were hierarchical in nature, ensuring that real power remained in the hands of elite male oligarchies. They also produced published subscription lists that put pressure on people to contribute according to their means. By contrast, the anonymity and apparent frivolity of bazaars, run as they were by women and with no way of keeping track of who was spending what, appeared to undermine this system.[56] This could sometimes give rise to tension, as was the case during preparation for the Leeds Mechanics' Institute Bazaar of 1859. On this occasion the women's committee clashed with the men's committee over unauthorised publication of the women's names in the local press and also over the date of the bazaar. It is clear in this instance that the women felt the men were trespassing on what was essentially female ground. At the same time the dispute allowed the women to represent themselves as having the true interests of the Mechanics' Institute at heart, while they accused the men of a vainglorious and wasteful pursuit of publicity.[57]

Relations between the men's and women's committees of the Covent Garden Bazaar appear to have been more harmonious. However, at least one conflict of interest seems to have arisen which elicited a collective response from the women. After the opening day of the bazaar, the Council of the League had decided to lower the entrance price to a shilling, in order to allow access to the commonality. Unfortunately, according to *Punch*, the lady stallholders were concerned about being 'stared out of countenance' by the low characters able to afford the new charge. In response, the women refused to work until a deputation from the Council of the League agreed to raise the entrance price to half a crown.[58]

Perhaps more importantly, bazaar committees provided the institutional space within which women could debate the issue at hand on their own terms and explore the possibilities of female action in support of the cause. This may have compensated to some extent for the lack of permanent women's auxiliaries in the Anti-Corn Law movement (in contrast to the anti-slavery campaigns after 1825). Although evidence of what went on at the meetings of these committees is scant, some light is shed on the question by a report in the *Manchester Courier*. It refers to a resolution passed by the Women's Committee of the Manchester Anti-Corn Law Association to abstain from all produce on which government duties were laid – a tactic which had previously been employed by the rejuvenated Birmingham Political Union in 1837.[59] Although the *Courier* ridiculed the motion, it is significant in that it demonstrates the potential for independent action which bazaar committees gave (abstention was never officially adopted as a tactic by the League), and shows that the kinds of issues discussed at their meetings were not necessarily restricted to the immediate business of the bazaar itself. Moreover, it is proof that the politicisation of women's economic position within the home was not just empty rhetoric, but instead included the potential for a wide range of practical action.[60]

To conclude, the achievement of the League was to provide discursive and institutional spaces within which women could operate. A viable political identity was constructed around the idea of 'Woman's Mission', which helped to protect the reputations of potential female supporters from censure in the press.[61] However, this rhetoric coexisted with discourses which politicised women's role in the *domestic* economy by drawing direct connections with the state's economic policy. These connections were encouraged by a well-established tradition of female authors writing on political economy in the decade or so before the foundation of the League, and by the anti-slavery traditions which the League was so anxious to appropriate for its own purpose. Such discourses were significant in that they introduced an embryonic language of 'women's issues', albeit closely linked to family interests, into a broad-ranging political campaign. This view of female political citizenship as an extension of women's domestic position may be related to later crystallisations of women's politics around issues of property and household suffrage (although there was clearly a change of emphasis from the sense of *duty* appealed to by the League, and the later concentration on the *rights* of women).

Institutionally the adoption of specifically feminine modes of campaigning and fundraising, especially bazaars, allowed women to form their own committees and so circumvent the increasingly bureaucratic machinery of the League. Moreover, the Covent Garden Bazaar, widely recognised as the forerunner of the Great Exhibition, played a major role in bolstering the League's claim to be a truly nationwide organisation. In particular it encouraged the formation of a national community of women working for a common object while retaining their local identities and loyalties. In the optimistic words of *The League*, 'Collected together from all parts of the British islands, those who had never seen or heard of each other in their lives found themselves encircled by friends though surrounded by strangers, community of feeling becoming the basis for community of affection.'[62] By placing women at the forefront of such an enterprise, the League momentarily made them the standard-bearers of a national middle-class political culture.

Notes

1. Helen Blackburn, *Women's Suffrage: A Record of the Women's Suffrage Movement in the British Isles with Biographical Sketches of Miss Becker* (Oxford and London: Williams & Norgate, 1902), pp. 15–18, esp. p. 17. Later historians have reaffirmed the importance of the League in the origins of early feminism without examining women's activities in great detail. For example, Constance Rover, *Women's Suffrage and Party Politics in Britain, 1866–1914* (London: Routledge and Kegan Paul, 1967), esp. p. 61; Jane Rendall, *The Origins of Modern Feminism: Women in Britain, France and the United States, 1780–1860* (Basingstoke: Macmillan, 1985), pp. 244–5; Sandra Stanley Holton, 'From Anti-Slavery to Suffrage Militancy: The Bright Circle, Elizabeth Cady Stanton and the British Women's Movement', in Caroline Daley and Melanie Nolan (eds), *Suffrage and Beyond: International Feminist Perspectives* (New York: New York University Press, 1994), pp. 217 and 229.
2. Alex Tyrrell, ' "Woman's Mission" and Pressure Group Politics (1825–1860)', *Bulletin of the John Rylands University Library*, 63, no. 1 (1980), pp. 194–230.
3. This view of the importance of the Corn Laws is described in Robert Stewart, *The Politics of Protection: Lord Derby and the Protectionist Party, 1841–1852* (Cambridge: Cambridge University Press, 1971), esp. pp. 4–8. More recently it has been argued that protection was part of a more nuanced Conservative ideology: 'conceived as a way of representing and re-balancing interests in a tariff which could identify propertied interests with a constitutionally conservative state. In this way it was considered to be a mechanism which could preserve the virtual representation of interests within the reformed constitution'. Anna Gambles, 'Rethinking the Politics of Protection: Conservatism and the Corn Laws, 1830–52', *English Historical Review*, CXIII (1998), p. 949.
4. The standard history of the League is Norman McCord, *The Anti-Corn Law League, 1838–1846* (London: George Allen and Unwin, 1958). See also Archibald Prentice, *History of the Anti-Corn Law League*, 2nd edn, 2 vols (London: Frank Cass, 1968).
5. See, for example, the account of the sugar boycotts in Clare Midgley's *Women against Slavery: The British Campaigns, 1780–1870* (London and New York: Routledge, 1992), pp. 60–2.
6. This development may be followed in McCord, *The Anti-Corn Law League*.
7. Prentice, *History of the Anti-Corn Law League*, vol. i, pp. 194–230.
8. Ibid., pp. 296–301.

9. *Anti-Bread Tax Circular*, 17 November 1842.

10. See the League periodicals for 1843.

11. Quoted in Prentice, *History of the Anti-Corn Law League*, vol. ii, pp. 137–8.

12. See ibid., pp. 315–41 for a full account of the Covent Garden Bazaar; see also Tyrrell, 'Woman's Mission', p. 217.

13. *Anti-Corn Law Circular*, 12 November 1839.

14. Ibid., 7 January 1840. After this the practice of chapel meetings became widespread.

15. *Leeds Mercury*, 22 January 1842.

16. Ibid., 5 February 1842.

17. Ryland Wallace, 'Wales and the Anti-Corn Law League', *Welsh History Review*, 13 (1986), pp. 8–9.

18. Sydney Smith to the League, 12 December 1839, Anti-Corn Law League Letters, Manchester Central Library, microfilm MF 502.

19. Ibid., James Acland to the League, 18 September, 1840. For the potential influence of landed women during election contests see Sarah Richardson, 'The Role of Women in Electoral Politics in the West Riding of Yorkshire During the 1830s', *Northern History*, 32 (1996), pp. 133–51.

20. *Anti-Corn Law Circular*, 11 February 1841.

21. David Stanley to J. B. Smith, 11 February 1841, J. B. Smith Election Papers, Manchester Central Library. The fund was to raise money for a piece of plate to be presented to Smith in recognition of his stand.

22. Biographical sketch of J. B. Smith, in J. B. Smith, Corn Law Papers vol. 1, pp. 21–2, Manchester Central Library. The role of women in elections more generally is examined in Elaine Chalus, '"That Epidemical Madness": Women and Electoral Politics in the Late Eighteenth Century', in Hannah Barker and Elaine Chalus (eds), *Gender in Eighteenth Century England: Roles, Representations and Responsibilities* (London: Longman, 1997), pp. 151–78.

23. *Anti-Bread Tax Circular*, 1 July 1841. The League registration committees could prove contentious where they upset the balance of existing political alliances and arrangements. See, for example, F. M. L. Thompson, 'Whigs and Liberals in the West Riding, 1830–1860', *English Historical Review*, 74 (1959), pp. 214–39.

24. Until the end of 1845 neither of the main political groupings was prepared to make repeal their official policy.

25. Catherine Hall, 'Private Persons Versus Public Someones: Class, Gender and Politics in England, 1780–1850', in Catherine Hall, *White, Male and Middle Class: Explorations in Feminism and History* (Cambridge: Polity Press, 1992), p. 152.

26. *Quarterly Review*, (1842) pp. 261–2.

27. *Anti-Bread Tax Circular*, 13 January 1842.

28. *Anti-Corn Law Circular*, 10 December 1839.

29. Ibid., 24 December 1839.

30. Midgley, *Women Against Slavery*, pp. 60–2.

31. *Anti-Corn Law Circular*, 14 January 1841.

32. *The League*, 12 April 1845. See also editorial of 15 March 1845.

33. *Anti-Bread Tax Circular*, 31 January 1843.

34. The League also tried to involve working-class women. The first mention of a female petition may be found in the *Anti-Corn Law Circular*, 31 December

1839, in a report on a petition from the Kendal Working Men's Anti-Corn Law Association, which claimed that 'The wives of the operatives have been most eager in their solicitations to add their names, and finding that it is contrary to usage, express the strongest wish that a petition should be originated for themselves.' The same issue carried an appeal for women to petition the Queen, which argued 'This is emphatically a mother's question. It is a mother's duty to take it up.' Unlike 'Woman's Mission' with its implications of middle-class virtue and superiority, appeals to motherhood transcended class boundaries.

35. Lady Kinnaird to George Wilson, 1 October 1841, Wilson Papers, Manchester Central Library, M/20.
36. Mrs Staunton to George Wilson, 20 October 1841, ibid.
37. Mrs Seville to George Wilson, 16 October 1841; William Brown to George Wilson, 20 January 1842, ibid.
38. Hannah Day to George Wilson, 5 October 1841; Mrs Gaskell to George Wilson, 7 October 1842, ibid.
39. Jane? to George Wilson, 18 October 1841, ibid.
40. Mrs Beardsall to George Wilson, 19 October 1841, ibid.
41. Prentice, *History of the Anti-Corn Law League*, vol. i, p. 296. For a similar interpretation of the Covent Garden Bazaar, see ibid., vol. ii, pp. 335–7.
42. Robert Stewart to George Wilson, 23 October 1841; see also Peter Rylands to George Wilson, 18 October 1841, and C. W. Robberds to George Wilson, 23 October 1841, Wilson Papers.
43. Prentice claims that there were 360 women on the committee of the Manchester Bazaar in 1842: Prentice, *History of the Anti-Corn Law League*, vol. ii, p. 298.
44. Mrs Clure to George Wilson, 29 October 1841, Wilson Papers.
45. Juliana Gifford to Richard Cobden, 26 August 1841, Cobden Papers, Microfilm MF 1311, Reel 2, Manchester Central Library.
46. *Manchester Times*, 8 February 1845.
47. *The League*, 21 December 1844.
48. Ibid., 15 March 1845.
49. Ibid., 12 April 1845.
50. 'We have tickets for the monster meeting at Covent Garden Theatre on Wednesday, when all the great heroes of the League will meet. It is a noble battle that they have fought. And now, thank Heaven! they are just on the eve of their great glorious, and bloodless victory' (Margaret Howitt (ed.), *Mary Howitt, An Autobiography*, 2 vols (London: W. Isbister, 1889), vol. ii, p. 36). Also quoted in Rendall, *The Origins of Modern Feminism*, p. 353, n. 48.
51. Minutes of Halifax Anti-Corn Law Association, 6 December 1841, West-Yorkshire Archive Service (WYAS), Calderdale District, MS HAS/B:11/1. The reorganisation of 1841–2 and the increasingly bureaucratic nature of the League are described in McCord, *The Anti-Corn Law League*, pp. 133–5 and 163–87.
52. *Anti-Corn Law League Bazaar Gazette*, no. 8 (London, 1845), pp. 3–6.
53. See Toshio Kusamitsu, 'Great Exhibitions before 1851', *History Workshop Journal*, 29 (1980), pp. 70–89.
54. *Leeds Mercury*, 3 May 1845.
55. See R. J. Morris, 'Voluntary Societies and British Urban Elites 1780–1850', *Historical Journal*, 26 (1983), pp. 95–118. The ideas expressed here are

elaborated in his book *Class, Sect and Party: The Making of the British Middle-Class, 1830–1850* (Manchester: Manchester University Press, 1990), esp. Chapters 7 and 8.

56. Some of these implications have been explored by S. J. D. Green, 'The Death of Pew Rents, the Rise of Bazaars, and the End of the Traditional Political Economy of Voluntary Religious Organizations: the Case of the West Riding of Yorkshire, *c.* 1870–1914', *Northern History*, 27 (1991), pp. 198–235. The social and financial implications of bazaars have been described in F. K. Prochaska, *Women and Philanthropy in Nineteenth Century England* (Oxford: Oxford University Press, 1980), Chapter 2.

57. See especially the Minutes of the Bazaar Committee, 18 March 1859, WYAS, Leeds, Leeds Institute MSS. 32. This case is explored in more detail in an unpublished paper given by the author to the York Women's History Group, November 1997, entitled 'Women, Bazaars and Public Identities *c.* 1840–1868'.

58. *Punch*, 8 (1845), p. 234.

59. *Manchester Courier*, 19 February 1842; Hall, 'Private Persons Versus Public Someones', pp. 161–2.

60. The tactic of 'selective shopping', or exclusive dealing, was a further manifestation of the politicisation of household duties, and was practised in particular by Chartist women. See M. Thomis and J. Grimmet, *Women in Protest, 1800–1850* (London and Canberra: Croom Helm, 1982), p. 131.

61. Tyrrell, 'Woman's Mission'.

62. Quoted in Prentice, *History of the Anti-Corn Law League*, vol. ii, p. 336.

7
'Our Several Spheres': Middle-class Women and the Feminisms of Early Victorian Radical Politics
Kathryn Gleadle

In the official records of the organisations formed by middle-class radicals in the early years of Victoria's reign, women are most notable by their absence. This is particularly striking, given that many of the radicals concerned in middle-class Chartist activity and in the promotion of European nationalism professed an ambitious feminism.[1] This chapter, by focusing upon two reforming communities – the radicals associated with the Ham Common Concordium and the Ashurst circle – considers how we are to understand this apparent inconsistency and asks how middle-class women might themselves have perceived the seemingly restricted nature of their political involvement. Central to such a discussion is an understanding of how contemporary radicals variously negotiated with Victorian discourses on gender, most notably the ubiquitous notion of 'separate spheres'.

There has been a recent historiographical trend to dismiss the concept of separate spheres as proscriptive rhetoric – a reactionary trope which reflected not women's containment, but rather fear as to the increasing scope of their extra-domestic activities. This chapter will suggest that such readings neglect the way in which the discourses of separate spheres contributed to the construction of individual subjectivities. It was a language which was consumed, discussed and digested by its audiences and which men and women actually used between themselves when they tried to make sense of their own lives. It will also be seen that the new 'optimistic' accounts fail to take into account radical readings of the discourse.[2] Barbara Taylor's pioneering treatment of the early socialist movement revealed that the Evangelical languages of separate spheres and 'woman's mission' were not confined to the mores of polite, middle-class society, but strongly informed the feminism of Owenite activists.[3]

The chapter begins by examining an aspect of the Owenite story which was not central to Taylor's account: the influence of Saint-Simonian and Fourierite theories.[4] Sharing with the Owenites a vision of a brave new world, emancipated from the ills of capitalism through the application of science and societal reorganisation, Fourierism and Saint-Simonism attracted considerable interest among the radical intelligentsia. The French Saint Simonians and Fourierists prophesied that only when woman had thrown off the shackles of her existing position would society truly be able to regenerate and reform.[5] The Saint-Simonians, in particular, became known for their eulogistic vision of woman's loving and moral nature. In the philosophy of Prosper Enfantin (the leading exponent of Saint-Simonism), women's supposedly emotional and eirenical sensibilities were to become privileged in a new value system which would herald a world order of peace and cooperation. Many Saint-Simonian disciples went so far as to proclaim the imminent arrival of a female Messiah. Following Enfantin's lead, French Saint-Simonian feminists often practised 'free-love' lifestyles, something that was also explicit in some of Fourier's work. Within France these philosophies produced a sustained early feminist movement, which derived much inspiration from Enfantin's insight that women's oppression stemmed not only from the subordination of their private lives, but also from their exclusion from public and political activity.[6]

The evangelising campaign of Saint-Simonian missionaries in Britain in the early 1830s failed to produce the concerted feminist movement which had sprung up in France. Those, such as the Irish feminist, Anna Wheeler, who had the personal conviction to deliver impassioned public lectures on the need for female emancipation remained exceptional.[7] Yet the theories did exert a considerable influence upon the emergent feminist discourses of the day. Throughout the 1830s and 1840s British radical journals, particularly those inspired by Owenism or Unitarianism, publicised the ideas of Fourier and Saint-Simon to draw attention to the need for divorce reform, women's economic independence and changes to women's legal position.[8]

However, the influence of Gallic Saint-Simonism and Fourierism upon British radicals was complex and often contradictory, derived as it was from a multiplicity of readings and emphases. This is amply illustrated by the career of James Elishama Smith. From the 1830s Smith made a significant contribution to the dissemination of Saint-Simonian ideas, not least through his publication of Anna Wheeler's translations from the journals of French Saint-Simonian feminists.[9] In his own lectures during this period Smith followed closely a Saint-Simonian view of female emancipation. Smith's commitment to the Saint-Simonian feminist vision was also evident in his translation of Saint-Simon's *New Christianity* in 1834, which featured a colourful frontispiece of 'La Femme Libre'.[10] However, Smith's own journal, *The Shepherd* (the leading organ for Saint-Simonian ideas in Britain), demonstrated that his feminism was becoming increasingly filtered through more conventional British concepts, in particular that of 'separate spheres'. The growing modification of British Saint-Simonianism and Fourierism was seen equally in the *London Phalanx* in the early 1840s – a publication founded by the Irish Fourierite, Hugh Doherty, but over which Smith also had influence. Both these publications articulated a belief in what was described as the 'two distinct spheres for the sexes'. The *London Phalanx* looked to a time when men and women, united by intellectual marriages, might come together in a 'joint co-operation in the government of society'.[11] However, Smith argued that this did not imply that 'political authority shall ultimately fall in the hands of woman'. He claimed that, 'Woman will never rule politically; for politics, to the very end of time, are the physical department, which does not belong to woman.'[12] Such declarations were, to their authors, compatible with a broadly feminist, reforming agenda – an agenda which can only be understood with reference to their efforts to redefine the very meaning of politics. As another Fourierite journal, the *Morning Star or Phalansterian Gazette* explained, 'It is not so much *political rights* as *social freedom* which is necessary'.[13] Political measures were seen as insignificant compared to their dream of creating a new moral government of both sexes in which men would 'hold the political sceptre' whilst women's moral authority would increase daily over both public and private conduct.[14] The *London Phalanx* rejected the possibility of women becoming more involved in electoral politics, explaining that they wished to 'introduce domesticity ... into politics, and perfect the one by intermarriage with the other.' It explained that they endorsed Fourier's plan to redefine the very meaning of politics by 'widen[ing] the sphere of domesticity'.[15]

Therefore, the journals with which 'Shepherd' Smith was associated during the late 1830s and early 1840s, whilst continuing to proclaim the need for women's emancipation, envisaged that this might be achieved by extending conventional gender differences, rather than overturning them. The possible implications such arguments may have had upon the political subjectivities of these journals' female audience may be reconstructed by turning to a forgotten aspect of the work of J. E. Smith – his reliance upon female patrons. That Smith was able to launch a new series of *The Shepherd* in 1837 and embark upon his ambitious lectureships was thanks to the financial support of two little-known Gloucestershire widows, S. C. Chichester and Mrs G. F. Welch, who acted as key patrons to some of the leading radical reformers of the day. During the late 1830s and early 1840s, by positioning themselves as radical patrons, they sought to be not political reformers in their own right, but rather to create a sphere of influence, (much as the pages of the *London Phalanx* and *The Shepherd* had advocated). By adopting (and urging upon their protégés) such causes as animal rights the two women found ways to fulfil Fourier's injunction that women form a new moral government.

During the late 1830s Chichester and Welch drew a tight cordon around the extent of their campaigning activity. They did not meet Smith during these years, their relationship remaining purely epistolary and their role regarding the journal, proprietorial.[16] The limits which they imposed upon their political activity were made evident when Welch suggested that Smith might help to promote vegetarianism, 'through the medium of the Press', whilst Chichester and herself would propagate such principles, 'in our more limited private circle'.[17] Chichester and Welch forged a similar relationship with Richard Carlile during this period. This patronage, which ran to hundreds of pounds, was absolutely essential to the continuation of Carlile's lecture tours and journals. Yet even in his private correspondence Carlile did not identify his two benefactors by name for almost two years, presumably at their insistence.[18] Once again they evidently wished to keep their involvement strictly private.

It was, however, to the radical transcendentalism of James Pierrepont Greaves, a Pestalozzian mystic, well-known in Owenite circles, that Chichester and Welch were increasingly drawn.[19] This connection (probably made through J. E. Smith) became of primary importance to the two patrons. It is also of significance in that it brought the two women into contact with a number of radicals, including Anna Wheeler, Richard Hengist Horne and Goodwyn Barmby, who placed far more emphasis upon the need to secure women's *political* rights. Greaves himself presided at the centre of a formidable coterie, who called themselves the 'Aesthetic Institution'. This society included J. E. Smith and the feminists mentioned above, as well as lesser-known female reformers, such as the writer Harriet Downing and Miss Ronalds (a relative of Harriet Martineau and friend of Lady Byron).[20] By 1839 Welch was explaining to James Smith that she and Chichester shared Greaves's views, in particular the 'vicious and demoralizing' nature of contemporary marriages. Chichester settled a life annuity of £100 upon Greaves and, with Welch, became a central patron of 'Alcott House' school (named after the

American educationist Bronson Alcott). This was the group's radical experiment in education run by Greaves's disciple, H. G. Wright, and his daughter at Ham Common in Surrey.[21]

The ideas of Fourier were central to these reformers. By the early 1840s Chichester was also attempting to further the cause of Fourierism in Britain. She requested the educationist, Samuel Wilderspin, to circulate Fourierite tracts for her and, with Welch, urged him to include in his lectures not only the cause of humanity to animals, but 'some ideas upon the associated system instead of the present wretched *isolated* system'.[22] In 1841, she published anonymously an idiosyncratic translation of Zoe Gatti de Gamond's exposition of Fourier's works, *The Phalanstery*.[23] Chichester's accompanying notes to the volume pointed to her interest in practising a radical political lifestyle. She argued for the value of alternative therapies – phrenological medicine, for example – and insisted upon the importance of 'harmonic' (vegan) cookery.[24] By politicising domestic issues, Chichester was following Fourier's call to erase the boundaries between the political and the domestic. Later that year, perhaps frustrated by the lack of detailed feminist discussion within the British Fourierite movement,[25] Chichester published the chapter on the position of women separately. This pamphlet underlined Fourier's concern to ensure the 'proper and real emancipation' of women, largely through the realisation of associated housing schemes to free women for employment by relieving them of domestic chores. It reiterated that Fourier's feminist vision might be attained, 'Without changing the legislation, or proclaiming new rights' and it was argued that woman's 'mission' was 'to vivify noble sentiments, by glowing faith.'[26]

Fourier's vision of women's potential provided, for Chichester, a politicisation of the views of contemporary writers such as Sarah Lewis, whose *Woman's Mission*, she eagerly endorsed.[27] For Chichester, the language of woman's mission could be appropriated to a radical political viewpoint. She desired a radical reformation of the existing political system by infusing the polity with the spiritual and loving values she believed to be practised by womanhood in the domestic setting. Chichester claimed that, 'Woman's mission is celestial', explaining that her 'peculiar duty', by dint of her holy nature, was 'to prevent the transgression of celestial laws' (sentiments which Chichester also espoused in her private correspondence).[28]

Meanwhile, in 1841, the Alcott House school was reorganised into a small, ascetic community, drawn from Greaves's circle. This became known as the First Concordium and was under the directorship of

William Oldham. It proved to be an extraordinary venture which excited considerable interest (and sometimes humour) among the Owenite community at large. Central to the Concordium was an uncompromising animal rights' philosophy. This, combined with the community's belief in the values of abstention (believed to be essential for the formation of spiritually-pure citizens to aid in the social and political regeneration of society) led to the observance of a strict vegan regime.[29]

S. C. Chichester was intimately involved with this community and was certainly residing there in 1843, if not before. She was also active in recruiting female members to the community, including Eliza Sharples (Carlile's widow) and other young protégées such as Emma Wilderspin.[30] However, the most striking evidence of Chichester's leading role in the life of the community is her involvement in the establishment of the British and Foreign Society for the Promotion of Humanity and Abstinence from Animal Food. This was founded at Alcott House in the autumn of 1843, in order to spread veganism among the wider reforming community. Unlike many radical associations, women were open not only to membership, but also to hold office in the society. In due course, its president was declared to be Mrs Chichester herself – making her probably the only woman to head a mixed-sex reform society at this time.[31] This was a major step for Chichester, who had previously masked her support for causes behind a veil of anonymity. Whilst not all the Concordians had equally progressive views on women, for Chichester to take the limelight in this way suggests perhaps, that she was moving closer to the principles of some of the feminist-minded within the Concordium. It included men such as Alexander Campbell (the society's secretary) a prominent Scottish trade unionist and enthusiast of Fourierism, who had campaigned for female suffrage during the 1832 reform agitation, and William Galpin who had attempted to persuade the Chartists to adopt female suffrage.[32]

The gradual evolution of Chichester's career indicates the way in which different feminisms blurred and overlapped within these circles, occasionally creating the space for more progressive possibilities for radical women. Indeed, it was in the fusion of an 'equal rights' philosophy, combined with Fourierist ideas on the particularity of women and the importance of the domestic sphere, that middle-class radical women did find ways to make an impact upon the public platform of reforming politics in the 1840s. This is demonstrated by feminist women such as Eliza Meteyard (who was asked to head a cooperative community in the United States at this time), Mary and Margaret Gillies and Mary Leman Grimstone – all of whom had connections with the personnel of Greaves's

circle.[33] In the mid-1840s they embraced the challenge to reform politics by widening its signification. Their promotion of associated housing
schemes ran very close to the language and aspirations of Fourier. Radical bodies such as the Co-operative League were keen for these women
to be involved publicly in their activities. They invited them as guests of
honour to their soirées and organised public readings of their essays and
encouraged them to participate in the discussions at organised events.[34]
Foreshadowing the work of labour activists at the end of the nineteenth
century, these essays often focused upon the minutiae of domestic organisation which was seen as crucial if society was to be reconstructed along
rational, humanitarian lines.[35]

The strategy of redefining politics so that it might include women's
domestic and moral expertise was an agenda which seems to have been
more successful in giving women a voice and visibility in the public
sphere than that which drew more exclusively upon a liberal ideology
of equal rights. The next case study, concerning the reformers associated with the radical lawyer, W. H. Ashurst, suggests that unless such
femininities were harnessed to political objectives, they continued to
hamper women's access to public political activities.

Whilst Chichester and her associates were seeking to change the
world from their little community in Ham Common, across the capital
in Holborn, William Lovett's 'New Move' Chartist organisation, the
National Association, was seeking the path to reform through the more
conventional routes of education and democracy.[36] It soon attracted
the active participation of many of the young men who were beginning
to rise to prominence in radical unitarian circles – William H. Ashurst,
John Humphreys Parry, James Stansfeld, William Shaen, Sidney Hawkes,
William James Linton and Collet Dobson Collet. In addition to their
democratic principles these men were also known for their espousal of
feminist ideas.[37] Indeed, Parry immediately took the opportunity, in his
capacity as editor of the *National Association Gazette*, to use the organisation as a vehicle with which to push for the political rights of women.
In the first edition, he promised to 'bring her rights into the same
prominence as those of man'.[38] The *Gazette* insisted, 'we shall do all in
our power to impress upon the generous and unprejudiced, the urgent
necessity of making the rights of woman as constant a theme of medita-
tion and examination as the rights of men.'[39] The publication continued to argue throughout its short life that the National Association was
different from other Chartist organisations in that it 'has manfully determined to make the rights of woman as much the object of its attention
and advocacy, as the rights of man.'[40] One article, 'The Duty of Woman',

threw convention on its head by arguing that women's duty lay in using the press, convening meetings and addressing political gatherings to help the Chartist cause.[41]

The National Association's regulations appear, at first glance, to ally with Parry's hopes of attracting a new, politically active female membership. Full membership was open to both men and women – all of whom had to undergo a formal electoral procedure for admission.[42] In practice, most of the female members were proposed for membership by male relatives, thus suggesting a desire on the part of the male members to share with their wives, daughters or sisters the activities and aspirations of the National Association.[43] Such sentiments were no doubt enhanced by the familial nature of the society's cultural activities – which included singing and dancing classes, tea parties, lectures and children's Sunday schools. Nevertheless, the association continued to function as a male-dominated institution. It was assumed from the beginning that its officers would be male and there is no mention of female participation at committee meetings.[44] Official statements often ignored the political rights of women and Lovett, writing his first annual report for the association, was at pains to thank the 'Noblemen' and 'Gentlemen' who had generously contributed to its running.[45] It seems probable that Parry, one of the staunchest of contemporary feminists, and who had consented to undertake the editorship of the Gazette only under 'certain conditions'[46] attempted to promote a radical line on the issue of women and politics, one that was only taken up sporadically by the body as a whole. This created a potential source of disunity within the society which was to flare up periodically.[47]

While rank-and-file members appear to have been successful in involving their female kin in the movement's activities, as do prominent lower-middle class and upper-working class activists such as William Lovett and Thomas Wade,[48] this was not true of its middle-class organisers, although Sophia Dobson Collet, (whose brother, Collet Dobson Collet was closely involved with the movement), did lend her assistance by playing the piano at some of its functions.[49] Yet the richer Ashurst women – daughters of W. H. Ashurst Senior – do not appear at all in the society's records, even though their family networks were intimately involved with the association. It was during James Stansfeld's period of activity with the National Association that he married Caroline Ashurst; William Shaen was close to all the Ashurst sisters, but was particularly intimate with Eliza Ashurst at this time. Shaen and Stansfeld's great friend, Sidney Hawkes, was similarly involved in the direction of the organization and married a third of the Ashurst sisters, Emilie (later

Emilie Venturi) during these years. W. H. Ashurst Jnr, the brother of Caroline, Emilie and Eliza was also active in the National Association.[50]

The absence of the Ashurst women from the National Association – a movement which their menfolk had hoped would promote feminism and female political activity – is striking: particularly as these young reformers formed a tight-knit group who, as Eliza Ashurst reported, agreed on 'the *perfect* equality of the sexes, morally, intellectually and politically'.[51] What were the Ashurst women doing, whilst the men closest to them were promoting the National Association? In 1841, Eliza Ashurst wrote to her American friend, Elizabeth Neall Gay, explaining that the young men in her circle, such as her brother William and Sidney Hawkes, were 'most energetic in endeavouring to rouse the attention of the young men in London' to the Anti-Corn Law cause (indeed, these men were also active in raising the priority of the issue within the National Association). She and her sister Emilie, she wrote, were also 'most exceedingly interested in the subject' and were to attend one of '*their* meetings' that evening [my italics]. Whilst a third sister, Matilda, was active in a Ladies' Anti-Corn Law association in Leicester, these women tended to position themselves outside the campaigning activities organised by their male friends. Eliza went on to recount in detail how she had given her three-year-old niece her 'first political lesson': giving the child a penny to give to Sidney Hawkes's fund and coaching her to memorise the phrase: 'knock down the Corn Laws, and give poor people cheap bread'.[52] Whilst her brother and brothers-in-law were active in setting up public meetings, debating on the councils of radical organisations and editing progressive journals, Eliza Ashurst's contribution consisted in translating stories from French and German which the men in her circle might use to flesh out their publications; collecting goods for the anti-slavery cause, acting as her father's secretary in his liaisons with the American abolitionist press and attempting to inculcate a political sensibility into her little niece. Whilst some of her literary projects had an explicitly feminist agenda, and indeed she and her sisters lent considerable support to early feminist projects during the 1840s, this did not translate into a desire to participate in public political activities. It was not until the 1860s that they began to take a prominent and public role in the women's rights movement.[53]

One reason for the lack of middle-class female input into the National Association may have been their reluctance to engage in the cross-class socialising which was demanded of such democratic reforming societies. The female philanthropic tradition provided no experience of meeting with classes on equal terms. William Shaen was convinced this was why his own sister, who called herself a 'Chartist' did so little to actively involve herself in the cause. He argued that to be a true social reformer it was necessary to acquaint oneself fully with a wide range of social classes. 'Some strong feelings in your mind *are* unfriendly to this spirit', he remonstrated, 'all those feelings which together constitute your aristocracy are so, which makes you prefer to remain at home even when your time hangs heavy on your hands rather than go and drink tea with vulgar, unpolished or even unintellectual people.'[54] Eliza Ashurst, writing wistfully in early spring, 1846, of her quiet life, and complaining of the extent to which she was missing her now married sisters, was similarly reluctant to throw herself into the thick of radical politics.[55]

If democratic politics did not succeed in rousing such women to activity, then from the mid-1840s, the issue of European nationalism, which was based upon the same Enlightenment premise of the individual right to self-determination, met with greater success. Women apparently had little hesitation in participating in the soirées and lectures which typified the British campaigns for Italian emancipation.[56] This was a movement in which the Ashurst sisters became fully engaged, largely through various domestic-centred activities. The great Italian revolutionary, Giuseppe Mazzini, became an intimate member of the 'Muswell Hill Brigade' (as the Ashurst set was known) from the mid-1840s and was enormously influential in drawing both the Ashursts and their wider associates into the movement for Italian self-determination. Exactly ten years after the National Association was first formed, many of those reformers associated with it now established the Friends of Italy Society, to raise public awareness and support for the cause of Italian nationalism. From the start, the Friends of Italy Society positioned itself as a 'male' pressure group. One of its key aims was to influence Members of Parliament; as such it was particularly concerned with winning over men of power and influence. The society made much of the fact that its members were made up of such dignitaries as magistrates, councillors, professors and commercial magnates.[57]

Females constituted just under 10 per cent of the society's membership and it attracted generous subscriptions from many high-profile women, such as Elizabeth Reid, Elizabeth Pease and Clementia Taylor.[58] Yet, there is barely any record of the organisation officially attempting to woo female support, as had been the case with the National Association. In his lectures upon the Italian movement, William James Linton did attempt to construct a new concept of nationhood – one which would include men equally with women. Another radical unitarian, Sophia Dobson Collet, was similarly concerned to draw women into the movement.[59]

However, such calls were exceptional. Despite the Friends of Italy Society's comparative silence on the subject of female involvement, behind the scenes the Ashurst circle of women worked tirelessly for the cause. Leading figures in the movement, such as the Tyneside MP, Joseph Cowen, as well as Mazzini himself, relied considerably upon Caroline Stansfeld (née Ashurst) and her sister, Emilie Hawkes, for much of the organisational work associated with the movement. Caroline Stansfeld was particularly intimate with Mazzini, acting as his personal secretary for the bulk of his personal, domestic and literary affairs in Britain. Both Emilie and Caroline were responsible for the publication of many of the written works and pamphlets which the movement produced, as well as taking on much of its accounting.[60] Matilda Ashurst Biggs was instrumental in keeping the issue alive in the Northern provincial press.[61] Emilie coordinated subscriptions and donations to the Ladies' Committee of the Free Italian School, as did Susanna Milner Gibson, another prominent radical. Caroline Stansfeld and her female associates also proved adept at exploiting and adapting conventional avenues of upper-middle class female activity to assist in radical causes – an obvious example being the organisation of large-scale bazaars to raise money for the cause. Emilie undertook portraits of revolutionary figures such as Mazzini and Ledru Rollin, which she then raffled to boost the movement's funds.[62]

All such activities were entirely in keeping with the particular model of female emancipation that had also been promulgated by J. E. Smith – one that was shorn of direct political action in the public arena. This appears to have been a popular formulation among the wider reforming community. In a public lecture in 1848, George Dawson, a favourite preacher of these circles, drew explicitly, if inaccurately, upon Saint-Simonism to argue (to much applause) that wishing to secure women's social and political rights did not necessarily mean condoning female 'legislators or preachers'.[63] Mazzini's view of female emancipation was often perceived to be in this vein. As one of Mazzini's female followers later said of him, '[he] invariably defended the Rights of Women. He used to say it was useless for men to talk of freedom while half the human race was enslaved. But I do not think that his idea of the Rights of Women included their taking an active part in public politics.'[64] However, Mazzini's private correspondence suggests that he wished for women to take a more public role in the movement for Italian Emancipation. The following comments, written to Matilda Ashurst Biggs, were perhaps designed as a powerful hint for Matilda and her sisters to push themselves forward more – 'I am as convinced as you are that the Christian myth of the woman crushing the head of the snake is concealing a great truth; and an association of women for all our purposes has long been my dream. But it would require a little nucleus of four and five women free and daring to stand before the public with circulars, appeals, etc. Where are they to be found?'[65]

Yet, despite the reputation which the Ashurst women had for flouting social conventions, it would seem that even in this enlightened family the notion of women fulfilling their radical activity without straying beyond certain limits was a consciously held belief. On the death of his daughter, Eliza, in childbirth in 1850, William H. Ashurst Sr recalled in his grief that she had 'ardently promoted *in her sphere* everything that she thought tended to promote truth and goodness' (my italics).[66] Nevertheless, this was an ambiguous and elastic concept. Eliza herself, when explaining both her own activities and the work of the young men in her circle, had referred in the plural to 'our several spheres. . . . [in which I hope] we are all doing some good & spreading good ideas'.[67] Meanwhile, her brother-in-law, James Stansfeld, argued that women should be allowed to extend their present 'confined sphere' by involvement in contemporary causes.[68]

In any case, what might have been deemed as 'woman's sphere' by a Hannah More or a Sarah Ellis, was very different from its interpretation in the hands of radicals such as these. These 'ministering angels' (as Mazzini referred to Caroline Stansfeld[69]) were not the traditional nurturers of domesticated womanhood. The Ashurst sisters, (two of whom professed a dislike for children[70]) were prepared to undertake highly unconventional and extremely dangerous activities for their cause. Emilie, for example, oversaw the accounts for the Emancipation of Italy Subscription Fund, which was instituted to raise money for the purchase of canons and muskets, as well as organising the Mazzini Fund in 1859. James Stansfeld had to resign a government post in 1863 after being implicated in an assassination plot on Napoleon III – because of the activities of his wife, the evidence suggests Matilda Ashurst Biggs was also implicated in the plot. Caroline and Emilie acted together to set up a private postal system between Italian insurrectionists in Paris and London and provided secret places of refuge for them. They also forged passports for Mazzini.[71]

For such women to actively support militarism and illegal activities was in itself a contortion of many of the prevalent concepts of 'woman's sphere' as nurturing and morally pure. The desire to actively engage in the armed struggles of European nationalism was not uncommon. For Harriet King (a close friend of Emilie Ashurst) and Harriet Meuricoffre (the sister of Josephine Butler), one means of doing this was through nursing. They saw caring for the wounded and dying men who fought 'on the side of liberty' in the Italian struggle as a means of turning a traditional female activity into a political gesture.[72] The first British woman to try and gain entrance to take a medical degree did so out of purely political motives: Jessie White Mario wished to become a doctor so that she might go out to Italy and treat the wounded soldiers fighting for liberty.[73]

Such examples suggest the need to be sensitive to the different personal meanings which ideologies of women's 'sphere' might hold (even for women within the same family). Caroline Stansfeld appeared content to fulfil her political sentiments through home-based activities. For women in such positions this could be a very meaningful and fulfilling option at a time, when, as Margot Finn has lately observed, 'Houses and the home lay at the heart of bourgeois radical culture . . . the practice of mixing politics and social life through nationalist activity was pervasive in middle-class reform circles'.[74] The role of the radical political hostess was one which Caroline's close friends such as Clementia Taylor and Susanna Milner Gibson were to exploit to the full in the 1850s and 1860s.[75] Others, such as those wishing to nurse the Italian revolutionaries in battle, were attempting to expand contemporary significations of women's caring nature to political purposes. For Emilie Ashurst Venturi, however, the domestic-centred activities she pursued with her family in the 1840s were merely the apprenticeship for her more radical assault on reforming sensibilities. In 1852 she smashed through conventional proprieties by rising in a theatre to make an appeal on behalf of Italian exiles.[76]

Emilie's transgressions are illustrative of the wider problems facing female political agency within this milieu. An unconventional background and personal self-confidence might lead to individual acts of public demonstration; but the political ideals of the Ashurst circle could not formulate an equal role for women in their reforming societies. One woman, Jessie White Mario, did assume a public role in the movement in the mid-1850s through her popular lecture tours. But her activities remained the work of a particularly forthright individual – they failed to signify wider public political involvement amongst other female supporters.[77]

For the 'Muswell Hill Brigade', separate spheres ideology was a part of their cultural make-up rather than an explicit part of their politics. Whilst they were very close to Owenite circles, whose work they often supported, their own political agenda followed in an Enlightenment tradition of rights. The National Association did pay lip service to the need to secure women's 'social' as well as 'political rights', but this was not fully elaborated. Women's contribution was not invoked in the name of the peculiar qualities which they might bring to the political agenda, nor was the basic understanding of the political challenged – as it was within those circles more influenced by utopian theories. This meant that their support for women's rights was based upon a vulnerable premise, for it was merely an extension of the liberal programme, rather than being fundamental to it. Indeed, many of those associated with the bid for female suffrage within the National Association had, by 1848, made a pragmatic shift to organisations such as the People's League for Obtaining *Manhood* Suffrage.[78] And, as we have seen, there was far less enthusiasm in these circles for women's political activity in 1851 than there had been in 1841. This apparent decline of male enthusiasm for the female cause may be one reason why the women's rights movement began to coalesce with renewed female energies in the early 1850s.

The two case studies presented here suggest the need for sensitive and subtle approaches if we are to fully comprehend the ways in which women constructed and understood their own political agency. The language of spheres was an important medium through which the subjectivities of even extremely progressive women were negotiated. The particular strand of Saint-Simonian and Fourierite feminism promulgated by J. E. Smith and his associates in the late 1830s and early 1840s illustrates the dangers of constructing monovalent readings of the language of separate spheres. The politicisation of the concept of spheres enabled women such as Chichester and Welch to construct fulfilling political identities. As patrons, and as promoters of alternative educational, medical and dietary agendas, they managed to satisfy both their political ideals as well as their self-identity as respectable, genteel women. In the case of the Ashurst women, the concept of spheres was clearly evident in the roles they felt able (and were permitted) to fill. Yet, as we saw, their own understanding of the concept bore little relation to more conventional formulations. Within their boundaries the Ashursts found a multitude of ways to express their political interests: as writers, translators, fund-raisers, committee members, secretaries, accountants, child-rearers and salonnières. For radical women, the discourses of spheres did not imply the denial of female political identity, for the expression of political ideas and agency could take a multiplicity of forms.

Notes

1. This was especially true of those connected to Unitarianism and Owenism. See Kathryn Gleadle, *The Early Feminists: Radical Unitarians and the Emergence of the Women's Rights Movement, 1831–1851* (Basingstoke: Macmillan, 1995).
2. See A. J. Vickery, 'Golden Ages to Separate Spheres: a Review of the Categories and Chronology of English Women's History', *Historical Journal*, 36 (1993), pp. 383–414. For a consideration of the limitations of such concepts when applied to aristocratic women, see K. D. Reynolds, *Aristocratic Women and Political Society in Victorian Britain* (Oxford: Clarendon Press, 1998).
3. Barbara Taylor, *Eve and the New Jerusalem: Socialism and Feminism in the Nineteenth Century* (London: Virago, 1983).
4. Saint-Simonism originated with the Comte de Saint-Simon (1760–1825), often considered the founder of French socialism. Fourierism originated with Charles Fourier (1772–1837), a French reformer who wished for society to be reorganised into 'phalansteries' – large communities run on joint stock principles.
5. For the influence of Saint-Simonism and Fourierism on British feminism, see Gail Malmgreen, *Neither Bread Nor Roses: Utopian Feminists and the English Working Class, 1800–1850* (Brighton: John L. Noyce, 1978); Taylor, *Eve and the New Jerusalem*, pp. 28–9, 45–6, 168–9 and Gleadle, *The Early Feminists*, pp. 48–52.
6. Claire Goldberg Moses, *French Feminism in the 19th Century* (Albany, NY: State University of New York Press, 1984), Chapters 3–5.
7. See Dolores Dooley, 'Anna Doyle Wheeler', in Mary Cullen and Maria Luddy (eds), *Women, Power and Consciousness in 19th-Century Ireland* (Dublin: Attic Press, 1995), pp. 19–54.
8. These included journals such as *The Crisis* (1832–5), *Howitt's Journal of Literature and Popular Progress* (1847–8) and the *Spirit of the Age* (1848–9).
9. Taylor, *Eve and the New Jerusalem*, pp. 167–72 and J. Saville, 'J. E. Smith and the Owenite Movement, 1833–4', in Sidney Pollard and John Salt (eds), *Robert Owen, Prophet of the Poor: Essays in Honour of the 200th Anniversary of His Birth* (London: Macmillan, 1971), pp. 115–44.
10. *The Crisis*, 3, no. 12 (16 November 1834), p. 6; R. K. P. Pankhurst, *The Saint Simonians, Mill and Carlyle: A Preface to Modern Thought* (London: Sidgwick and Jackson, 1957), p. 114.
11. *London Phalanx* (30 October 1841), p. 494.
12. *The Shepherd*, 1, no. 37 (9 May 1835), p. 303.
13. *The Morning Star or Phalansterian Gazette*, no. 10 (13 January 1841), p. 80.
14. *The Shepherd*, 1, no. 37 (9 May 1835), p. 304.
15. *London Phalanx* (30 October 1841), p. 494.
16. Details of the relationship between Chichester, Welch and Smith may be found in William Anderson Smith, *'Shepherd' Smith the Universalist: The Story of a Mind, Being a Life of the Rev James E. Smith* (London: Sampson Low, Marston and Co., 1892), pp. 165, 191, 198–9, 205–7.
17. Mrs Welch to James Smith, 16 December 1838, cited in ibid., p. 199.
18. It was thanks to their financial aid that Carlile was able to set off on an ambitious lecture tour of the provinces, issue several pamphlets from Man-

chester during winter 1837–8, and establish a new weekly journal, *The Church* in 1838. Joel H. Weiner, *Radicalism and Freethought in Nineteenth Century Britain: The Life of Richard Carlile* (Connecticut: Greenwood Press, 1983), pp. 225–30, 239.

19. Greaves had been a disciple of the educationist Johann Heinrich Pestalozzi in Switzerland. Greaves's own interpretation of infant development placed a considerable emphasis upon the individual's innate and spiritual capacities. A memoir of Greaves was composed by one of his followers: A. F. Barham, 'A Memoir of the Late James Pierrepont Greaves Esq', in *An Odd Medley of Literary Curiosities* (London, 1845). Useful insights may be gained from *Letters and Extracts from the MS Writings of James Pierrepont Greaves*, 2 vols (Ham Common, Surrey: Concordium Press, 1843).

20. William Henry Harland, 'Bronson Alcott's English Friends', p. 4, typescript document in the possession of Fruitlands Museum, Harvard, Massachusetts. I am grateful to the curators of the Fruitlands Museum for providing me with a xerox of this document.

21. F. B. Sanborn, *Bronson Alcott at Alcott House, England and Fruitlands, New England (1842–4)* (Cedar Rapids, IA: Torch Press, 1918), pp. 29ff. Philip McCann and Francis A. Young, *Samuel Wilderspin and the Infant School Movement* (London: Croom Helm, 1982), pp. 264–5. An attempt to elucidate the school's educational philosophy was made in Mr and Miss Wright, *Retrospective Sketch of an Educative Attempt at Alcott House, Ham Common, Near Richmond, Surrey* (London: V. Torras, 1840).

22. S. C. Chichester to Samuel Wilderspin, 14 January 1840, and 20 February 1842, University College, London, Wilderspin Collection, MS 917 (hereafter Wilderspin papers).

23. *The Phalanstery; or Attractive Industry and Moral Harmony: Translated from the French of Madame Gatti de Gamond, by an English Lady* (London: Whittaker, 1841).

24. *The Phalanstery*, p. 79n.

25. See Malmgreen, *Neither Bread Nor Roses*, p. 10.

26. *The Phalanstery*, pp. 116, 124, 122.

27. S. C. Chichester to Samuel Wilderspin, 14 January 1840, Wilderspin papers.

28. S. C. Chichester to Mrs Carlile [i.e. Eliza Sharples], 13 April 1841, Richard Carlile papers, RC 86, Huntington Library (hereafter Carlile papers). Chichester's religious viewpoint, in common with many of her associates, was highly idiosyncratic. It was a transcendental faith, which focused upon the spiritual properties believed to reside within each individual.

29. Details on this community may be found in W. H. A. Armytage, *Heavens Below: Utopian Experiments in England, 1560–1960* (London: Routledge and Kegan Paul, 1961), pp. 171–83; Sanborn, *Bronson Alcott*, passim; Odell Shephard, *Pedlar's Progress: The Life of Bronson Alcott* (Boston, MA: Little Brown, 1937), pp. 320–6. See also Thomas Frost, *Forty Years' Recollections: Literary and Political* (London: Sampson Low, Marston, Searle and Rivington, 1880), p. 41ff., and Harriet Jay, *Robert Buchanan: Some Account of His Life's Work and His Literary Friendships* (London: T. Fisher Unwin, 1903), p. 10. For a recent study of vegetarianism among contemporary reformers see John Belchem, '"Temperance in All Things": Vegetarianism, the Manx Press and the Alternative

Agenda of Reform in the 1840s', in Malcolm Chase and Ian Dyck (eds), *Living and Learning: Essays in Honour of J. F. C. Harrison* (Aldershot: Scholar Press, 1996), pp. 149–62.

30. Wilderspin was furious at his daughter's decision to join Chichester at the community, J. M. Young to Samuel Wilderspin, 17 September 1843, Wilderspin papers. Another of Chichester's protégées, Elizabeth Hardwick, caused a major rift within the community by secretly marrying H. G. Wright – to the betrayal of the society's stance on celibacy. Harland, 'Bronson Alcott's English Friends', p. 11.

31. *New Age*, 1, no. 10 (1 October 1843), p. 111 and no. 12 (1 December 1843), p. 138.

32. Taylor, *Eve and the New Jerusalem*, p. 338 ; Jutta Schwarzkopf, *Women in the Chartist Movement* (Basingstoke: Macmillan, 1991), pp. 60–1.

33. Eliza Meteyard, *Nine Hours Movement: Industrial and Household Tales* (London: Green and Co., 1872), p. xi. Many of Greaves's outer circle – including Barmby, Wheeler and Horne – moved in radical unitarian circles during the 1840s.

34. See, for example, *Howitt's Journal*, 1, no. 2 (9 January 1847) ['Weekly Record', p. 3] and 2, no. 27 (3 July 1847), ['Weekly Record', p. 15]; *People's Journal*, 4, no. 100 (27 December 1847), pp. 359–60.

35. For women's attempt to put domestic issues on the political agenda in the later period see C. Rowan, 'Women in the Labour Party, 1906–20', *Feminist Review*, 12 (1982), pp. 74–91, and Alistair Thomson, ' "Domestic Drudgery will be a Thing of the Past": Co-operative Women and the Reform of Housework', in Stephen Yeo (ed.), *New Views of Co-operation* (London and New York: Routledge, 1988), pp. 108–27.

36. For brief discussions of the National Association see I. J. Prothero, 'Chartism in London', *Past and Present*, 44 (1969), pp. 76–105; F. Goodway, *London Chartism, 1838–1848* (Cambridge: Cambridge University Press, 1982), pp. 40–2; J. T. Ward, *Chartism* (London: B. T. Batsford, 1973), p. 150.

37. Gleadle, *The Early Feminists*, particularly pp. 75–82.

38. *National Association Gazette*, no. 1 (1 January 1841), p. 4.

39. Ibid., no. 2 (8 January 1842), p. 13.

40. Ibid., no. 11 (12 March 1842), p. 84.

41. Ibid., no. 6 (5 February 1842), pp. 44–5.

42. National Association, *First Annual Report* (1843), p. 6.

43. See the MS minutes of the City of London National Association, British Museum Add MSS 37, 774 (hereafter 'Minutes') *passim*.

44. National Association, *Plans, Rules and Regulations of the National Association of the United Kingdom for Promoting the Political and Social Improvement of the People* (n.d.).

45. National Association, *First Annual Report*, p. 3.

46. Minutes (14 December 1841), vol. ii, p. 14.

47. See, for example, the heated meeting at which a proposal to enlist the aid of female members in resolving a financial crisis within the society was eventually lost (ibid., 25 September 1843, vol. ii, pp. 104–5); for another example see Gleadle, *The Early Feminists*, p. 81.

48. Minutes, (9 August 1842), vol. ii, p. 49 and (30 August 1842), vol. ii, p. 54.

49. Sophia Dobson Collet to George Jacob Holyoake (17 February 1846), George Jacob Holyoake Collection, Co-operative Union, Manchester, 157.

50. Further details on this group may be found in Gleadle, *The Early Feminists, passim.* See also the excellent biographical accounts by Eugene Rasor in J. O. S. Baylen and N. J. Gossman (eds), *Biographical Dictionary of Modern British Radicals* (Hassocks: Harvester Press, 1979).
51. Eliza Bardouneau-Narcy (née Ashurst) to Elizabeth Neall Gay, October 1841, Sydney Howard Gay papers, the Rare Book and Manuscript Library, Columbia University Library (hereafter Howard Gay papers), quoted in Gleadle, *The Early Feminists*, p. 40.
52. Eliza Ashurst to Elizabeth Neall Gay, October 1841, Howard Gay papers.
53. Details of Eliza Ashurst's activities may be gleaned from her correspondence with Elizabeth Neall Gay, Howard Gay papers; Gleadle, *The Early Feminists*, pp. 60–2, 114, 132, 134, 136, 175–6.
54. William Shaen to his sister, 20 November 1845, Symington Papers, Box 19, Leeds Archives.
55. Eliza Ashurst to Elizabeth Neall Gay, 6 March 1846, Howard Gay papers.
56. The young George Eliot, who mixed in these circles, attended such functions – Gordon S. Haight (ed.), *The George Eliot Letters*, 9 vols (Oxford: Oxford University Press, 1954), vol. i, pp. 91–2. See also Chapter 3 in this volume.
57. *First Annual Report of the Society of the Friends of Italy: Read at the Society's Annual Meeting. June 19 1852* (1852), p. 3; see also printed circular of the Friends of Italy, (25 July 1851), Joseph Cowen papers, Tyne and Wear Archives, (hereafter Cowen papers) A78.
58. For example, *First Annual Report*, p. 3; *Monthly Record* (1851), p. 138, Cowen papers, A118.
59. *Reasoner*, 4, no. 88 (1848), p. 137; *Reasoner*, 13, no. 14, (1852), p. 215.
60. See Kathryn Gleadle, 'Caroline Stansfeld', in the *New Dictionary of National Biography* (Oxford: Oxford University Press, forthcoming); J. W. Mario, *The Birth of Modern Italy* (London: T. Fisher Unwin, 1909), p. 87.
61. Elizabeth Adams Daniel, *Jessie White Mario: Risorgimento Revolutionary* (Athens, OH: Ohio University Press, 1977), p. 36. In 1859 she also wrote a letter to the *Newcastle Guardian* on the issue of women's suffrage; see Rasor in Baylen and Gossman, *Biographical Dictionary*.
62. The Cowen papers are the best source for reconstructing such activities. See, for example, A659, 487, 476, 634. See also Mario, *The Birth of Modern Italy*.
63. George Dawson, 'Second Lecture on Social Reformation – its Apostles and Systems', 18 December 1849, George Dawson Collection, vol. xi, p. 450, Birmingham Public Library.
64. Harriet E. King, *Letters and Recollections of Mazzini* (London: Longmans, Green and Co., 1912), p. 126. Mazzini himself was highly critical of utopian and communitarian theories.
65. G. Mazzini to Matilda Ashurst Biggs, December 1855, cited in Daniel, *Jessie White Mario*, p. 40.
66. W. H. Ashurst to George Jacob Holyoake, 4 December 1850, George Jacob Holyoake Collection, Co-operative Union, Manchester (hereafter Holyoake collection), 392.
67. Eliza Ashurst to Elizabeth Neall Gay, 6 March 1846, Howard Gay papers.
68. 'The Present State of the Law by a Barrister', *Female's Friend*, no. 4 (April 1846), p. 73, cited in Gleadle, *The Early Feminists*, p. 138. Stansfeld's

comments related to encouraging women to join the Associate Institution, a body campaigning for the laws regarding prostitution to be reformed.

69. E. F. Richards (ed.), *Mazzini's Letters to an English Family, 1844–54*, 3 vols (London: John Lane, 1920–2), vol. i, p. 25.

70. Eliza Ashurst to Elizabeth Neall Gay, 6 March 1846, Howard Gay papers.

71. Barbara Hammond and J. L. Hammond, *James Stansfeld: A Victorian Champion of Sex Equality* (London: Longmans, Green, 1932), pp. 58, 71; see also the biographical accounts of the sisters by Rasor in Baylen and Gossman, *Biographical Dictionary*; Daniel, *Jessie White Mario*, p. 38; Cowen papers, A871, 476, 634.

72. King, *Letters and Recollections*, p. 12 (King, who had not then reached her majority, was prevented by her father from fulfilling her ambition); Josephine E. Butler, *Memoir of John Grey of Dilston* (Edinburgh: Edmonston and Douglas, 1869), pp. 296, 392.

73. Daniels, *Jessie White Mario*, p. 41.

74. Margot C. Finn, *After Chartism: Class and Nation in English Radical Politics, 1848–1874* (Cambridge: Cambridge University Press, 1993), p. 160.

75. See ibid. and also Alan Ruston, 'Clementia Taylor', *Transactions of the Unitarian Historical Society*, 20 (1991), pp. 62–8.

76. Richards, *Mazzini's Letters*, vol. i, p. 211. She was also prepared to risk her life by disguising herself as a man and travelling across the Alps to find Mazzini's camp.

77. For the work of Jessie White Mario (who was later imprisoned for her part in the Pisacane expedition) see Daniel, *Jessie White Mario*.

78. Some details on this organisation may be found in the Lovett Collection, Birmingham City Archives, MS 753.

8
'Jenny Rules the Roost': Women and Electoral Politics, 1832–68

Matthew Cragoe

Anyone familiar with newspaper accounts of nineteenth-century elections will recognise the standard nodding reference made to the presence of women at election time. By far the most common observation made by contemporary reporters was, as in the following example from 1837, of the way in which the 'windows of many houses were open, displaying the fashion and beauty of Canterbury, waving small banners and colours' as the rival candidates' parades wound through the streets below.[1] Less frequently, it was recorded that a group of women had got together a subscription in order to present their favoured champion with some token of their esteem – a snuff-box, perhaps, or his party banners.[2]

On occasion, however, it is possible to obtain a more detailed glimpse of women's involvement with the political drama unfolding around them. At the general election of 1868 in Liverpool, for example, as Viscount Sandon went canvassing through the fish market, he was seized by a buxom fishwife who marched arm in arm with him through the market, where they were joined by another who kissed him and his fellow candidate, Mr Graves – an action which, apparently, was 'applauded to the echo'.[3] In western Scotland in the same year, the *Rothesay Chronicle* recorded how, on nomination day, upon the Sheriff calling for a show of hands 'a large majority, including all the mill girls, held up their hands for Mr Burns', the Liberal candidate. An angry letter to the newspaper from 'A Rothesay Elector' demanded that the mill owners prevent their girls attending such events in future, as not only did they put their hands up to vote, but they also babbled, rendering the candidates' speeches inaudible.[4] Rather more tempestuous were the women of Carmarthen in South Wales: a fisherman who had voted for the Conservative party was set upon and assaulted by what one newspaper described as 'a band of female viragos' and 'beaten & scratched in the face with the greatest cruelty'.[5]

All three stories suggest a larger truth than that revealed by the standard newspaper accounts: that, at election time, women all over Britain might be conspicuously involved in the fun and fury of the contest. Until very recently, however, the role of women in electoral politics has eluded historians. For all that the work of scholars such as Frank O'Gorman and John A. Phillips has deepened our understanding of both the symbolic and practical aspects of elections and electioneering during the eighteenth and early nineteenth centuries, the role of women is scarcely mentioned.[6] And where attention has been paid to their activities, it is the tendency of changes in the culture of politics to circumscribe their opportunities for involvement in organised protest that has been emphasised. Dorothy Thompson, for example, has argued that the attitudes of women to political action 'were often brought about more by changes in the style of politics than by the changes in political programmes'.[7] Thus women's withdrawal from politics after the mid-1840s was due not to the decline in Anti-Poor Law agitation alone, but also to 'the rationalization of the crowd, the reduction of the role of the mass demonstration [and] the replacement of participatory politics by the politics of the committee and representative delegations'. More recently, James Vernon has adopted a similar line, arguing that the radicals' search for respectability led them to create a new cultural context for political activity.[8] Whilst this policy, which involved taking politics out of the pub and away from the mob, had the potential to increase female participation in politics, the practical consequence was to emphasise women's roles as supportive wives, mothers and sisters: it was the husbands whose respectability was defined by political activity.

Whilst the absence of women from organised radical politics is a notable feature of the mid-century, to deduce from this that women had no political role would be mistaken. Indeed, another historiographical current has recently emerged which demonstrates clearly that women possessed an influence in politics independent of the fortunes of particular popular movements. The role of elite women, in particular, has been subjected to new and searching forms of enquiry. Elaine Chalus, for example, in a persuasive study of eighteenth-century elections, has argued that elite women exercised a 'multi-faceted and flexible' political influence.[9] In some circumstances they might direct campaigns and control the family's electoral influence; more frequently they routinely coordinated the social politics of elections, managing people and social activities for political ends, and participated in the hectic business of canvassing. K. D. Reynolds has uncovered a similar pattern in the nineteenth century.[10] She argues that although the most common form of involvement for women might have been simply following the campaign of a 'husband, son or friend', it was by no means unheard of for women to take an active part in the campaign themselves, mobilising family networks of support or influencing those within her sphere in favour of a particular candidate.

As a result of the work of Chalus, Reynolds, Richardson and others,[11] we now possess a more complex and subtle picture of elite women's political activity across the eighteenth and nineteenth centuries. For a few, power might be directly attainable. As owners of land they might possess power, whilst the wives of a few leading politicians exercised immense sway through their roles as political hostesses in the great London salons.[12] Many more, however, as members of family networks, had access to an influence which might be brought to bear at election time. In this chapter an attempt will be made to extend our understanding of women's electoral role by examining the actions of elite women alongside those of women from lower social groups. To provide a focus, two themes have been selected. The chapter begins with an examination of the role of women in the canvassing process, and attention then turns to their more surprising role in the mire of electoral corruption. This latter section relies heavily on a hitherto untapped source of information about women's conduct in elections, the reports of Select Committees established by the House of Commons to investigate controverted election returns.[13] In both areas, however, the same point will be argued: that, despite the changing cultural context of politics highlighted by historians like Vernon, women remained an important part of the electoral equation.

Canvassing was a key feature of nineteenth-century elections and provided women with many opportunities to become involved in the political process.[14] The nature of these opportunities varied, however, from class to class. Elite women were often active canvassers, engaged on behalf of relations or friends to canvass those within their sphere of influence; women from lower social status groups were more frequently the recipients of canvassing attentions.

Women of the elite, as both Chalus and Reynolds have shown, played an active part in elections. In some, but by no means all cases, the wives of the candidates became heavily involved. Mrs Gwynne Holford, whose husband, J. P. Gwynne Holford, contested the Breconshire election in 1837, was said to have 'canvassed for her husband far more energetically and successfully than he did himself'.[15] When her son came out to contest the borough seat at a by-election some thirty years later, she 'canvassed every elector for him', despite the fact that she was nearly blind from the effects of cataracts. Apparently, she paid her visits in full state, arriving at each poor cottage in a barouche drawn by four big bays, ornamented by white liveried postilions, and attended by two powdered footmen. Her secretary, carrying the Canvass book, travelled with her. The ground thus prepared, she entered the dwelling,

> and sat with each poor man and his wife, and talked about her char-
> ities, how she maintained this one, buried that, kept the widow of
> another, and how no one who served a Gwynne *ever* had cause to
> repent it.

To complete the effect, her butler followed shortly after with gifts of grapes, pineapples or trout.[16]

Canvassing on this scale, in which carrot and stick were so nakedly waved before the voter's eyes, was hardly common, however, and many elite women conducted their campaigns by letter. Lady Drummond, received a series of missives 'from the Cawdors (*male & female*)', urging her to deploy her interest in favour of two Conservative candidates at the Carmarthenshire election of 1868.[17] Women with tenants, mean-while, generally let them know their wishes by letter. Mrs H. E. Bruton addressed the following note to all her tenants on the eve of the 1868 election: 'SIR – I request you will vote for my father, J. W. S. Erle-Drax, Esq., on receipt of this.'[18]

For women outside the elite, canvassing was normally something experienced rather than actively participated in. Despite the fact that women did not possess the vote, candidates expended a great deal of energy in wooing them, and the appeal of a candidate to the women of the constituency was an important consideration. Mr Jordan summed up their importance for a meeting of working men at Marlow in 1868, saying 'if the man was the head of the family, the woman was the neck, and often turned the head which way she liked'.[19] Jordan earned a hearty laugh for his comment, but his wit merely made palatable a truth that all active participants in elections understood. Indeed, one highly experienced electoral agent went so far as to tell the journalist, Justin McCarthy, that 'when he had secured the wives, he cared nothing about the husbands'.[20]

The consequence was, as McCarthy continued, that candidates spent much of their time 'flattering and winning wives'. In this process, charm and good looks were purported to count for much. Thus Sir

James Hamilton wrote of Henry Lavellin Puxley, a candidate for the county seat of Carmarthenshire, that not only was he rich, 'decidedly clever and fluent of speech' and 'of irreproachable Private Character', but had also 'a Personal Appearance that could make him a *Favori des Dames*, and conciliate their support'.[21] According to McCarthy, there were few women of 'that class of wives who are above the money bribe' who could resist the 'sweet condescension of rank' involved in a young, aristocratic candidate offering them a 'smiling salutation' or a 'gracious word'.[22] Women, or their children,[23] were thus ritually admired and made a fuss of. As one editor put it in 1868: 'Kissing ... formed no unimportant part in political canvassing. A candidate for political honours was as much expected to kiss the butcher's wife and fondle her children as he was expected to issue an address.'[24]

On occasion, the women of a constituency were courted *en masse*. At Peterborough, in 1852, the Liberal candidate, George Whalley, took the relatively unusual step of hosting a tea meeting for the ladies of the town at the Temperance Committee House. Mrs Anne Scholley, wife of the keeper of the House, later admitted that, having heard him speak and recommend, among other things, that women should be allowed to vote, she began using her influence with her husband to ensure that he voted for Whalley.[25] At Boston, meanwhile, the Conservatives held a 'ladies' evening' during the general election campaign of 1868 at which one of the candidates, 'by happy coincidence a bachelor', as the *Warwickshire Chronicle's* reporter noted, was present. Nearly one thousand women turned out to hear an address, which presumably dealt with the political questions of the election, and then a selection of popular readings and vocal and instrumental music. The Liberals were said to be planning a rival evening the following week.[26]

The deliberate courtship of voters' wives reflected the fact that women were widely perceived by contemporaries to have an important influence over the way in which their husbands cast their votes. At one level, the weak-spirited man, as subject to his wife in the public sphere as he was in his own home, was a target for laughter and mockery. Justin McCarthy, in his article on 'The Petticoat in the Politics of England', reported the story of the 'worthy matron' who, being pressed by the friends of a particular candidate to procure for him her husband's 'plumper', 'promptly replied that if he hesitated a moment about doing so she would give him a "plumper"!'[27] And newspapers made regular comment upon the extent to which some men were subject to 'the petticoat influence' in such matters. In 1832, when the Tory, Wyndham Lewis, received fewer plumpers than expected at the Maidstone election, the *Maidstone Gazette* denounced the town's 'Blue Devils': 'Many of those who had promised Tory plumpers', it noted, 'were married to "blue devils"...Succumbing to marital lobbying, these men compromised and cast their second votes as their wives demanded'.[28] Whilst humorous and anecdotal evidence such as that contained in these two examples cannot stand as historical 'evidence' for the perceived influence of women in electoral politics, other sources can be used to indicate the importance attached to it by contemporaries, and to underscore its reality as a factor in the electoral process.

The canvassing books drawn up at the start of an election campaign provide much evidence of this sort. When planning their canvassing campaigns, each candidate's central committee routinely analysed the list of registered voters, noting any information which might assist them in their bid to secure votes. The opportunities presented by such a source can be seen in the comments made by the committees established to secure the return of the Conservative candidate for the borough of Caernarfon in the general elections of 1837 and 1847. On each occasion, their candidate, William Bulkeley Hughes, came up against a representative of the Paget family of Plasnewydd.

The committee's notebooks identified a number of voters with whom women's influence was likely to be crucial.[29] That influence had a variety of sources. In some cases, it was clear that the wives' personality was the crucial element. William Davies, victualler, was considered sure to vote for Hughes: 'the wife is a decided Conservative and she wears the Breeches!!!', noted the committee. The same was true of Griffith Williams, a gardener, of Mount Pleasant whose wife, Jenny, had been employed many years earlier in the household of Hughes's uncle: 'Jenny rules the roost', the committee recorded, 'and the squire may possibly prevail upon her to keep the old cock from voting which she did at one Election by locking him up in her Bedroom.' The link forged by employment was thus also a source of potential influence, and the committee similarly despaired of securing the vote of Owen Hughes, a sawyer, of South Penrallt, because his wife was a charwoman at the house of a hostile baron. The wife's place of birth represented a third factor which might influence the husband's vote. The committee concluded that it was impossible to win over William Williams of Treflan because his wife was 'a native of Amlwch and is much attached to the Plasnewydd family'. She was accordingly classed as 'a violent Paget'. Finally, female relations could also influence the way in which voters chose to cast their ballots. It was reported that David Evans, a currier, had promised his vote to Mr. Hughes's canvassers 'but voted in consequence of his sister being [a] Tenant of Admiral Lloyd, for Paget'. Contemporary electoral activists thus clearly recognised the manifold ways in which women's influence could secure a vote on polling day.

An examination of canvassers' notebooks during a contested election reveals much else besides the strength of some women in their own homes. It also reveals that women had considerable contact with the canvassers themselves. It was often the wife who received the canvasser, since the husband was out at work. This was clearly considered acceptable by those who organised the canvassing, since no attempt was made to shift the canvassing ritual to times, such as evenings or weekends, when it might be expected that the menfolk would be at home. The consequence was that women were often allowed the opportunity of a direct input into the political process, bringing important matters to the candidate's attention. Even when their menfolk were present, women seem often to have taken the opportunity to speak directly with the candidate on matters of interest to them. Sir Harry Verney, MP for the borough of Buckingham, gave the following example. 'At Preston Bissett', he said:

> I went into a cottage and sat down; the mother of a family said to me 'There is my son; he went away many years ago, a fine, stout, healthy fellow, as a soldier – now his health has failed, and they have granted him a pension for a year and a half; I think if he has lost his health, so as to prevent his earning his livelihood for all the rest of his life, that his pension ought to be for life too.'

'That', continued Verney,

> was perfectly fair and good logic, and if I am returned to parliament, when the Army Estimates are moved, I shall recollect that old woman in her cottage, and shall endeavour to persuade the House of Commons, that whenever a man is disabled for life from earning a livelihood, the pension should be for life [*cheers*].[30]

Verney saw this case as a perfect illustration of the utility of canvassing in the political process: it allowed, he commented, every 'man' access to his representative. What it also allowed, of course, was an opportunity for many women to voice their concerns.

Canvassing calls were not always as friendly as Verney's, however. George Howell, the working men's candidate at Aylesbury in 1868, claimed that the vicar of Haddenham 'went into the cottages in the absence of the husbands, and threatened the poor wives with the loss of the half or quarter of an acre of the glebe or Church land' let to them if they did not vote for the Conservatives.[31] At Peterborough, this time in 1859, the wife of a publican who kept an additional piece of land, Elizabeth Dalton, received a similar canvassing call from a Mr Morris. 'Mrs. Dalton', he told her, 'you must talk to your husband well, and you must tell him the consequence that if he did not vote for Mr Whalley that he will lose all his friends in the borough ... and he is sure to lose his land, and then it will be a very bad job for him.'[32]

Such threats were not mere talk: the punishment of voters for wrong votes was not unknown in this period, and the wives and families of those punished naturally suffered along with the errant voters themselves.[33] Sarah Milner, whose husband had a vote for the borough of Bridgenorth, told a Select Committee that 'if there was any gift at Christmas for people with heavy families I could not have it. The minister would not give us the burgesses loaf [though] we had asked for it ... He told me the reason was because we voted for the opposite party, and we must look for no favours from him.'[34] Forfeiting access to Christmas largesse was one thing, but the effects could be even more severe. Mary Toleman of Caernarfon wrote to the borough's recently elected MP, Sir Charles Paget, for whom her husband had voted, with a singularly pathetic appeal after the 1835 election.

> Lord Newborough and his agent took offence, and we have been driven from our House, have lost all our business, and have been pursued to ruin and wretchedness with the most bitter hostility. My husband has been in prison, has taken the benefit of the insolvent act, and since that, Mr. Lloyd Roberts, for his expenses, 25*l*., has sent the bailiffs into the house, and sold everything, without leaving us even a miserable bed to lie upon, and we are now utterly helpless and forlorn.

She reminded the member that his son, 'the gallant Capt Paget', had patted her husband on the back during the election and assured him that 'if he was true to you, he should never be a sufferer'. Sir Charles, however, turned a deaf ear to the appeal: he 'felt the hardship of the case', he replied, but concluded, regretfully, that it was 'not in his power to do anything'.[35]

Women, therefore, often played an important role in that most crucial aspect of electioneering, the canvass. This was not their only involvement in the political process, however: women also played a role in the darker side of electioneering, in overt 'influence' and corruption. Women who owned land could, if necessary, coerce their tenants in precisely the way that male landowners were said to do.[36] The note addressed to her tenants by Mrs E. H. Bruton, quoted earlier, was short and to the point and, though it contained no direct threat, neither did it admit that the tenants themselves had any leeway. In practice, few tenants would have risked disobeying so direct an order from their landlord.[37] This example supports the work of Sarah Richardson. Her examination of the activities of two independent female landowners in Yorkshire, Anne Lister and Elizabeth Lawrence, shows them combining the traditional female role of 'family networker' with the activities normally associated with men: the proper management of the estate's political interest; the eviction of tenants who did not toe the party line; and participation in discussions with other politically active landowners as to who should stand as candidate for Parliament.[38]

Illegitimate influence, that is influence that involved coercion, bribery or intimidation and was not as a result of 'natural' influence emanating from family property, was not, however, by any means confined to women of elite status.[39] Middle-class women were also guilty. Mrs Rowland, owner of the Uxbridge Arms in Caernarfon, apparently threatened Richard Hughes of North Penrallt with dismissal if he did not vote for Paget in 1837, and also threatened to withdraw her custom from David Parry, a smith, and John Davies, a wheelwright, if they refused to vote as she wished.[40] Middle-class women, especially the wives of Conservative voters, apparently notoriously prone to threatening 'exclusive dealing,' as a correspondent of G. W. Norman, a leading Kentish Liberal, remarked in 1834. He argued that any election in which women had been seen to canvass should be declared void: 'their mode of proceeding is worse than direct bribery', he declared, 'for the threat of withdrawing their custom & that of their friends is too ruinous to the tradesman & he must comply or be ruined.' And he continued: 'Tell it not again, but Ladies, especially if they be Tories, are very violent animals when they step forward to display their political feelings.'[41] Exclusive dealing was a favourite strategy for those excluded from the franchise and, as recent work on women and Chartism has revealed, it was women who controlled the family budget and therefore found such tactics effective.[42]

If upper-class and middle-class women can be shown to have taken a clearly distinguishable part in the seamier side of electoral politics, what of those in a lower station of life? Evidence on this subject can be found in the reports of the Select Committees of the House of Commons established in response to petitions alleging foul play on the part of the victorious side at an election. Every general election produced its own crop of petitions and subsequent investigations, and, although women did not at this time possess a vote, Select Committees regularly called them as witnesses. Eight of the fifty-two witnesses (15 per cent) called before the Select Committee on the 1852 Peterborough election, for example, were women, as were seven of the fifty-seven (12 per cent) called before the Committee adjudicating the Cockermouth petition in the same year. Sometimes the proportion of female witnesses was higher: at the hearing on the Bury St Edmunds election, for example, 25 per cent (five out of twenty) of those called were women. The Select Committees thus provide an interesting, and hitherto untapped, source for examining the behaviour of non-elite women in elections at this time. And evidence drawn from this source suggests that the wives of enfranchised shopkeepers and skilled tradesmen were no strangers to bribery and corruption. This can be conveniently demonstrated by following the bribing process through all its stages, from its negotiation, to its distribution and collection and, finally, to its spending.

The prominence of women in the negotiation of bribes seems to have been reasonably common, judging from the Select Committee evidence. During the Liverpool election of 1852, Mrs Mary Brown, who ran a tobacconist's shop, assured a canvasser that he should have her husband's vote if he could provide her spouse with work at the local sailors' home, where there were several posts vacant for which she considered him qualified: 'I had a large family, and business was very dull', she explained.[43] Another example is provided by Mrs Elizabeth Graham, wife of a beerhouse-keeper from Carlisle. At the election of 1859, a Mr Nanson had come with a group of gentlemen to ask for William Graham's vote and met the couple in the yard outside their shop. Mrs Graham described what took place:

> 'I turned round and said, "Well, gentlemen, if you want his favour," 'I said, "he will want one from you perhaps." ... Mr Nanson turned round, and said, "What was his favour;" and I said, "He was wanting a spirit licence for the house;" and he said, "We will look after it".'[44]

This bold intervention on the part of the wife, confirmed by her husband in his evidence, was not ultimately rewarded with success: the Grahams' application for a license was ultimately turned down by the magistrates. Nevertheless, the promise of it to the wife proved enough to secure her husband's vote.

If, on this occasion, the wife was a keen participant in electoral mal-practice, in other examples, women found such behaviour more repre-hensible. At Berwick-upon-Tweed, William Purves, who kept the Cannon Tavern, was called upon by two canvassers, John Wilson, the leading ironmonger in the town, and George Young, a fishmonger. They pressed him for his vote, signalling that he might expect a financial reward, and, when he refused, as he reported in his evidence to the Committee, they suggested that he 'go down to my mistress and my daughter, and consult with them about whether I was to change my mind or not'. He duly did so and said 'Jane, I think I may get 10*l*.' His wife, however, was horrified. 'Not for 20*l*. William', she claimed to have said, adding that her daughter had rushed to her support, crying: 'Honour before money, father.'[45] Once again, the women were involved in the negotiation sur-rounding the disposal of a vote that all parties (canvassers, the holder of the vote, and his spouse and daughter) seem to have regarded as a piece of family property.[46]

When voters did decide to take money for their votes, women might perform a number of roles. In some cases, they received the money on behalf of their male relations. When one of the Tory agents wanted to bribe a Mr Stimpson during the 1859 election in Peterborough, he paid the money to the wife, saying, 'There is a present, Mrs. Stimpson, if you like to take it'.[47] At Berwick-upon-Tweed in the same year, Catherine Keen took her father down to the George public house on the morning of the election; whilst there, some unknown person pressed two sover-eigns into her hand, after which she left, her father going on to the polling booths.[48] And Mrs C. Nurrish, wife of a coal porter at Caius College, Cambridge, received ten sovereigns from the Tories for her husband's vote, delivered to her on five separate occasions by three dif-ferent men.[49]

Women also provided the conduit through which bribe money passed. At Bridgenorth, in 1852, it was left to Martha Jones, daughter of a clerk at Mr Pritchard's bank in the town, to distribute the agreed bribe money of £4 per voter on behalf of the candidate.[50] At the Dover election of 1859, a considerable amount of bribery seems to have been handled by women. Mrs Elizabeth Barton, the wife of C. T. S. Barton, a Folkestone barber, was involved not only in the collection of bribe money, but was originally intended to have been involved also in its distribution. Barton was to organise a group of voters from Folkestone who were qualified to vote at Dover, and to arrange their bribe money. The £20 supplied for the purpose was to have been paid to Mrs Barton by a man named Dodd. On one visit, Dodd said 'I will give your wife . . . 20*l*.; and you are to say that it is to put a new shop front in your window'. There were thirteen men to be paid, however, and it was Mrs Barton who pointed out to Dodd that £20 'will not pay 13 men 2*l.* each'. For reasons unclear, the money was eventually distributed by Mrs Bromley at the Bricklayer's Arms. Under the new arrangement, Mr Barton had been promised 30*s.* for his expenses to Dover and duly sent his wife to collect the money; after several unsuccessful visits, he was ready to give up the money, but Mrs Barton insisted they should have it. She finally went to see Mrs Bromley in her bar; 'She says, "Oh, you want to borrow a little money." I laughed', said Mrs Barton, 'and said, "Yes", because I knew what it was for . . . and she went back into the next room behind the bar, and she came to the bar again, and she says, "There is 30*s.*, that will do, will it not?"'[51] In all these examples, women demonstrated a practised ease in their accommodation with the corruptions of the electoral system.

Once the money had been secured, women were again to the forefront. One of the most interesting features of the evidence given to the election petition committees is the repeated assertion that the money, or at least the bulk of it, was handed over to the woman. Both Catherine Keen at Berwick and Anne Stimpson at Peterborough claimed to have kept the bribe money they collected, whilst Anne Giles's husband gave her £2 of the £3 he had been paid during the Dover election.[52] The example of Henry Allen, who was alleged to have accepted ten gold sovereigns and a gold watch from the Whigs in Berwick-upon-Tweed, and concealed part of his booty on top of his five canary cages, unbeknownst to his wife, is almost unique in this respect.[53] In the corrupt exchanges surrounding many election contests, therefore, women appear to have played a prominent part, acting as willing particpants in the shady drama. At all stages, from the negotiation of a bribe to its collection, women might have a role to play.

Sarah Richardson has recently remarked that, 'apart from the, admittedly important, ability to exercise the franchise, . . . [women] were not politically impotent and were able to participate in other aspects of political and electoral life'.[54] Indeed, as many contemporaries recognised, the polling booth was not the only source of influence in politics.[55] If the work of historians like Elaine Chalus, K. D. Reynolds and Sarah Richardson has helped to explain the mechanisms by which the informal influence exercised by women was brought to bear among the elite, it is hoped that this chapter has shed some light upon the ways in which women of lower social groups made their presence felt at election time.

The forum for the exercise of that influence was often the family. Women of the elite worked through family social networks, and Elaine Chalus's comment that aristocratic women's political activities should be viewed as 'logical extensions of traditional female roles in a familial political culture'[56] can be extended to women outside the aristocracy. Thus middle-class women threatened their tradesmen with a withdrawal of their family's custom, whilst those of a lower class seem to have treated the vote as yet one more commodity that might be turned to the advantage of the family budget. To this extent the vote was something that the whole family possessed, and over the disposal of which men and women alike might have a say. As a consequence, the fact that women were being forced out of participation in organised politics by a newly respectable, mid-Victorian political culture figured around the respectable man and his domesticated family, did not necessarily diminish their practical influence in electoral politics. The court paid them by canvassing candidates and their entourages was a recognition of this. Thus it seems reasonable to conclude that, in many households, the vote was a piece of family property whose disposal was negotiated between husband and wife, and that in many cases, where 'Jenny ruled the roost', the woman's influence was paramount.

Notes

1. *Canterbury Weekly Journal*, 22 July 1837; Sarah Richardson, 'The Role of Women in Electoral Politics in Yorkshire During the 1830s', *Northern History*, 32 (1996), p. 140, n. 32.
2. *Canterbury Weekly Journal*, 2 December 1837.
3. *Monmouthshire Beacon*, 31 October 1868.
4. *Rothesay Chronicle*, 28 November 1868.
5. *Carmarthen Journal*, 20 November 1868.
6. Recent works include two books by John A. Phillips, *Plumpers, Splitters and Straights: Electoral Behaviour in Unreformed England* (Princeton, NJ: Princeton University Press, 1983) and *The Great Reform Bill in the Boroughs: English Electoral Behaviour, 1818–1841* (Oxford: Clarendon Press, 1992); Frank O'Gorman, *Voters, Patrons and Parties: The Unreformed Electoral System of Hanoverian England, 1734–1832* (Oxford: Clarendon, 1990) and 'Campaign Rituals and Ceremonies: the Social Meaning of Elections in England, 1780–1860', *Past & Present*, 135 (1992), pp. 79–115; Jon Lawrence and Miles Taylor (eds), *Party, State and Society: Electoral Behaviour in Britain since 1820* (Aldershot: Scolar Press, 1997); Norman Gash, *Politics in the Age of Peel: A Study in the Technique of Parliamentary Representation* (London: Longmans, Green, 1952); H. J. Hanham, *Elections*

and *Party Management: Politics in the Time of Disraeli and Gladstone* (London: Longman, 1959) provide detailed treatments of Victorian electioneering history.

7. Dorothy Thompson, *The Chartists: Popular Politics in the Industrial Revolution* (London: Templesmith, 1984), pp. 121–2.

8. James Vernon, *Politics and the People: A Study in English Political Culture, c. 1815–1867* (Cambridge: Cambridge University Press, 1993), p. 249.

9. Elaine Chalus, '"That Epidemical Madness": Women and Electoral Politics in the Late Eighteenth Century', in Hannah Barker and Elaine Chalus (eds), *Gender in Eighteenth-Century England: Roles, Representations and Responsibilities* (London: Longman, 1997), p. 153.

10. K. D. Reynolds, *Aristocratic Women and Political Society in Victorian Britain* (Oxford: Oxford University Press, 1998), pp. 129–52.

11. Amanda Foreman, *Georgiana, Duchess of Devonshire* (London: HarperCollins, 1998); Nicholas Rogers, *Crowds, Culture, and Politics in Georgian England* (Oxford: Oxford University Press, 1998), pp. 215–20; Richardson, 'The Role of Women in Electoral Politics'.

12. Peter Mandler, *Aristocratic Government in the Age of Reform: Whigs and Liberals, 1830–1852* (Oxford: Oxford University Press, 1990), pp. 56, 106.

13. For eighteenth-century examples, see Chapter 1.

14. Matthew Cragoe, *An Anglican Aristocracy: The Moral Economy of the Landed Estate, 1832–95* (Oxford: Oxford University Press, 1996), pp. 155–62, for an overview of canvassing.

15. National Library of Wales [NLW], Mayberry MSS/6784, 'Parliamentary Elections Act 1868 – Borough of Brecon . . . Brief for the Petitioners', f. 17.

16. NLW, Mayberry MSS/6784, 'Parliamentary Elections Act 1868 – Borough of Brecon . . . Brief for the Petitioners', f. 5.

17. NLW, Dolaucothi MSS/L6006, E. Ferguson-Davie to Bee Jones, no date [1868].

18. *Bucks Advertiser*, 5 September 1868.

19. *Bucks Advertiser*, 14 November 1868, working men's meeting at Salem chapel schoolroom. See also Parliamentary Papers [hereafter PP] 1860, XI, Sub-Committee on Carlisle Election Petition, pp. 417–20, evidence of Mary Thompson.

20. Justin McCarthy, 'The Petticoat in the Politics of England', *Lady's Own Paper*, 9 July 1870, p. 20. McCarthy's comments in this article closely reflect those of Alexis de Tocqueville, *Memoir, Letters, and Remains of Alexis de Tocqueville*, trans. H. Reeve, 2 vols (Boston, MA: Ticknor and Fields, 1861), vol. ii, p. 351, letter to Madame Swechtine, 20 October 1856.

21. Cragoe, *An Anglican Aristocracy*, p. 127.

22. McCarthy, 'The Petticoat in the Politics of England', p. 20.

23. *Northamptonshire Mercury*, 10 October 1868. United Liberal Association meeting, speech of Charles Gilpin: '"If you please (that's a very pretty little child) will you give me your vote?" (*loud laughter*)'.

24. *Monmouthshire Beacon*, 31 October 1868.

25. PP 1852–3, XVII, pp. 2340–5.

26. *Warwickshire Chronicle*, 10 November 1868.

27. McCarthy, 'The Petticoat in the Politics of England', p. 20; a 'plumper' in a two-member constituency involved the voter giving a single vote to just one candidate, thus wasting one of his two votes but giving his one, favoured candidate the clear advantage of his whole support.

28. Quoted in Phillips, *The Great Reform Bill*, p. 58. For another example, PP 1852–3, VIII, SC on Berwick-upon-Tweed Petition, pp. 735–7.
29. This paragraph is based upon University of North Wales, Bangor [UNW], Plas Coch MSS/2828, 'Check Book for Booth No. 2 at the Election of W. Bulkeley Hughes, esq.,... Carnarvon Borough 26 July 1837', and Plas Coch MSS/2836, 'A Register of Persons entitled to vote... for the Borough of Carnarvon', 1847.
30. *Bucks Advertiser*, 7 November 1868, meeting at National School, Padbury; see also Richard W. Davis, *Political Change and Continuity, 1760–1885: A Buckinghamshire Study* (Newton Abbot: David and Charles, 1972), pp. 225–6.
31. *Bucks Advertiser*, 7 November 1868, meeting at Princes Risborough. The vicar, Henry Meeres, strongly denied the charge: *Bucks Advertiser*, 14 November 1868.
32. PP 1860, XI, SC on Peterborough Election Petition, pp. 1953–4.
33. The precise extent to which voters might be punished is difficult to establish since many well-publicised cases do not bear close scrutiny. See Matthew Cragoe, 'The Anatomy of an Eviction Campaign: The General Election of 1868 in Wales and its Aftermath', *Rural History*, 9 (1998), pp. 175–91.
34. PP 1852–3, VIII, SC on Bridgenorth Election Petition, pp. 357–8.
35. UNW, PN/II/368, Mary Toleman to Sir Charles Paget, 25 May 1835.
36. For the debate on the use of landlords' coercion at election time, see Cragoe, 'The Anatomy of an Eviction Campaign'.
37. But see J. R. Fisher, 'The Limits of Deference', *Journal of British Studies*, 21 (1981), pp. 90–105.
38. Richardson, 'The Role of Women in Electoral Politics', pp. 133–51.
39. For example, in 1793 a survey by the Friends of the People, entitled 'A Report on the State of Representation', attempted to differentiate between legitimate and illegitimate influence, categorising the latter as nomination. Nomination occurred only in rotten and pocket boroughs and arose from the unequal distribution of the franchise. Influence on the other hand was acquired by wealthy candidates or those with wealthy sponsors and was found in all types of constituency. The report deplored nomination as corrupt but drew a distinction between influence that entailed an immoral use of power and should be suppressed and influence that was a natural consequence of wealth and power and should be maintained. For a further discussion see O'Gorman, *Voters, Patrons and Parties*, pp. 18–22 and Gash, *Politics in the Age of Peel*, Introduction.
40. UNW, Plas Coch MSS/2828, 'Check Book for Booth No. 2 at the Election of W. Bulkeley Hughes, esq.,... Carnarvon Borough 26 July 1837'.
41. Centre for Kentish Studies [CKS], U 310/ C 209/4, W. B. Traill to G. W. Norman, 3 January 1834.
42. For further examples of exclusive dealing see Chapter 6 in this volume and Thompson, *The Chartists*, pp. 137–9.
43. PP 1852–3, XV, SC on the Liverpool Election Committee, pp. 4896, 4907–8.
44. PP 1860, XI, SC on Carlisle Petition, pp. 610–11.
45. PP 1860, X, SC on the Berwick-upon-Tweed Election Petition, pp. 8853–4, 8894, 9082.
46. PP 1860, XI, SC on the Great Yarmouth Petition, pp. 158–412, evidence of Charles and Hannah Botwright who surrendered to a Magistrate the fifteen sovereigns a Tory agent slipped into the husband's pocket as a bribe.

47. PP 1860, XI, SC on Peterborough Election Petition, p. 1743.
48. PP 1860, X, SC on Berwick-upon-Tweed Election Petition, pp. 3383–598.
49. PP 1860, X, SC on Cambridge Borough Election Petition, pp. 642–97.
50. PP, 1852–3, VIII, SC on Bridgenorth Election Petition, pp. 470–81.
51. PP 1860, XI, SC on Dover Election Petition, pp. 462–86, 501–11.
52. PP 1860, X, SC on the Berwick-upon-Tweed Election Petition, pp. 3594–5; PP 1860, XI, SC on Peterborough Election Petition, p. 1704; PP 1860, XI, SC on Dover Election Petition, p. 2923.
53. PP 1860, X, SC on Berwick-upon-Tweed Election Petition, pp. 84–93. It might be noted, that his wife hotly denied that such a sum, secreted in such a place, could possibly have escaped her attention!
54. Richardson, 'The Role of Women in Electoral Politics', p. 151.
55. Quoted in Brian Harrison, *Separate Spheres: The Opposition to Women's Suffrage in Britain* (London: Croom Helm, 1978), p. 81.
56. Chalus, 'That Epidemical Madness', p. 153.

Index